"Do Your Job!"

The historic launching of four submarines in a single day occurred on January 27, 1944, with the christening of Redfish *(center), flanked by* Razorback *(left) and* Ronquil *(right), followed an hour later by the launch of the* Scabbardfish *from the Building Ways. PNSMVC*

"Do Your Job!"

An Illustrated Bicentennial History of the Portsmouth Naval Shipyard, 1800–2000

Richard E. Winslow III

With a Foreword by Vernon T. Williams, Captain, USN
Shipyard Commander, Portsmouth Naval Shipyard

The Portsmouth Marine Society
Publication Twenty-Six

Published for the Society by

Peter E. Randall
PUBLISHER

Designed and produced by
    Peter E. Randall Publisher
    Box 4726, Portsmouth, NH 03802

A publication of
The Portmsouth Marine Society
Box 147, Portsmouth, NH 03802

ISBN: 0-915819-26-0

1926 foldout photograph of the Portsmouth Naval Shipyard from the National Archives.

To the memory of
Joseph G. Sawtelle Jr.
Founder and Benefactor of
The Portsmouth Marine Society

Other Portsmouth Marine Society Publications:

The Portsmouth Marine Society is grateful to the following Shipyard employees and and Sponsors whose support helped to make this publication possible.

Joseph W. Hammond
George & Jeanne Snell
Daniel H. Vickery
In memory of William J. White,
    Retired PNS Shop 67 1991
    and USN ETC 1967
Troy and Maura Kaichen
David B. Gooch
Joseph and Jean Sawtelle
Capt and Mrs. Vernon
    T. Williams, USN
Roger A. Putnam
Stephen Laurenti
Naval Civilian Managers
    Association, Portsmouth
    Naval Shipyard Chapter
Joseph W. P. Frost

Capt. Ray P. Jones
Russ Van Billiard
Frank and Irja Cilluffo
Cor. Barbara Ellis, Ret.
Charles B. Doleac
Chuck Petlick
Ferris G. Bavicchi
Ray W. Fernald
Richard E. Winslow III
Bruce W. Hazelton
Valerie Cunningham
J. Dennis Robinson
Geoffrey and Martha Clark
James and Sandra Wakefield
Harry Tagen
Peter and Judy Randall

Foreword

Two Centuries of Freedom

This book chronicles the people, events, ships, and submarines that have collectively defined Portsmouth Naval Shipyard over the past two centuries. Reflect on the principles that these facts bear witness to as you scan its pages, read its stories, and look back through its historical photographs. Principles are truths, timeless and unchanging.

Our founding fathers' principles created the very foundation of our Nation's greatness, and throughout our history, these principles have been passed to successive generations. The truths of life, liberty, and the pursuit of happiness as proclaimed in our Declaration of Independence are synonymous with freedom of opportunity and choice. Prior to the American Revolution, these freedoms were restricted, rights and liberty were withheld at will. The Divine Right of Kings was the order of the day. Through the Magna Carta, this philosophy was challenged. Our American philosophy heralded that our rights are God given and only with the consent of the governed, are rights surrendered to a central authority.

Today we find that throughout the world freedom, faith, and family are values held most dear. Freedom, two centuries of freedom, is what Portsmouth Naval Shipyard and its people represent. Freedom and sovereignty, both individual and national, based on the principles set forth by our founders, are worth fighting for, not only with our pocket books, but with our lives if need be.

In the last half of the 20th Century, a most implausible cloud has risen over our people. Many of us have willingly given up more and more of our freedom to the central government while at the same time becoming reluctant to accept or enforce individual accountability. Benjamin Franklin wrote, "They that can give up essential liberty to obtain a little temporary safety deserve neither liberty or safety." We have lost the will to call evil behavior evil, except in the most egregious cases. Many of our citizenry have become lazy and complacent. A nearly irreversible cancer has developed. Untreated it will continue to grow and take over our lives until that day arrives when our freedom will be gone, lost forever. Thomas Jefferson wrote, "God who gave us life, gave us liberty. Can the liberties of a nation be secure when we have removed a conviction that these liberties are the gift of God? Indeed I tremble for my country when I reflect that God is just, that his justice cannot sleep forever." Indeed, how we sew, so shall we reap.

This book honors the efforts and the sacrifices of those who have served the Navy and the Nation through the Portsmouth Naval Shipyard. It should serve to motivate us to preserve our freedom and continue to hand down our forefathers' principles to our future generations. It is my hope that you will reflect on the freedom that has been dearly purchased and given to you; and it is my prayer that you will jealously guard and preserve this freedom.

It is your *Opportunity* and your *Choice!*

VERNON T. WILLIAMS
Captain, USN
Shipyard Commander

Contents

Preface

THE UPCOMING BICENTENNIAL OF THE PORTSMOUTH NAVAL SHIPYARD marks a special occasion, culminating in a two-day Open House celebration June 10-11, 2000. For two hundred years, the Yard has persevered—through wars, technological changes, appropriations cuts, closure orders, political neglect, accelerated wartime production schedules, boundary disputes, downsizing, new inventions, fluctuating employment levels—not only to survive but also on occasion to show the way for the rest of the Navy team. For an institution, either public or private, that is able to maintain its longevity for two centuries, such tenacity demonstrates that the Yard has indeed proven its worth in the defense of the United States. Otherwise the Yard would have closed its gates long ago. By any yardstick, the Portsmouth Naval Shipyard has been an asset to the local community and to the nation at large.

This book seeks to recount and interpret the Yard's rich history—its military, economic, social, political, and diplomatic significance. No stranger to chroniclers of its history, the Yard has been the subject of four earlier books, each carrying the narrative to its date of publication. In 1876, Walter E.H. Fentress, drawing upon his experience and knowledge as a former Union naval officer and subsequently as Yard clerk, published the first study, *Centennial History of the United States Navy Yard at Portsmouth, N.H.* Less than two decades later (1892), Rear Admiral George Henry Preble's updated manuscript was published posthumously as the *History of the United States Navy-Yard, Portsmouth, NH*. In 1978, the profusely illustrated and well-written *Portsmouth Naval Shipyard, Portsmouth New Hampshire: Cradle of American Shipbuilding* was published under the auspices of Captain William D. McDonough, then shipyard commander. In 1992 came the fourth and last volume: *Portsmouth-Kittery Naval Shipyard: In Old*

Photographs, collected and edited by Robert H. Whittaker, a pictorial effort with images and captions.

What then, one might ask, is the purpose of producing yet another history of the Yard? My response is threefold. First, in addition to updating the entire range and scope of the Yard's complete history, I have gathered fresh material while treating the same subjects and events described in the earlier books. Second, this book contains many previously unpublished photographs, paintings, sketches, maps, and newspaper-article reproductions. Third, this volume is designed to commemorate fittingly the Yard's bicentennial.

Even before I began the research for this book in the fall of 1995, I fully realized that the Yard's history is a huge, almost insurmountable topic, considering the hundreds of ships and subs built, repaired, and overhauled; the millions of people (naval and marine officers, enlisted personnel, their military dependents, Yard employees, off-base contractors, visitors, and military prisoners) who have passed through its gates; and the billions of dollars of defense appropriations. Faced with this staggering amount of material, I have been compelled to touch upon only the highest of the high points and to leave specialized aspects of this immense story to other writers. For example, an excellent topic for a future book-length legal-history study would be the ongoing New Hampshire–Maine boundary controversy, with its many ramifications—still unresolved as this book goes to press. Whole books have already appeared—and will continue to appear—on such perennially favorite topics as the Portsmouth-built submarine exploits during World War II, the technology of submarine construction, and the 1905 Treaty of Portsmouth, to say nothing of the massively researched investigations of the 1939 USS *Squalus* sinking and rescue, and the 1963 USS *Thresher* tragedy. Some of these subjects, indeed, have generated two or three books each. Given the space limitations and realistic coverage of this survey book, I have generally not repeated information that appears in my earlier Portsmouth Marine Society books on the Yard. Thus, I have been obliged to select judiciously what to include and (regrettably, in many cases) what to leave out.

While this book is not an official publication sponsored and endorsed by the United States Navy or the Portsmouth Naval Shipyard, I do not write from a vacuum or a sense of detachment. Above and beyond a hometown feeling of loyalty, I maintain a positive, even patriotic, attitude toward the topic, writing from the vantage point of having visited, observed, and read about the Yard for almost fifty-five years. The Yard has played a meaningful role in the seacoast area—

providing employment, bolstering the national defense, and nurturing a decent livelihood for thousands of people, both in and outside of the Yard. Without the Yard's presence for the last two hundred years, the entire region would have been the poorer.

I shall emphasize a couple of points from the outset. The vast preponderance of the Yard's history has been played out in peacetime. In its two hundred years, the Yard has faced the exigencies of war during only twenty-nine years (less than fifteen percent of the total). These conflicts (the War of 1812, the Mexican War, the Civil War, the Spanish–American War, World War I, World War II, the Korean War, the Vietnam War, and the Gulf War) have tested the Yard's resolve to produce the necessary military hardware for the defense of the United States. The rest of the time—171 years, more or less—the Yard has operated in a peacetime standby alert status, often developing nonmilitary inventions and concepts in advancing the public good.

In terms of regional influence and importance, the Portsmouth Naval Shipyard goes far beyond its mere military posture. The Yard has been an economic giant, the chief employer in the Piscataqua area for most of its two centuries, certainly during the last century. Its enormous payroll is subsequently circulated within the many communities outside its gates. One generation follows another—father to son and, more recently, mother to daughter—in working at the Yard, often as a career. Except for a necessary security perimeter, the Yard resembles a typical American industrial plant where employees work in shops and offices, eat lunch in a cafeteria, pursue hobbies in off-hours, read the Yard newspaper, attend apprenticeship classes, deposit checks at a federal credit union, seek medical care at a hospital clinic, and attend church services. Naval officers live in base housing, shop at the commissary and Navy Exchange, and walk to work. In every sense, the Yard is a self-contained community, providing the same services that would be found, for example, in a civilian company town.

In a political context, the Yard lends its name to the "Navy Yard District"—the designation for both New Hampshire's and Maine's First Congressional Districts, whose office-seekers and incumbents depend on Yard votes to win elections to their U.S. House and Senate seats. Once in office, they are expected to champion the Yard's interests and to elicit congressional support and appropriations—billions of dollars through the years—to operate the facility. Congressmen, senators, Navy secretaries, governors, and even U.S. presidents have routinely appeared at the Yard on inspection tours, when they often take the opportunity to stump for themselves or candidates of their political parties.

As a demographic and sociological factor in bringing new people to the area, the Yard has determined the course of thousands of lives. The influx of newcomers, in whatever capacity, has remained constant since the Yard was founded. As an employment magnet, the Yard currently draws its people, especially engineers, from throughout the country. As Yard naval officers, enlisted personnel, and employees enter into the social fabric of the community, they marry local citizens, buy homes, join civic organizations, send their sons and daughters to nearby colleges and universities, and send for their aging parents to join them. Once their active military service is over, many naval retirees take second-career jobs at the Yard to contribute their expertise and remain in an area to which they have become attached. In short, the Yard has been the catalyst for the seacoast area, almost synonymous with Portsmouth and Kittery, considering their close association and partnership through the years.

As the third century of the Yard approaches, the demands of the modern world necessitate adjustments. The Yard's motto, "Sails to Atoms," attests that the Portsmouth Naval Shipyard has been ever-adaptable to any challenge on the naval horizon. I trust this book captures the proud spirit of the Yard, an institution that mirrors the American experience.

Happy Two-Hundredth Birthday to the Portsmouth Naval Shipyard! And many more!

Acknowledgments

SINCE THIS UNDERTAKING IS MY THIRD BOOK dealing entirely or in part with the Portsmouth Naval Shipyard, many people who aided me in my earlier efforts have continued to provide their support. Scores of these contributors, along with their professional affiliations, have been mentioned in my previous extensive lists of acknowledgments, and I renew my thanks. For this latest book, I express my gratitude in particular to six stalwart veterans of my previous Portsmouth Marine Society books—Kathleen Brandes, James Dolph, Patricia Mullaney, Peter Randall, and Joe and Jean Sawtelle.

A seventh person, Fred Crawford, who guided my writing career for twenty years, is no longer with us. During the first four of the five years it took to bring this project to completion, Fred stood by me—section by section, page by page, and even comma by comma. Most of his exhaustive revisions remain intact in the final text. Thanks, Fred, for your dogged dedication to this book.

New people have come on board to advance the interests of this bicentennial history. Within the Portsmouth Naval Shipyard family, my debt is great. Since the beginning of my research back in 1995, three successive shipyard commanders—Captains Lance Horne, Carl Strawbridge, and Vernon T. Williams—have supported my efforts. Captain Williams also wrote the Preface to this volume, providing an overview of the Yard's commitment and sense of purpose to the United States Navy. Alan D. Robinson, Jan Hussey, and Deborah White—all in the Congressional and Public Affairs Office— coordinated my way around the Yard, arranging appointments with the right people and supplying updated information germane to my study. On a beautiful fall day, Yard photographer Curry Lashua escorted me around the grounds and the historic sites on a combined walking and auto tour, shooting many pictures, and a number of his outstanding images grace these pages. Dee Bissell of the Yard Library provided back issues of the *Portsmouth Periscope* and a pleasant place for research. Several editors of the *Periscope*—Philip Sanderson, James Mallen, Ruth Dow, and Mary Anne Mascianica—have written excellent articles that were invaluable in assessing and interpreting the Yard's history.

The Portsmouth Naval Shipyard Museum and Visitor Center, where I spent many productive hours over a four-year time period, is fortunate to have Director Jom Dolph at its helm. His personal and professional attention to this book has gone beyond the call of duty, especially in procuring photographs. Museum volunteers John Cowan, George Watson, Duncan Martin, Jack Miller, Gifford Wilcox, Michael Gletka, William MacLehose, Dave Davenport, Joe Frost, and Dan MacIsaac, many of whom are retired submariners, have enlightened my thinking on numerous points, along with regaling me with their World War II "war stories."

Designer Tom Allen and word processor compositor Sandra Frechette lent their skills in providing an attractive appearance to this book.

Larry Favinger of the *Portsmouth Herald,* dean of the Yard reporters, and Clare Kittredge, reporting for the *Boston Globe,* have faithfully covered the Yard for years. Their incisive articles have represented journalism at its best in compiling an accurate record of the Yard's activities. D. Allen Kerr and Jennifer Saunders of Dover's *Foster's Daily Democrat* are also perceptive reporters on Yard matters.

Three naval scholars—Paolo Coletta, Annapolis, Maryland; Raimondo Luraghi, Torino, Italy; Mike Crawford, Naval Historical Center, Washington, DC; and Terry Foenander, Toowoomba, Queensland, Australia—have contributed their expertise.

Captain Vernon T. Williams, Russell Van Billiard, John Cowan, Howell Russell, and Richard E. Winslow, Jr., read and clarified questions in the text.

I would be remiss not to mention the late Admiral Jeremy ("Mike") Boorda for his efforts to save the Yard in 1995. I heard his stirring speech at the Yard auditorium, and, along with everyone else who was there, will never forget his presence and oratory.

Many others, although unnamed here, have enhanced this book through conversation, clippings, and artifacts. To all again, many thanks.

RICHARD E. WINSLOW III
Little Harbor
Rye, New Hampshire
September 5, 1999
(ninety-fourth anniversary of the signing
of the Treaty of Portsmouth, in Building 86,
Portsmouth Naval Shipyard)

List of Abbreviations

THE ABBREVIATIONS BELOW appear within the text as well as in illustration captions and the Notes at the end of the book.

ACAB	*Appletons' Cyclopaedia of American Biography*
ANB	*American National Biography*
DAB	*Dictionary of American Biography*
DANFS	*Dictionary of American Naval Fighting Ships*
DNB	*Dictionary of National Biography*
FDD	*Foster's Daily Democrat*
NA	National Archives
NCAB	*National Cyclopaedia of American Biography*
NHC	Naval Historical Center
NHG	*New-Hampshire Gazette* (Portsmouth, New Hampshire)
NHHS	New Hampshire Historical Society
NYT	*New York Times*
PA	Portsmouth Athenaeum
PC	*Portsmouth Chronicle*
PEM	Peabody Essex Museum
PH	*Portsmouth Herald*
PJ	*Portsmouth Journal of Literature and Politics*
PNSMVC	Portsmouth Naval Shipyard Museum and Visitor Center
PNSY	Portsmouth Naval Shipyard
PP	*Portsmouth Periscope*
PPL	Portsmouth Public Library
PT	*Portsmouth Times*
SU	*The States and Union* (Portsmouth, NH)
UNH	University of New Hampshire
USN	United States Navy
USS	United States Ship

During the War of 1812, an 1814 Navy Yard signal chart was prepared to offer safeguards against attack. Night and day signals included both flag and gun firing warnings. UNH

I *1800–1900*

Establishment of the Yard, 1800–1812

THE ESTABLISHMENT OF THE PORTSMOUTH NAVY YARD on June 12, 1800, was directly precipitated by a national crisis. For years, the American merchant marine had been ravaged by French privateers and other freebooters, and in 1798, the fledgling United States became embroiled in the so-called Quasi-War, an undeclared war against France. To put an end to brazen seizures on the high seas, U.S. Secretary of the Navy Benjamin Stoddert sought to build up America's pitifully weak navy. Initially, he bought vessels built at private yards, and he contracted for others. In time, Stoddert managed to acquire a fleet of fifty ships. Among them was the USS *Portsmouth*, built at Badger's Island in the middle of the Piscataqua River, the boundary between New Hampshire and Maine (the latter was part of Massachusetts until 1820). When Captain Daniel McNeil and his crew sailed aboard the *Portsmouth* with twenty-four guns on Monday, January 30, 1799, to carry the war to the enemy, the local *New-Hampshire Gazette* commented, "They go to protect our rights, to secure commerce from depredation, to support the honor of the American name, and may they return with the glory of well done, good and faithful, in the cause of an injured and insulted country."[1]

But the mere acquisition of ships from private yards proved to be insufficient. Procurement of land to develop government yards, Stoddert contended, was the best solution to this problem, and he acted accordingly. In Stoddert's official report, dated January 12, 1801, he announced, "Ground has been purchased at Portsmouth, New-Hampshire, Charlesto[w]n (near Boston), Philadelphia, the city of Washington and Norfolk; and measures have been taken to procure ground at New-York, for capacious building and dock-yards; and progress is making [has been made] in preparing docks for the receiving of timber and wharves for the building of ships."[2]

All the necessary land at these various locations was purchased during 1800 and 1801. The Portsmouth site, probably the earliest acquisition, can claim to be the first government-owned navy yard. Bought for $5,500 in 1800, fifty-eight-acre Fernald's Island, in the Piscataqua River, proved to be an excellent choice. It was soon renamed Navy Yard Island. The boundary demarcation of the island has long been in dispute. Generally acknowledged at the time as part of Maine, a district of Massachusetts, the Portsmouth Navy Yard name derived from its proximity to the nearest post and customs office of Portsmouth, to which U.S. Navy mail was directed. In 1800, Kittery (Maine) lacked such a post office. At any rate, the island, now federal property in Portsmouth Harbor, had all the prerequisites for a military facility. The proposed yard site was well situated for adequate defense, with outer-harbor forts, access to the sea, and nearby resources of stone, wood, and naval stores.

Still another advantage was the availability of an experienced workforce—Portsmouth shipwrights had been building well-crafted vessels for almost two centuries. The economic benefits of gaining a local Navy shipyard were not lost on its citizens. In 1801, the *Gazette* editorialized: "What will those who live by the 'sound of the axe and the hammer,' say on perusing the above list [of American naval ships]? And what consolation must it afford to the farmer who furnishes ship-timber, the ship-carpenter, blacksmith, ship-joiner, painter, rigger, boatbuilder, mast-maker, block maker, sail-maker, rope-maker, caulker, carver, and in short many other mechanics who have experienced constant employment and ready pay, in furnishing our country's best hope, and Commerce's sure protector, a respectable and progressive NAVY?"[3]

But the anticipated frenzied shipbuilding at the Yard never materialized during the early 1800s. In a pattern that has repeated itself throughout the history of the Yard, wartime projections were quickly dashed by peacetime realities. The Quasi-War ended in the autumn of 1800, with the formal treaty being signed in 1801. By September 1802, the Yard was selling at public auction surplus articles "belonging to the U. State Navy Department, consisting of A quantity of Russian Iron; Cordage; Junk; Oakum; Old Iron; Nails . . .[;] Copper, Sheet Lead; Saws; Iron Anvils; Scales; Beams and Weights; Leather Fire Bucketts; Glass; Twine; Blankets, two Boats; one large Gondola. . . ."[4]

A 1978 map shows the cluster of islands in Portsmouth Harbor that subsequently evolved as the Portsmouth Navy Yard. Over the years, landfill has joined the various islands into one 278-acre land mass. PNSY

In the end, little was done at the Yard during the early 1800s except the construction of a few sheds and workshops and the Marine Barracks. Impressment of American seamen, however, resumed as the Napoleonic Wars between England and France convulsed most of Europe, spilled over across the oceans, and led to an American embargo. Despite these difficulties, however, the United States remained at peace until 1812.

After a decade of impressments, lost trade, and repeated violations of American territorial waters, the American Congress—unwilling to be humiliated any longer—declared war on Great Britain on June 18, 1812.

Commodore Isaac Hull and
The War of 1812, 1812–1816

The War of 1812–15 stimulated the Portsmouth Navy Yard into action. But the odds appeared slim that the stripling U.S. Navy could defeat the Royal Navy, almost double its size. Yet the U.S. Navy, bolstered by the Portsmouth Navy Yard (among others) and the leadership of such naval officers as Commodore Isaac Hull, proved to be a formidable opponent.

The Portsmouth Navy Yard responded well to meet this national crisis. On October 31, 1812, Yard Purser Tunis Craven notified Secretary of the Navy Paul Hamilton that the Yard needed waterproof sheds to protect wood, frames, and other timbers, and that the Yard could obtain "Oak . . . Spruce, Pine . . . Ball and powder from nearby sources for ship construction."[5]

Bold action was vital to counteract British bravado about the superiority of their fleet. In September 1812, the *British Quarterly Review* had declared: "We will not stoop to degrade the British Navy by condescending to enter into a comparison between the high order, the discipline and comfort of an English man of war and an American frigate. We disdain any such comparison." In March 1813, the *Gazette* accepted the challenge in its retort: "Since the declaration of war, the U.S. Frigate *Constitution* has *invited* the crews of two British frigates on board that vessel, and in both instances the *invitation* was accepted; those of the *Guerrière* were welcomed on board by Capt. Hull. . . . We never heard that any of these men passed the ceremony of asking what accommodations of comfort they would find on board the Yankee frigates—or stopped to *enter into a comparison!*"[6]

Hull had defeated the HMS *Guerrière*, whereupon her British commander and crew had surrendered in a celebrated sea battle 700 miles east of Boston. Hailed as a national hero, Hull was reassigned the next year as commandant of the Portsmouth Navy Yard. As the *Gazette* reported, "Commodore HULL, who first taught the boasting bullies of Britain that 'twas their duty to knock under,' when AMERI-CANS were their foe, arrived in this town with his lady, on Wednesday afternoon last [March 31, 1813]. He is to superintend the building of a 74 gun ship at the Navy Yard in this harbor. He was welcomed with the discharge of cannon, and reiterated cheers of the citizens."[7]

As commandant of the Navy Yard from 1812 to 1815, Commodore Isaac Hull supervised the building of the USS Washington. *During Hull's tenure at the Yard, workmen built a residence, now known as Quarters A, for the commodore and his wife. PNSY*

Hull wasted no time directing the building of the 74-gun ship-of-the-line throughout 1813, despite a shortage of live-oak timber (white oak was substituted for it). He also addressed the issue of ensuring year-round construction by proposing the erection of a shiphouse to cope with severe Portsmouth winters.

On July 24, 1813, Hull wrote Secretary of the Navy William Jones: "As the Winters here are very cold and large quantities of Snow falls, may I be permitted to suggest the idea of covering the Ship after she is framed. The cost to build a permanent cover, would probably be two thousand dollars. . . ."[8]

Hull's proposal was approved, and in time the shiphouse became a reality. But it was not until September 1814 that the building was erected to cover the 74-gun ship, providing protection for both the ship and her workmen.[9]

More pressing before then was the Yard's response to the "Great Fire" of Portsmouth, which broke out on the night of December 22, 1813. Commodore Hull, Captain John Smith of the USS *Congress* and other naval officers personally and immediately responded with crews and equipment to fight the blaze. Despite major damage to the town, the Yard firefighters saved much property. The *Gazette* praised the officers and crews "for their exertions at the late destructive fire."[10]

By the end of that month, as Portsmouth was recovering, the Yard advertised: "WANTED, at the United States Navy Yard, Portsmouth, Thirty Ship Carpenters, first-rate workmen—to such will be given good wages, and constant employ under cover."[11]

The keel of the still-unnamed 74-gun ship was laid in March 1814, at a time when the British blockade of the Atlantic coastline between Portsmouth and Boston prevented American vessels from entering or leaving Portsmouth Harbor. Rumors circulated that the British intended to send boats from their blockading squadron to set fire to the ship on the ways, but the alarm proved unfounded. In September, as launch time approached, Secretary Jones ordered the ship to be named the *Washington*. Finally the ship was ready, and the *Gazette* announced: "LAUNCH. On Saturday last [October 1, 1814] the *WASHINGTON,* 74, was launched from the Navy-Yard in this harbor. The spectators were very numerous. . . . Salutes were fired on the occasion from the navy-yard, forts, and the private armed vessels [privateers] in the harbor. . . . The *Washington* is considered one of the finest vessels of her class ever built."[12]

In late October 1814, the blockade was lifted—not by American naval action but by the whims of nature. With the approach of winter, the increasing severity of the winds caused the British ships off Portsmouth to sail for Halifax. The Portsmouth Navy Yard and the *Washington* were left unharmed. On December 28, 1814, the War of 1812 ended with the Treaty of Ghent, amounting to a stalemate with no transfer of territory.[13]

Portsmouth recognition of the Navy, the Yard, and Commodore Hull for their steadfast wartime performance occurred at a public dinner on March 22, 1815. Just prior to Hull's transfer to Washington as one of the commissioners of the Navy, Portsmouth citizens hosted a well-attended, "without distinction of party" affair at a local hotel to honor him "as a public expression of their high sense of his brilliant achievements in the service of his country, of his correct and manly deportment while commanding here, and of his vigilance and activity in providing for the defense of this port." Many patriotic toasts conveyed the uplifted American spirit at the end of the war: "The American Navy—Its increase, with the increase of our national means, the surest protection of our commerce." The French consul saluted "the constructors of the Navy—May they bear in mind how much they are indebted to a strong and steady 'Hull.'"[14]

Yard Ships Bolster American Foreign Policy, 1816–1846

After the War of 1812, the Portsmouth Navy Yard again struggled to adjust to peacetime priorities. With reduced naval appropriations, the Yard fought for funds while Caribbean pirates and containment of the slave trade required scrutiny and attention.

In early 1816, New Hampshire Governor John Langdon, along with many prominent Portsmouth citizens, responded vigorously to a rumor that has prevailed off and on throughout the Yard's existence: that the Yard was slated to be abolished. In a petition addressed to Secretary of the Navy Benjamin Crowninshield, Langdon argued against such shortsighted thinking: "We have too much confidence in the wisdom and justice of our rulers to believe that they will give up this Yard without particular inquiry into the advantages it possesses. . . ." Crowninshield apparently did not respond in writing to this petition, but at least the Yard remained open. Further reinforcing the government's apparent commitment to the Yard's future, President James Monroe visited the facility on Monday, July 20, 1817, during a New England tour. The event was celebrated with the firing of cannon. "He [President Monroe] embarked from Langdon's wharf in an elegant gig," reported the *Portsmouth Oracle,* "and [inspected] the arsenal, warehouses, depots of ordnance and naval stores, and the various quarters and barracks," culminating in "a collation."[15]

Despite lean appropriations throughout the 1820s, the Yard succeeded in building a second shiphouse in 1820. In 1825, a bridge was built from the north side of Navy Yard Island to Kittery, enabling transportation and communication to flow more quickly and efficiently to and from Portsmouth. In the event of fire, the bridge also would allow fire engines to reach the Yard with less delay.[16]

Thanks to the various naval shops, timber sheds, and shiphouses, and the blacksmith's shop, the Yard completed two ships during the 1820s—the eleven-gun *Porpoise* and the eighteen-gun sloop *Concord*. The *Porpoise,* launched on December 2, 1820, sailed the following May 8. Under the command of Lieutenant James Ramage, the *Porpoise* cruised the West Indies in search of pirates.[17]

Ramage's mission accentuated a major thrust of American policy and the activities of the United States Navy from 1808 to 1898. The Latin American wars of independence caught the American merchant marine in the middle, as Spain sought to defend her colonies from liberators or insurgents who struck back at the Spanish paper blockade. The rebelling Latin American revolutionaries relied on privateers to harass their Spanish rulers. Many privateers simply turned pirate— the distinction often being very vague in their minds—and preyed on American shipping in the Caribbean, staging more than 3,000 incidents between 1815 and 1822.[18]

Ramage cruised aggressively to intercept pirates in the Caribbean. "On the 15th [of January 1822], having seen the vessels bound to Havana and Matanzas safe to their destined ports," Ramage reported to Secretary of the Navy Smith Thompson: "I made all sail to the westward, and on the following day boarded the brig *Bolina,* of Boston, Gorham master, from whom I received the following information. That, on the day previous, his vessel was captured by pirates, and robbed of every material they could carry away with them. . . ."

The next day, Ramage went in pursuit "of these enemies of the human race." Dispatching forty-man boats, Ramage discovered, chased, and captured "a piratical schooner, the crew of which made their escape to the woods." Continuing his pursuit, which erupted into a firefight, Ramage destroyed five vessels and the pirates' base, which turned out to be their chief depot. "The prisoners now on board," Ramage concluded, "are recognized by a seaman in my possession, who was one of the crew of the English ship *Alexander,* of Greenock, lately burnt by these pirates; and not content with destroying the vessel, they inhumanely butchered her unfortunate commander."[19]

A month later, the exploits of the *Porpoise* again reached the Portsmouth newspapers. Arriving in Charleston, South Carolina, on February 10, the *Journal* reported: "Capt. R. has recaptured the sch. *Charles* of Baltimore, which has been three days in the possession of pirates and destroyed in all three piratical establishments on shore, and twelve vessels, besides two on the stocks."[20]

The cruises of the *Porpoise*—among many undertaken by American naval ships throughout the early 1820s—led to a major American foreign-policy statement. On December 2, 1823, in his annual message to Congress, President James Monroe issued the famous doctrine that bears his name—stipulating that the United States would not tolerate any additional European colonization or even intervention in Latin America. This cornerstone of United States foreign policy thus defined the Caribbean as an American sea, and it required much attention, activity, and enforcement by the U.S. Navy during the next century.

Helping to meet these increased naval responsibilities, the Yard built and launched another ship in the late 1820s. "Another addition has been made to our gallant Navy in a beautiful ship," reported the *Journal* in September 1828, "destined, we trust, to do honor to her flag. . . . The Sloop of war *Concord* was . . . launched at the Navy Yard. . . . She is pronounced by judges to be one of the finest ships of her class in the navy—is 600 tons burthen and is pierced for 18 guns."[21]

With the advent of President Andrew Jackson's administration in 1829, a fresh wind of change, reform, and activity stirred for both the Navy and the Yard. In 1831, Levi Woodbury, a prominent Portsmouth resident, was appointed Secretary of the Navy. A close friend of Jackson's, Woodbury sought and received his chief's nod in Yard matters. In the words of a Philadelphia newspaper correspondent, "Through the influence of the Hon. Levi Woodbury . . . [who] manifested a becoming interest in behalf of the station at his native town," the Yard "received several large appropriations which have been wisely expended."[22]

During Woodbury's six years as secretary, the Yard expanded with a third shiphouse, timber sheds, enclosure of the timber dock (that "conveys to the mind some idea of the great wall of China"), mast house, and other buildings—all accomplished with an ample supply of labor and a company of Marines. "The island is ornamented by the residences and

The 1837 granite sail-loft building remains in service today as Building 7. Originally situated next to the Jenkins's Gut channel, where ships once were anchored, Building 7 now borders Dry Dock No. 2—a result of landfill and construction between 1899 and 1906. PNSY

gardens of the Commodore and other officers; and it is a delightful place of resort on a sultry day," wrote the same correspondent. "The present officers of the yard are distinguished for their punctual attendance to business, their temperance, and their politeness to strangers."[23]

In addition to securing Yard improvements, Woodbury heeded the various social-reform movements astir in the country and applied them to improving the caliber of Navy life. He disapproved of flogging and in late 1831 issued an official circular "that fines or badges of disgrace should be substituted for whipping for the offenses of seamen in the navy." Woodbury and his successor were under pressure to abolish liquor in the Navy—the example already having been set by the secretary of war, who had banned spirit ration in the U.S. Army.[24]

Attention to these nascent reforms languished while Jackson and Woodbury directed military and naval action in the Second Seminole

Located on a street behind Building 86, Officers' Row provides housing for the Yard's chief naval officers. Constructed in the 1830s, these quarters are occupied by the Executive, Production, Public Works, and other key officers. PNSY–Lashua Photo

War of 1836–38. The Seminole Indians of Florida, led by Osceola, bitterly objected to Jackson's proposed policy of moving them to the West. Violence broke out and the Jackson administration hastened to subdue the resistance by force. The Yard was called upon to send its entire Marine detachment, substituting civilians to guard government property. The Marines boarded the *Concord*, which sailed on February 26, 1836.[25]

By June of that year, an assembled detachment of 150 marines from the Boston, Portsmouth, and Brooklyn Navy Yards sailed from Charleston, South Carolina, for Fort Mitchell, Florida. Events proceeded rapidly. Accompanying army units to Tallahassee in early June was "a party of about 70 sailors and marines from the United States [USS] *Concord*. . . . These 'sons of the ocean' are encamped at the race course, which has been named Camp Concord in honor of the ship."[26]

The wooden sloop-of-war USS Portsmouth, *launched at the Yard in 1843, enjoyed a seventy-year career in naval service. In 1860, her commander negotiated a commercial treaty with West African tribesmen. UNH*

Dubbed "sailor soldiers" by the press, the men participated in engagements that drove the Indians into the swamps for refuge. In 1837, Osceola was seized at a conference under a truce flag, and he died less than a year later in a military prison. Not long afterward, resistance collapsed. Most of the Seminoles were removed in 1842. Their punitive mission over, the Marines returned to the Yard.[27]

To respond to potential domestic or foreign crises, the Navy launched three new vessels at the Yard during the early 1840s: the frigate *Congress* in 1841, the sloop *Saratoga* in 1842, and the sloop *Portsmouth* in 1843. A launching inevitably was a major event, with extensive press coverage along the Portsmouth waterfront. On August 16, 1841, the *Congress*'s launch drew many spectators to the banks of the Piscataqua. "At about half-past ten the guns at [Navy Yard] Island called the public attention," noted one reporter, "and every store and workshop in town was deserted. At a quarter past eleven she began to move—and majestically dipping and plunging into the foam of her own creation . . . the frigate *Congress* in a few moments sits like a 'thing of

The sail plan of the USS Congress, *as depicted here, was realized in 1841 at the Yard. On March 8, 1862, during the Civil War, the* Congress *was sunk by the CSS* Virginia (ex–USS Merrimack), *with great loss of life. UNH*

life.'" Praise for her beauty and performance accompanied her voyage across the Atlantic. On August 7, 1842, a boatswain wrote from Madeira: "We have fallen in with a great many vessels ahead of us, but we soon passed them. She is so easy to her rigging that she would not chafe a rope-yarn."[28]

Not so fortunate during sea trials was the sloop USS *Saratoga*. Sailing from the Yard on Thursday morning, March 16, 1843, the *Saratoga* was overtaken by a storm that evening. Sleet and snow raged, forcing Captain Josiah Tattnall to let go his anchors and cut away the masts to save the ship. "There was no confusion, no violence either of action or language," commented local ship captain William Neal, who shortly thereafter went on board to talk to the naval officers and crew. "The orders were promptly given and as promptly executed." On Friday morning, the dismasted *Saratoga* lay at anchor off Wallis Sands, Rye Beach, south of Portsmouth, with all hands safe. Two days later, the disabled vessel was towed to shore—with the rigging and sails salvaged—

The sloop-of-war USS Saratoga, *the third U.S. Navy ship to bear that name, was commissioned at the Yard on January 4, 1843, and dismasted in a gale on her sea trials two months later. The most notable service of the* Saratoga's *long career occurred in the Far East as part of Commodore Matthew Perry's squadron in the 1854 opening of Japan. PNSMVC*

and transported overland to the Yard. By May 2, the repaired *Saratoga* again set sail, this time successfully, bound for service off the west coast of Africa to suppress the slave trade. En route to her station, the *Saratoga* docked in New York, causing a local reporter to comment that the ship "is perhaps the finest vessel of her class in the world."[29]

The effort to stamp out the slave trade was one reform undertaken by both the American and the British navies. Another human evil that needed redress had festered for years within the United States Navy itself—flogging. At the hands of a number of tyrannical naval captains who insisted that lashings promoted shipboard discipline, many sailors suffered severe disfigurement, even death, from flogging—mostly administered at sea but occasionally also at navy yards. For years,

American editorial writers railed against the inhumane practice. In a major article, "Flogging in the Navy," in late January 1843, the *Journal* attacked this cruelty: "This practice is wholly unworthy of the American Navy, the pride and boast of the nation. . . . In this day of reforms, the Navy of this Republic ought to have its anti-Republican features blotted out. Flogging is done away with in the Army, by law—Why not in the Navy also[?]"[30]

Less than a week later, the Portsmouth Navy Yard was itself the scene of such a whipping. The Yard's log for February 2, 1843, reads: "Samuel Seggel, ord[inary] sea[man], receives 12 lashes for desertion." Despite opposition to this barbarous practice, flogging continued.[31]

In a more positive development, the Maine and New Hampshire congressional delegations toured the Yard in the fall of 1843 to become "acquainted with the situation of the Yard, its advantages for building and repairing vessels of war." The visitors saw for themselves the new stone wharf, more than a thousand feet in length, used for tying up vessels. A five-year project, the construction required blasting rocks twenty or thirty feet under water to prepare the foundation. Bearing "the marks of system and good order," the Yard appeared shipshape for the official congressional party.[32]

In 1841, the well-known English travel author William Buckingham made an extensive tour of the United States and Canada. Including the United States Navy in his observations, Buckingham grasped its sense of purpose when he wrote: "And yet small as it [the United States Navy] is in the number of its ships, its efficiency is so great, and the skill of its officers and seamen so conspicuous, that it is superior in actual force to any other navy in the world, except that of Great Britain, and would not shrink, single-handed, from a contest with it, gun for gun, and man for man, with a probability of being victor."[33]

Foreign Wars and Social Reforms, 1846–1860

Foreign affairs—wars, diplomacy, and unexpected incidents—required the United States Navy and the Yard to remain vigilant in the 1840s and 1850s. The Navy on the domestic scene also kept abreast and adjusted to social reforms and technological change.

American efforts to suppress the slave trade continued. This international crusade by the American and British navies off the west coast of Africa meant a high cost in lives. The Yard sloop *Preble,* one of the ships in the African Squadron commanded by Commodore Matthew Perry, patrolled off the coast during 1844 and 1845. "Our ship was anchored near the shore," wrote a *Preble* officer, "and on that side [village of Bissao] heretofore attacked by natives [in revolt against the Portuguese colonial government]." When the *Preble*'s heavier guns fired back, the clash ended. Of a more serious nature was the appearance of yellow fever, which temporarily halted the mission. The disease spread, sparing no one. "The Captain had the fever and delivered the command of the ship to the first lieutenant." The latter in turn became ill, and the second lieutenant took charge. Ultimately, the captain became "raving mad," and the *Preble* had eighty cases of yellow fever on board. The ship then sailed to St. Vincent, deemed the safest and most healthful of the Cape Verde Islands. Before the epidemic ended, the *Preble* lost seventeen men to the fever, with seventy on the sick list.[34]

A more serious situation for the United States Navy, however, was developing much closer to home. War with Mexico seemed imminent, and the Navy's Pacific Squadron, including the sloop *Portsmouth,* was anchored off Mazatlán on the west coast of Mexico. Writing from that port on January 28, 1846, a squadron officer reported: "We are anxiously awaiting the arrival of the President's [James Knox Polk's annual] Message, to learn his views about Oregon and Mexico. . . . Our active commander-in-chief [Commodore John D.] Sloat has lost no time in preparing himself to meet any emergency that may arise, having already assembled in this port or very near at hand, the largest force ever collected at one time in this region. . . . We live in hope that our troubles with the Mexicans will speedily be settled, and that we shall soon be allowed to return home. . . ."[35]

Events proved otherwise. On May 12, 1846, over an alleged border dispute, the U.S. Congress declared war on Mexico. The conflict was fought primarily by opposing armies on land. Because Mexico did not have a navy, there were no sea battles. The United States Navy, however, was assigned several vital functions, including transporting and supporting American troops, blockading and capturing Mexican ports, and being on the lookout for Mexican privateers. The latter never materialized.

Perhaps the most historically significant aspect of the war regarding American vessels involved the seizure by the United States of the

Custom House   *U. S. Sloop of War "Portsmouth"*
THE RAISING OF THE AMERICAN FLAG AND TAKING POSSESSION OF YERBA BUENA (SAN FRANCISCO), CAL.
By Commander John B. Montgomery, U. S. N., of the U. S. Sloop of War "Portsmouth", on the morning of July 9, 1846, by order of Commodore John Drake Sloat, U. S. N.
See Life of the Late Rear Admiral John Drake Sloat, U. S. N., by Major Edwin A. Sherman, Editor and Compiler, Secretary of the Sloat Monument Association, Oakland, Cal.
[Subscription Price for the Monument, Three Dollars.]

In one of the most historic events in the Mexican War, the USS Portsmouth *on the morning of July 9, 1846, sends several five-man-boat crews ashore to take possession of Yerba Buena (later San Francisco), California, and to raise the American flag. Portsmouth Plaza in modern-day San Francisco commemorates the ship. UNH*

Mexican province of Alta California, soon to be renamed California. The sloop *Portsmouth* played the most active naval role in this mission. Skippered by Commander John B. Montgomery, the *Portsmouth*, at anchor off Yerba Buena Cove, landed a party on the morning of July 9, 1846. At a square in front of Yerba Buena's Customs House, Montgomery's men raised the American flag as a twenty-one-gun salute from the *Portsmouth* echoed about the hills. After a short speech, Montgomery returned to the ship and issued a proclamation, stating in part: "In the event of an attack by the Mexicans or other forces upon Yerba Buena, all necessary assistance will be immediately landed from the United States ship *Portsmouth;* and in the meantime, your country expects . . . that every man will . . . defend the flag of the United States." In October 1846, the plaza was renamed Portsmouth Square, in honor of the ship. On March 10, 1847, the town of Yerba Buena was officially renamed San Francisco, employing the same name the Spanish had given the bay two and a half centuries earlier.[36]

When the Treaty of Guadalupe Hidalgo ended the Mexican War on February 2, 1848, the United States annexed a huge tract of northern Mexico, including California. The work of Montgomery and the *Portsmouth* remained intact; the United States Navy Yard on Mare Island in San Francisco Bay was established less than a decade later, becoming the first and most vital naval base on the Pacific coast.

During the 1850s and 1860s, other incidents and events vis-à-vis Mexico and Central America involved Portsmouth ships—notably relating to American filibusterer William Walker's meddling in Nicaragua, and an 1860 clash between the USS *Saratoga* and Mexican steamers south of Vera Cruz. But the most significant contribution of Portsmouth Navy Yard ships involved Japan. In 1849, the Yard ship *Preble* arrived in Nagasaki to rescue American seamen confined to a Japanese prison after the wreck of their ship, the whaler *Lagoda* of Plymouth, Massachusetts. The original fifteen prisoners were reduced to thirteen—one by suicide and another through natural causes. The *Preble* made a defiant show of strength, and the Japanese released the survivors.[37]

This incident increased pressure—which had been building since 1839—for the opening of Japan to the West. The American State Department, seeking to avoid subsequent squabbles in repatriating stranded or imprisoned American seamen, wanted to establish normal diplomatic relations and inaugurate commercial trade. Commodore Matthew C. Perry led this famous mission to Japan with seven warships, including Portsmouth's *Saratoga,* and negotiated the Treaty of Kanagawa in March 1854. Three months later, the *Journal* published a letter written by a naval officer who mentioned the *Saratoga*'s role in this mission and described the abundance of raw material and manufactured goods relative to "the purpose of commerce."[38]

Commerce was Portsmouth's economic lifeblood, and news of this treaty favorable to American business and shipping interests was received with great local acclaim. Perry returned to the United States as a national hero.

The Yard already had been forging ahead with the latest technology to remain competitive in a changing world of international commerce. In 1848, the year the Mexican War ended, the USS *Saranac,* the first Yard steamer, was launched amid great fanfare. "Let her go," cried the shipyard commander, as the ship slid down the ways and "set like a swan upon the water." In January 1850, her boilers were fired up and her engines started. Of this "chef d'oeuvre of Vulcan, dedicated to Mars," the *Journal* noted, "her engines are about of the same power as those used in Cunard steamers—700 horsepower . . . and will require from twenty-five to thirty tons of coal to keep them in operation twenty-four hours."[39]

Portsmouth Navy Yard ships and commandants also remained in the forefront in embracing and implementing naval social reforms. The issue of flogging finally was resolved, prompted by the efforts of Watson G. Haynes, a former seaman with nineteen years of service in the Navy, who lobbied Congress to elicit action. On September 25, 1850, the House of Representatives finally abolished the flogging of seamen.[40]

The benefits of the reform quickly became evident. *Journal* readers learned in early 1851 that the USS *St. Mary's,* the first naval ship to sail from the United States under the new law, experienced no difficulty in maintaining discipline: "Thus far our crew have shown that seamen are capable of being better governed by kindness than by the degrading severity of the old law." A report from an officer aboard the Yard ship *Congress,* writing from Montevideo, Uruguay, on April 23, 1851, reaffirmed the wisdom of this new policy: "Our ship is in high order and discipline, and it is gratifying to know that the new system of governing sailors, rendered by the 'doing away' with the lash has been found on board the *Congress* signally successful."[41]

Efforts to eliminate the grog ration aboard ship then gained momentum. The *Journal,* in "Spirit Rations and Flogging in the Navy," editorialized: "The free use of the liquor rations, which are given out at 8 and 12 o'clock every day, is the prime cause of most of the offenses which require punishment." Slowly this reform rid the Navy of inefficiency and indeed danger on the high seas. In 1855, Lieutenant David Dixon Porter, commanding the U.S. store-ship *Supply* on a voyage to the Near East to obtain camels, arranged that no grog would be permitted on board. Instead, the men received compensation for the liquor at a rate of six pence a day. The following year, the Yard ship USS *Portsmouth,* commanded by Andrew H. Foote, advanced this reform even further. "The *Portsmouth* is the first United States vessel that ever left Norfolk," reported the *Journal* on May 17, 1856, "having

entirely dispensed with the spirit rations by the voluntary arrangement of the crew."[42]

Try as they might, however, Yard and other naval ships could
make little headway against the long-festering evil of the slave trade.
In 1858, as reported by the *Journal,* a naval officer aboard the USS
Cumberland off the west coast of Africa observed: "Contrary to expec-
tations . . . the slave trade had been resumed with redoubled activity of
late, and most of it was done by American vessels under the American
flag; and most if not all in American-built ships—Boston doing rather
more than her share of the business."

While on her two-year cruise (1859–61), the *Portsmouth* compiled
an impressive list of accomplishments—sailing 50,000 miles, capturing three slavers, and, perhaps most important, negotiating a commercial treaty with a West African tribe. As a naval officer empowered
to conduct diplomacy in distant places in the absence of American
ambassadors or consuls, Commander John Colhoun of the *Portsmouth*
anchored off Ambrizette, Angola, in the spring of 1861. He went ashore
to conduct negotiations with the local tribal queen—an event attended
with great ceremony by many of the tribal elite. In quick order, "Articles of Agreement" were drafted, duly signed, and sealed. The treaty
consisted of four provisions. The first established that there would be
"peace and friendship between the Queen, her successors and subjects, and the U.S. and citizens." The second permitted American citizens to build factories there and granted trading rights with the
guarantee of protection "from assault by the subjects of the Queen."
The third allowed American ships to procure water from the river; the
fourth articulated the right of American merchants or agents residing
there to be fully protected from thieving and stipulated that articles
stolen would be returned or "compensation made for them." While the
one-sided treaty was slanted to protect American commercial interests, the document nevertheless represented a positive attempt to
respect the mercantile integrity and independence of the local people
and to conduct business matters honorably, not by seizure or intimi-
dation. Despite the treaty, however, the efforts of the *Portsmouth* and
other American warships failed to eradicate the slave trade. Resolution of that national problem would wrack the United States in the
1860s.[43]

The Yard remained a beehive of activity during the 1850s and into

Developed as a public works project by Lieutenant David D. Porter between 1858 and 1860, Gun and Shot Park displayed cannonballs and other ornamental weaponry. The park was opposite the Ordnance Building (right center), and the iron objects eventually were removed as scrap-metal salvage for the World War II military effort. UNH

1860, preparing for any eventuality. Its mission could not have been better stated than in an editorial, "The National Defenses—The Navy," which first appeared in the *Philadelphia Inquirer* and subsequently (March 8, 1856) was printed in the *Journal:* "The nation is constantly growing, its interests are constantly increasing, and its commerce is already of formidable extent. The Navy should be augmented accordingly. It should keep pace with the progress of the nation. . . . [W]e should . . . remember that wars do still occur among civilized nations, and that preparation is therefore a work of duty." The Yard accepted this ever-present challenge, its work of duty, by building and repairing ships and constructing new facilities.

"The whole island," commented the *Journal* in 1858, "has the appearance of a temple of industry." A three-story brick ordnance building was erected in 1857 at a cost of $21,000. A gun carriage shop was attached in 1860, prompting the *Journal* to comment on June 2: "Here may be seen all parts of the heavy gun frames, broadside gun carriages, sponges, rammers, powder buckets, shot bearers, artillery percussion locks, and a multitude of other articles now in common use on board of our national ships, all neatly arranged, and marked with the name of the vessel for which they are intended. A more beautiful display of the enginery of war cannot be found." That same year, an office building and a powder magazine were completed, the latter with walls forty inches thick and with a capacity of 5,000 casks of powder. A "submarine lantern" was tested in 1860. Anticipating modern trends, the Yard enforced a strict regulation: "It is an excellent rule of the Yard, that no smoking is allowed any where [sic], outside of private residences. Even the great smithery, where eight or ten forges are in fiery operation, seems under the smoking restrictions; for though without a visible chimney, yet not a puff of smoke is seen rising in the great room. Through subterranean avenues it escapes to some Vulcan parlor, such as smokers might inhabit without injury or annoyance to the outside world."[44]

In June 1855, the USS *Constitution,* better known as "Old Ironsides," sailed to the Yard. Condemned as unseaworthy, she was decommissioned shortly thereafter. In 1857, however, the Navy reversed its earlier decision and ordered the vessel overhauled and returned to active service. Restoration was to be done with the new facilities of the Yard. "The 'iron sides' are being stripped of most of their planking, the copper being entirely taken off," reported the *Journal* on August 29, 1857: "But little remains of the cherished old frame which has brought so much honor to the U.S. Navy. A few timbers and a piece of the keel of the old ship are all, besides the model, which warrant the name. A few more series of repairs, and all but the model will be gone." Finally,

U.S.S. FRIGATE SARANAC, off San Juan del Sur, NICARAGUA.

Built at the Yard in 1848, the frigate USS Saranac *is shown at San Juan del Sur, Nicaragua, en route to California, in late 1857. During the Civil War, the* Saranac *protected American commerce along the Pacific coast. UNH*

in 1860, the essentially rebuilt and recommissioned *Constitution* sailed from the Yard.[45]

For years, newspaper reporters and local people debated whether the government facility should be called the Portsmouth Navy Yard or the Kittery Navy Yard, occasioning a good-natured rivalry between the partisans of Portsmouth, New Hampshire, and Kittery, Maine. During the nineteenth century, such a distinction meant little and created no financial concern, since Yard workers paid no state income taxes. But having two names for the one Yard proved most inconvenient for one distinguished visitor in 1859, according to a narrative in the *Journal* reprinted from the *New York News:* "An English commander of the Royal navy has recently had a singular adventure here. Having visited several navy yards, among others Portsmouth, N.H., he returned to this city [New York], but found that the navy yard at Kittery, Maine, had escaped his notice. Accordingly he retraced his steps to Portsmouth, which city, he was surprised to find from the guide book, was quite near Kittery. On arriving at Portsmouth he ordered a cab to drive him to Kittery, and was still more astonished to be driven into the same navy yard which he visited some weeks before. On investigating the matter he found that Portsmouth, N.H., and Kittery, Me., were one and the same place, and his time and money were lost."[46]

The Civil War Transforms The Yard, 1861–1865

Two years later, there would have been little or no difficulty realizing that the Portsmouth Navy Yard and Kittery, Maine, were one installation. With the outbreak of the Civil War in 1861, the United States was changed—politically, constitutionally, and militarily—and transformed forever, as the federal North attempted to crush the Southern Confederacy that had seceded from the Union. Union navy yards expanded rapidly—Portsmouth in particular—to confront this national emergency.

During the four years of war, the Portsmouth Yard built twenty-six new ships, repaired many others, manufactured gun carriages, and maintained a receiving ship for recruiting. The Yard's civilian workforce jumped from 207 employees in 1860 to 2,563 in May 1865. Yard Marines assisted in quelling a major draft riot in Portsmouth in 1863. Newly liberated black sailors, known as contrabands, were stationed at the Yard as part of the Union naval force. The Yard built an ironclad ship and either pioneered or adopted technological innovations. A ring of forts around Portsmouth Harbor protected the Yard from surprise attack. The stirring times catapulted the Portsmouth Yard into the forefront as a major naval base for the Union cause.

"The large gang of workmen at the Navy Yard here," reported the *Portsmouth Chronicle* on May 6, 1861, "were employed on Sunday. War knows no Sabbaths." This frenzied boom time remained a concerted effort until war's end. Work commenced on the steamers *Kearsarge* and *Ossipee.* "This Station," commented the *Journal* in August, "so long

Built at the Boston Navy Yard in 1839, the USS Marion *was homeported at the Portsmouth Navy Yard intermittently for many years thereafter. "In ordinary" when the Civil War broke out in 1861, the* Marion *was repaired and recommissioned at the Yard that same year for blockade duty. PNSMVC*

neglected by the Government, now assumes its proper importance, as ships are built, fitted, repaired and sent to sea in as short a time, and as well as at any other Government establishment, and, if quality of work is considered, perhaps at less cost." On September 7, the *Journal* further described the Yard's erection of new buildings and ship construction, "which could hardly have been excelled at the erection of the ancient Temple at Jerusalem." To man these ships and facilities, Secretary of the Navy Gideon Welles issued directives to the Navy recruiting offices in Portsmouth and other northern seaports: "The travelling expenses of recruits from their residences to the rendezvous [receiving ships]," stated Welles, as reported in the *Chronicle* on December 28, "are allowed by the Government and an outfit valued at $31.27 furnished on board and charged for. Three months' advance [in salary] to seamen, and two months' advance to landsmen is allowed."[47]

The next year, the critical need to fill ship complements resulted in the adoption of a new naval policy. On April 30, 1862, Secretary Welles issued an order to accept blacks in the U.S. Navy: "The large number of persons known as 'contrabands' flocking to the protection of the U.S. flag affords an opportunity in every department of a ship especially for boats' crews, [and] acclimated labor. The flag-officers are required to obtain the services of these persons for the country by enlisting them freely in the navy, with their consent, rating them as boys, at $8, $9, or $10 per month, and one ration." Medical care, education, and furloughs were also included. It has been calculated that eventually black sailors comprised eight to twenty-five percent—estimates vary—of the total Union naval force. In November 1862, twenty contraband sailors arrived at the Yard aboard the USS *Minnesota*. During furloughs, at the request of the New Hampshire governor, they were housed in suitable Portsmouth boardinghouses. Local women acted as tutors, conducting reading classes for the men. Later in the war, black sailors built and garrisoned Fort Sullivan on Seavey's Island. Opening the Navy's ranks to contrabands proved successful. That same year of 1862 saw the passage of still another and long-sought-after reform—the abolition by Congress of the Navy spirit ration, thus ending the consumption of liquor aboard ship.[48]

Work continued throughout 1862 on various ships under construction, including the ironclad steamer *Agamenticus,* the steam sloop *Sassacus,* and the sidewheeler *Nipsic.* After a one-day strike in January 1862, labor relations improved at the Yard, and some 1,800 men were on the job by year's end. Defense of the Yard stiffened, with ever-tightening security from forts. News from the fishing communities on the strategically placed Isles of Shoals, six miles offshore, proved encouraging. A tax assessor making an official visit there "found the people loyal and patriotic, and . . . should a rebel dare invade Star Island, they would take him for fish-bait."[49]

Morale at the Yard remained high. "Some persons get the impression that the workmen on the Navy Yard," reported the *Chronicle* on October 17, "have no patriotism, and seek nothing but the attainment of their own selfish ends, but we will state that, to our personal knowledge, during the months of August and September scarcely a day passed, on which from one to a half a dozen persons did not request their discharge for the purpose of enlisting in the army. Many left places where there was a good prospect of a long job, and where their services were much needed. Some even left wages of $2.00 and $2.50 per day to enlist as privates at $13 per month."[50]

During 1863, acceleration of Yard improvements and ship construction continued unabated. Projects included numerous additions to existing buildings, a new reservoir, new machine shop and foundry, smithy, paint shop, boathouse, and carpenter's shop. A futtock saw mill for sawing crooked and beveled timber introduced mechanization, turning out ship's futtocks that previously had been worked out with an ax. The new buildings and technology had immediate results, as the *Chronicle* noted: ". . . the *Kearsarge,* carrying 7 guns and of 1031 tons burthen, which was constructed in 138 working days, the *Ossipee,* 9 guns, 1240 tons, building in 138 working days," and similar statistics for seven more ships. Twelve ships were repaired. Furthermore, these ships fulfilled their intended purpose: "Many of the vessels built . . . are now engaged in important duties—blockading southern ports and pursuing British rebel pirates." These impressive building statistics, and the resulting operations at sea, were still accomplished with the most efficient and cost-saving measures—subject to the watchful congressional eye and press criticism determined to make the Navy accountable for every cent expended. "If the stove pipe is lost from a cook's galley on a *man-of-war,"* reported the *Chronicle,* "certain [news]papers fall to abusing Sec. [Gideon] Welles."[51]

The diligence of Secretary Welles, the Navy, and the Portsmouth Navy Yard during 1864 was sapping the strength of the Confederacy through an ever-tightening blockade. Despite a yellow-fever epidemic at the Yard and environs in the summer of 1864, resulting in the deaths of about sixteen people, the work went on. The effort to build faster ships achieved success. "The first adventures of the [Southern raider CSS] *Alabama* so startled the commercial public," reported the *Journal,* "that there was a general outcry for fast war vessels. . . . [T]he Navy Department set at once to work to provide a fleet capable of overhauling and catching her." The Yard contributed the screw-sloop *Sacramento* and the sidewheel steamers *Sonoma, Mahaska, Conemaugh,* and *Sassacus.*[52]

Boston shipbuilder Donald McKay, a highly respected leader in maritime circles, publicly praised the Navy's effort: "The rebel coast

A mainstay in the United States Navy for more than half a century, the frigate Santee *was commissioned at the Yard in 1861. After Civil War blockade duty, the* Santee
served in Annapolis as a training ship for midshipmen from 1865 to 1912. UNH

has been held with a grasp of iron and nearly hermetically sealed. The
pirates of the enemy [Confederate raiders] have been followed round
the world and captured wherever they could be found."

To ensure adequate food supplies on the Union Navy's extended
cruises, the Yard maintained a storehouse—three floors of spacious
rooms to equip vessels fitting out and ready for sea. "We noticed several boxes labeled 'roast beef,'" noted the *Journal*. "These boxes are
filled with tin canisters hermetically sealed, each containing four
pounds of beef . . . which may be kept in this way for years. Other provisions, perishable on exposure to the air, are packed in like manner."
The Union blockade strangled the Southern economy, depriving the
Confederacy of food, war matériel, and diplomatic communication. Rel-

ative to the South's plight, an English military visitor commented on the appearance of Confederate General Pierre G.T. Beauregard, saying, "Beauregard's hair was getting very gray; the romantic attributed it to the anxiety of the last two years but the real reason is that the strictness of the blockade deprives him of dye."[53]

In addition to shutting off Beauregard's dye supply, the Union Navy and shipyards systematically destroyed the Confederate Navy, supply lines, and morale by capturing or sinking 1,504 Southern vessels. Yard vessels and naval captains participated in virtually every major and minor Civil War naval expedition—at Hampton Roads, Mobile Bay, Fort Fisher, and other locales much farther afield.

Perhaps the most important naval engagement of the Civil War occurred when the Yard's USS *Kearsarge* sank the British-built Confederate raider *Alabama,* commanded by Captain Raphael Semmes, in the English Channel off Cherbourg, France, on Sunday, June 19, 1864. "It was one of the greatest Naval engagement[s] on Record," wrote Carsten DeWit, a *Kearsarge* crewman, "as allowed by the Naval officers of the nations round here." In a letter written to his mother the day after the battle, *Kearsarge* Midshipman Edward E. Preble asserted: "One of the [Confederate] officers was a schoolmate of mine at the naval academy. He described the carnage on board his ship as terrific, and says she was a complete slaughter house." As the *Alabama* was sinking, Semmes and his men abandoned ship. Regarding Semmes's escape, Captain James S. Thornton, executive officer of the *Kearsarge,* recalled: "I was waiting impatiently for the order to come to fire on the English yacht *[Deerhound]* which had rescued Semmes from his sinking ship. I never for a moment doubted that such an order would be given. But it was not, and I felt so indignant that I almost lost self-control. I felt for awhile that it was a barren victory and that we had spent all our powder for nothing." Thanks to the skill of the *Kearsarge*'s gunners in this decisive battle, Semmes's naval career, despite Thornton's misgivings, was effectively over. Northern newspapers now referred to the once-proud Confederate hero as "Capt. Semmes of the British Neutral Service." With the loss of the *Alabama,* the Confederate Navy never recovered and the Union Navy grew stronger and more powerful.[54]

The Portsmouth Navy Yard's momentum continued during 1864. In addition to building and repairing ships, expanding the physical plant,

KEARSARGE

Undoubtedly the most renowned ship built at the Yard during the nineteenth century, the USS Kearsarge *in her post–Civil War career sailed to distant ports on diplomatic missions to advance American foreign policy. In 1894, she foundered on a reef and sank in the Caribbean. PNSY* and welcoming Secretary Welles during his September tour of inspection, the Yard achieved progress in other ways. The Yard frequently donated to charitable causes to aid the Union effort. During May 1864, as Grant's overland campaign was taking great casualties, the *Journal* reported: "The officers of the Yard, marines, seamen, workmen and laborers, have by general consent, without a dissenting voice, contributed one day's pay in aid of the sick and wounded soldiers of the Army in Virginia. This noble contribution will amount to nearly $5000." The Portsmouth Ladies' School, conducted on a voluntary basis to educate the contrabands stationed at Fort Sullivan, continued its successful efforts. Receiving two hours of instruction twice a week over ten months, the black sailors readily acquired proficiency in reading, writing, and arithmetic. "Your coming to us," said one of the men to his teachers, "has been like bringing us to the light from a dark room." For the Yard workers themselves, frigid temperatures resulted in a rare day off. Ever since 1841, if inclement weather occurred, a black ball would be hoisted on the flagstaff to notify the Yard workmen not to report for muster. On Friday morning, December 23, 1864, the thermometer read eight degrees below zero. "No work on the Navy Yard," reported the *Chronicle,* "the first ball-day for the winter." After a long stretch of uninterrupted seven-day weeks, the cold weather brought a well-deserved day of rest.[55]

The beginning of 1865 found the much-shrunken Confederacy, squeezed on land and at sea, on the verge of collapse as the Union Navy and the Yard continued to press without letup. Yard workmen repaired the USS *Minnesota*, damaged in the Fort Fisher fighting. The ironclad *Agamenticus* fired her engines and conducted outstanding sea trials. After the news of the surrender of Robert E. Lee's army reached Portsmouth on Monday, April 10, 1865, a spontaneous celebration seized the local populace and the Yard itself, "with vociferous cheers, the closing of stores, clanging of bells, booming of guns, and running hither and thither of everybody." Around noon, the Yard workmen assembled beneath the flagstaff and gave three hearty cheers for the Stars and Stripes. The Yard commandant thereupon informed them that work was suspended for the rest of the day. The Civil War had changed the Portsmouth facility almost beyond recognition, with many new buildings and facilities. Such a profusion in the number of ships sent to sea on blockade or cruising duty materially contributed to the Union naval victory and, in the process, transformed Portsmouth into a first-class yard.[56]

A popular literary and artistic theme in the North during the Civil War, the 1864 Kearsarge–Alabama sea battle was depicted in numerous paintings and lithographs. PNSMVC

A French painting, Combat du *Kearsage [sic] {right]* et de *Alabama [left], depicts the famed sea battle off Cherbourg, France. PNSMVC*

Hanging from the spars, the USS Portsmouth *ship's laundry dries in the opwn air. UNH*

In the 1870s or 1880s, the officers and crew of the USS Kearsarge *assemble on deck to observe Sunday services. During the post–Civil War era, the* Kearsarge *often returned to the Yard for repairs and overhaul between extended sailing voyages to foreign ports to advance American foreign policy. UNH*

HAIL TO THE KEARSARGE.

BY GEORGE W. BUNGAY.

Hail to the Kearsarge, castle of oak,
  And pride of the heaving sea!
Hail to her guns, whose thunder awoke
The waves, and startled with lightning stroke
  The nations that should be free!
          Hail to her captain and crew!
          Hail to her banner blue!
          Hail to her deathless fame!
          Hail to her granite name!

Haughty Britannia no longer can boast
  That she rules the ocean waves;
Her fame is dead, and its sheeted ghost
Stalks discrowned on her chalky coast,
  Mocked by Columbia's braves.
          Hail to the queen of the sea!
          Hail to the hopes of the free!
          Hail to the navy that spoke!
          Hail to our hearts of oak!

The British lion may cease his roar;
  For his darling privateer,
At sea a pirate, a thief on shore,
Now lies a wreck on the ocean floor,
  No longer a buccaneer.
          Hail to our Yankee tars!
          Hail to the stripes and stars!
          Hail to Winslow, chief of the sea!
          Hail to his victory!

Cheers!—"Two Ninety," the robber, is dead!
  And Semmes, the pirate-in-chief,
A swordless coward, defeated, has fled,
Bearing the curse of the sea on his head,
  To England, the home of the thief.
          Hail to our holy cause!
          Hail to our equal laws!
          Hail to our peace to be!
          Hail to our nations free!
                    —Independent.

After the Yard's USS Kearsarge *sank the CSS* Alabama *off the coast of France in 1864, Northern popular culture abounded with paintings, poems, and souvenirs celebrating the victory. "Hail to the Kearsarge"—patriotic, propagandistic doggerel typical of the time—commemorates the event.* Holyoke [Massachusetts] Transcript, *July 30, 1864.*

A Yard drover readies his oxen team, probably in 1865. Employed at the Yard from the earliest times, oxen power was standard for heavy work until as late as 1901, when a railroad spur into the Yard rendered such teams obsolete. PNSY

Desiring to preserve the image of the Yard for history, the Davis Brothers, well-known Portsmouth photographers, crossed the river in August 1865 to "this great manufactory of the paraphernalia of war." From the tower of the office building (now Building 13), they filmed the scene below, with panoramic views of the buildings "giving a picture of the entire Yard, together with the surrounding country for miles away."[57]

Victory brought peace to the nation, but it did not guarantee the economic stability of the military installations across the United States. A new battle loomed to maintain the active status of the Yard. Without a steady stream of contracts or appropriations from Washington, the Yard again was subject to closure. Less than two months after the end of the war, the *Journal* on May 27, 1865, grimly articulated this reality, as well as its impact on the community: "About seven hundred and fifty Navy Yard workers were discharged from the Yard on Monday and Tuesday [May 22-23] of this week. This number includes carpenters, borers, joiners, spar makers, calkers, gunner's riggers, machinists,

*View of Shot and Gun Park (left center) and the Ordnance Building (right center)
from the cupola of the Administration Building at the end of the Civil War in 1865.
PNSMVC*

watchmen, boat-builders, smiths, yard carpenters and sail makers. Discharges from other departments are soon to follow, which will reduce the force about 33 per cent. The suspension of so large a number of workingmen will necessarily affect the interests of this city, and a reduction in prices of rents must immediately ensue."[58]

The Beginning of the Doldrums, 1865–1877

The doldrums of the Yard persisted until 1898, when the Spanish-American War erupted. For more than three decades, the United States government, the average citizen, and the press—satisfied the Civil War had been won—had directed their attention elsewhere: to the westward movement, Reconstruction, industrial expansion, and the mania for making money. During the Gilded Age, the Navy and its yards battled for congressional appropriations, contracts, and even self-respect.

Without the exigency of a major foreign war, the Portsmouth Navy Yard struggled along, cutback by cutback, with a diminishing number of employees. On March 26, 1870, the *Journal* captured the mood that dominated this era of public indifference and neglect: "About 200 men have been discharged from the Navy Yard this week. The necessities of the [Navy] service always have and always will require these constant changes in the number of employees. When the government wants work done it hires men to do it and pays them good wages. When the jobs are finished the men are discharged. This has always been the case, no matter which political party is in power."[59]

Even before Secretary of the Navy Gideon Welles left his post in March 1869, he saw the erosion of his efforts to maintain an adequate navy. By May 1868, responding to congressional pressure that the U.S. Navy fleet be dismantled, he reported that 300 government vessels had been sold since the end of the war. In August of that year, the Yard sold at auction six steamers, including the blockading steamer *Maratanza,* for $32,000. In May 1869, the Navy Department advertised "the iron side-wheel steamer '*MUSCOOTA*' [sic] for sale at auction" at the Portsmouth Yard: "The vessels and their inventories can be examined at any time on application to the commandants at the respective yards. The whole amount of the purchase money must be deposited at the time of adjudication, and the vessels must be removed from the Navy Yards within two weeks from the day of sale."[60]

Gideon Welles's successor, Navy Secretary George M. Robeson, was an unfortunate choice for President Ulysses S. Grant's cabinet. Described in a widely quoted contemporary assessment as "a first-rate judge of wines, a second-rate trout-fisherman, and a third-rate New Jersey lawyer," Robeson, it was implied, would make a fourth-rate sec-

Commandant of the Yard between 1864 and 1867, Rear Admiral Theodorus Bailey (shown here as captain) and his wife Sarah Ann Platt hosted military and social functions at Quarters A. Bailey's tenure at the Yard coincided with post–Civil War reductions and downsizing. Frost Collection

retary. Believing in a "great repair" policy, Robeson managed to usher expensive overhaul programs through Congress to keep navy yards busy with plenty of work, especially Republican Yard employees during election years. Stockpiling also kept navy yard storehouses full of materials purchased from friendly Republican suppliers. Despite his extravagance, Robeson was for the most part favorably received around the New Hampshire seacoast area. He was a familiar figure on Portsmouth streets, maintaining a summer home nearby at fashionable Little Boar's Head. An 1871 official visit to the Yard reflected Robeson's style. Appearing with an entourage of senators and naval dignitaries, he arrived at Quarters A, the commandant's residence, for a gala reception. With officers in full-dress uniform and numerous visitors and ladies on the lawn, as the *Journal* reported, "The entire Marine Corps were [was] drawn up in line, and music furnished by the Marine Band. . . . An elegant entertainment was served at the residence of the Commandant."[61]

The press was not oblivious to Robeson's high-flying conduct. "There is some talk at Washington of combining the Secretaryships of War and Navy to one office," reported the *Journal* in 1870. "Of late years the Secretary of the Navy has done but little except draw his salary, and arrange for pleasant excursions in our national vessels." Suspicion of Robeson's management of his office resulted in a congressional investigation in 1876 that reported him "guilty of carelessness, extravagance, and lawlessness, but . . . no direct evidence of corruption." Despite the probe, and his alleged acceptance of $300,000 in bribes, Robeson served out his term. After he left office in 1877, the *Journal* defended Robeson's repair record, especially the money expended to repair the *Kearsarge*: "The cost, originally, certainly was not extravagant, and her *[Kearsarge's]* age and service doubtless required that repairs of an extensive character should be made on her. . . . [T]he noble vessel was a good investment. But the idea of charging the late ex-Secretary of the Navy with being responsible for 'the rotten hulks of the Navy,' built years before he was in office, seems indeed novel. Ships decay and wear out."[62]

Despite this awkward period in American naval history, a number of positive accomplishments improved the operation of the Yard. In July 1868, the federal eight-hour day went into effect at navy yards. Nearly a year later (June 1869), the Navy Department contacted Kittery, Maine, authorities to request the use of Wood Island in the harbor to quarantine arriving U.S. vessels.

The Kittery officials approved, thereby providing a safe area to curb the spread of yellow fever should a vessel arrive with infected passengers. In 1872, Secretary Robeson ordered an important reform: abolition of the long-established custom of putting seamen in irons for most offenses against naval discipline. Punishment by confinement in double irons was judged too severe and was to be carried out only in incorrigible cases.[63]

Physical improvements included the laying of slate walks around the Yard, with the stone coming from a Lebanon, Maine, quarry. During the early 1870s, the Yard built two new steam vessels, USS *Essex* and USS *Enterprise,* under contract by the noted ship construction architect John W. Griffiths.[64]

As the centennial of the United States approached, the Navy Department in 1873 selected Captain George H. Preble to write the his-

Launched at the Yard in 1874, the USS Essex, *a wooden screw steamer and sister ship to the USS* Enterprise, *was towed to the Boston Navy Yard for her machinery and commissioned there two years later. These two Yard vessels marked the end of the wooden ship construction era, soon replaced by the "Steel Navy." PNSMVC*

tory of the Portsmouth and Boston Navy Yards. Preble, however, failed to complete his manuscript in time, and Walter E.H. Fentress assumed the task. A Navy veteran, Fentress published his book in time for the national celebration in 1876, highlighted by the World's Fair in Philadelphia. On the last page of *Centennial History of the United States Navy Yard at Portsmouth, N.H.* (1876), Fentress stressed the importance of the Portsmouth Yard: "A station having so good a record, and possessing so many peculiar advantages, we doubt not will be cherished by the Government, till developed and furnished with means for constructing the finest of ships." Local newspapers praised the book for offering, in the words of the *Journal*'s reviewer, "a compilation of much that has never before been offered to the public. . . . The prominent part which this port took in the early naval history of our country will make

View of the Navy Yard waterfront in 1883 features the Franklin Shiphouse (center) and a forest of masts of wooden ships—a scene soon to be replaced by the "Steel Navy." PNSMVC

the perusal of the work a matter of much interest on this our Centennial year throughout this country, especially among naval people."[65]

But the nation's centennial year was not a holiday or a time of celebration for the Navy or its shipyards. Since March 1874, the legislative branch of the United States government had failed to support the Navy sufficiently, and Congress had tightened the purse strings. "THE PROPOSITION TO ABOLISH CERTAIN NAVY YARDS," read one 1875 *Journal* headline. "There is a bill now pending before the Committee on Naval Affairs of the House to abolish the Navy Yards at Kittery, Boston, and New London. It was introduced by Mr. [Washington C.] Whitthorne of Tennessee, and his theory is that, in time of peace, there is no necessity of these yards." Such lack of legislative support was reflected in Admiral David D. Porter's year-end report. "OUR NAVY RETROGRADING," headlined the *Journal's* story that deplored the situation at hand, "showing to what a wretched condition the navy has been reduced." By January 1874, Whitthorne raised the already lofty stakes. "Chairman Whitthorne," reported the *Journal* on January 8, "will recommend the abolition of the marine corps, the sale of all

Built at the Yard by John W. Griffith, a private contractor, the screw sloop-of-war Enterprise *was launched in 1874. Her most important naval service occurred between 1883 and 1886, when she sailed around the world on a three-year hydrographic survey. UNH*

wooden vessels, and the entire abolition of the navy yards at Kittery, Charlestown [Boston], New London, and Washington." Reacting to a threat to their area's economic livelihood, Portsmouth citizens were incredulous—indeed, angered—that a Southern congressman, an ex-Confederate Army officer, would be shaping and directing naval policy. The Portsmouth press hammered away at Whitthorne: "Why a man from Tennessee is made chairman of the Naval Committee . . . we cannot ascertain. Whitthorne's treasonable disabilities [Confederate service] were removed by an act of Congress a few years ago. . . . He thinks the Navy helped put down the rebellion, and now the reconstructed rebels should help to put down the Navy."[66]

Speeches in Congress, newspaper editorials, and much hot air on both sides of the issue continued through most of 1876. "The abandonment of so many navy yards," argued the *Worcester Gazette* in its May 27 editorial, "Penny Wise, Pound Foolish," as quoted in the *Journal,* "is

part of the shortsighted, weak-minded policy of pretended entrench-
ment which had gained control this year of so many legislative and
municipal bodies." In mid-July, shortly after the news of Custer's defeat
reached the East, the *Journal* sarcastically reported: "The recent vote
of the confederate House of Representatives at Washington to disman-
tle the Navy, is evidently an attempt to capture by indirection that
which they failed to obtain by open revolt." [67]

In his annual report in December, Secretary Robeson admitted:
"Our Navy at present cannot be regarded as large or powerful, but it is
at least respectable in extent, and seems to be in a fair condition. . . .
In the opinion of the Secretary, the Department has been unduly crippled by the scanty appropriations for the present year." It was not until
after Christmas in 1876 that Portsmouth citizens were relieved of the
anxiety under which they had been laboring. "RETENTION OF
PORTSMOUTH NAVY YARD," read the *Journal* headline on December 30, 1876. "The naval committee . . . recommended that this yard be
retained" for four reasons: its building and repair record, the ice-free
harbor, a quarantine station, and skilled workmen. "They [the commit-
tee] recommend that the yard should have a sufficient force of officers
and employees kept on duty to maintain it in the most efficient condition and ready for any emergency." The Yard workforce numbered 160
employees in 1876, but that figure dipped to a mere 71 in 1877.
Although reduced to its smallest workforce since 1851, the Yard survived the legislative cutbacks—but just barely.[68]

The "Steel Navy," 1877–1897

The short-range battle had been won, but the United States Navy, the
Portsmouth Navy Yard, and naval personnel realized that to ensure its
long-term survival, the service needed to adapt and adjust. Despite the
Panic of 1877, the Depression of 1893, and the changes of administration in Washington, the Navy moved forward to modernize with the latest technology. It also used shrewd public relations by entertaining the
incumbent secretary of the Navy, even the president of the United
States, on inspection tours. Thanks to the vision of New Hampshire's
William E. Chandler, Navy secretary during the Chester Arthur
administration, the Navy embraced a "steel navy" policy, thereby eliminating or retiring obsolete wooden vessels. As became increasingly

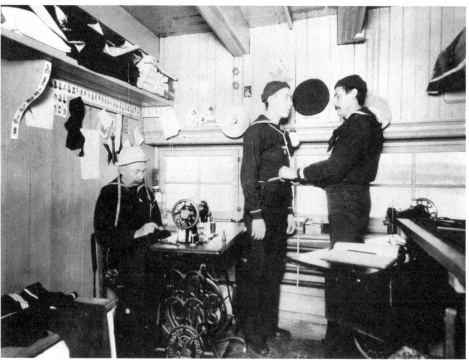

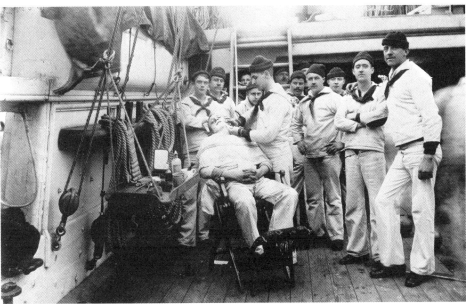

Posed images reflecting the good life aboard the Yard-built USS Enterprise in the 1880s seem to suggest a Navy recruiting campaign: tailors at their sewing machines provide a custom fit and instant service; berth-deck cooks ladle out soup; and a barber administers a close shave. UNH

apparent, the United States Navy, tending to fall asleep during a long period of peace, needed to expand its vision globally.

Even tracking the weather at the Yard had assumed international implications. In January 1878, a Yard officer each day at 7:35 A.M. made and recorded "proper and careful observations of atmospheric pressure, temperature, wind, rain, thermometer and the weather," for submission to the worldwide system of meteorological observations. American economic concerns were also linked to naval power. In "Present Condition of Our Navy," reprinted in the *Journal* on May 5, 1877, a *New York Tribune* analyst decried the weak condition of the United States Navy, touching on its economic ramifications: "As an illustration of the benefits to be derived from an efficient navy, it is mentioned that in 1848 our trade with Africa amounted to $12,000,000 per annum, while that of Great Britain amounted to about $5,000,000. In 1873 our trade had dwindled down to less than $1,000,000 per annum, while the English trade had increased to over £[probably $]12,000,000, and that trade owes its existence to the protection afforded by the British navy. A few days ago an American vessel . . . was attacked by natives at the mouth of the Congo River, and the crew were rescued by an English cruiser, there being no American vessels in these waters. Old officers argue that we are losing our commerce all over the world for the want of a navy to properly police the seas. The only commerce of any consequence we now have is with Cuba, and that is falling off every day."[69]

Worldwide American trade, with economic and military interests inexorably linked, prompted Republican and Democratic administrations alike to modernize the U.S. Navy. Rumors abounded that shipyards might be closed; appropriations occasionally were cut, but the Navy, seizing on the importance of public relations, overcame this shortsightedness, managing to place ships in the right place at the right time. Even ex-President Ulysses S. Grant, during his 1877–79 round-the-world tour, availed himself of the Navy's presence and hospitality. On December 25, 1877, he and his party had Christmas dinner on board the USS *Vandalia,* in Palermo, Italy. During the 1860s, the *Vandalia* had been the Portsmouth Yard's receiving ship, and the occasion was hosted by two naval officers formerly stationed at the Yard.[70]

During the early 1880s, modern technology provided major advances for the Navy and the Yard. In late January 1882, the Navy Department ordered the Yard connected to Portsmouth by telephone, uti-

Men's reading room at the Billiard Hall provided off-duty relaxation for enlisted men and officers. UNH

lizing the Boston & Northern exchange. By February 28, the telephone service was operational. The next month brought the first fledgling efforts to establish a steel navy. Congressman Benjamin Winslow Harris of Massachusetts, chairman of the Committee on Naval Affairs, presented the House of Representatives with a bill authorizing and directing Secretary of the Navy William H. Hunt "to construct six cruising vessels of war of open-hearth steel of domestic manufacture, having a tensile strength of not less than 55,000 nor more than 60,000 pounds to the square inch." On April 12, 1882, William E. Chandler of New Hampshire replaced Hunt as Navy secretary, to the acclaim of the Portsmouth press. On April 15, the *Journal* editorialized: "He [Chandler] is, we think, one of the brightest and most brilliant men New Hampshire has ever produced, and will make one of the ablest members of President Arthur's Cabinet. . . . He will prove a wise and faithful advisor, and administer the

Outside view of the USS Constitution.

affairs of the Navy Department in a manner creditable to himself, his native State, and the Administration."[71]

A shrewd, often calculating politician known as the "Stormy Petrel," Chandler proceeded to dive into his duties. By August, Congress authorized plans for two steel cruisers and seven months later voted appropriations for constructing them. For some time, the Portsmouth Yard sought to relocate the USS *Constitution,* "Old Ironsides," then laid up "in ordinary" at the Brooklyn Navy Yard. In May 1882, only two months after assuming his post, Chandler applied pressure to bring the ship back to Portsmouth. Upon receiving a petition presented by a Portsmouth businessman, New Hampshire Congressman Edward Henry Rollins responded to his constituent: "I presented it [the petition] to the secretary of the navy, and asked him to arrange to have the old *Constitution* go to Portsmouth. He says he will do something for the yard in that direction as early as possible. We will push the matter." The lobbying attempt was successful, and the *Constitution* ultimately arrived at the Yard on October 27 to be refitted and then retained as a receiving ship, anchored between Kittery and Pumpkin Island.[72]

The USS Tallapoosa *performed valuable service as a dispatch steamer for the Navy Department during the Gilded Age. On September 4, 1882, the* Tallapoosa *arrived at the Yard carrying Navy Secretary William E. Chandler, who conducted a thorough inspection of the naval facility. PA*

Chandler also believed in on-the-spot inspections, and he conducted frequent trips to the yards under his jurisdiction. In early September, he arrived at the Portsmouth Yard aboard the USS dispatch steamer *Tallapoosa,* the vessel flying the broad pennant of the secretary of the Navy for three days. Chandler conducted a thorough inspection, including calling out the fire department so he could judge its efficiency. He also went to Wood Island to inspect the quarantine hospital. On September 8, President Chester A. Arthur arrived in the Portsmouth Lower Harbor aboard the USS *Despatch.* Chandler, the Yard commandant, other Yard officers, and local business leaders entertained Arthur during the next two days, fully apprising him of Portsmouth's and the Yard's roles and activities. Following Chandler's tour of the northern navy yards, the *Army and Navy Register* commented: "It is said by the officers who accompanied him that it was

In 1884, crewmen of the USS Thetis *employed sled dogs to rescue members of the ill-fated Adolphus Greely expedition in the Canadian Arctic; the eight survivors were transported to the Yard. PNSMVC*

throughout a business trip and not a mere junketing excursion. A bureau officer says that it is doubtful whether the yards have been so thoroughly inspected as by Secretary Chandler this year. He has accumulated a large amount of valuable information, and we have no doubt that the result will be advantageous to the Navy." There were the usual rumors that several yards might close, but Chandler in his annual report refuted such misleading talk. The "Stormy Petrel" served until the end of Arthur's term in 1885. Although perhaps heavyhanded in his dealings, he had firmly established the new program of steel construction as his legacy.[73]

Perhaps Chandler's greatest achievement in the eyes of the general public was not his steel-navy promotion but rather his role in rescuing the American survivors of the ill-fated USS *Jeannette* expedition to the Arctic. In response to rumors that the explorers had been left

Greeley Cottage, Portsmouth Navy Yard

With his exploring party of twenty-five men reduced by starvation and exposure in the Canadian Arctic, Army Lieutenant Adolphus W. Greely and seven survivors were rescued and arrived at the Yard on August 1, 1884, via rescue ship. Their recuperation was speedy at the "Greely Cottage," the name given to their quarters on Seavey's Island. UNH

stranded without reinforcements of supplies and food, Chandler secured a supplemental appropriation from Congress and sent a three-ship rescue party to Cape Sabine to pick up the near-starving survivors—Lieutenant Adolphus W. Greely of the Army Signal Corps, leader of the expedition, and seven of his crew. Amid great fanfare, accompanied by national press coverage throughout the summer of 1884, the men arrived aboard the USS *Thetis* at the Portsmouth Navy Yard at 2 P.M. on Friday, August 1. During the days that followed, Secretary Chandler participated in the greetings, receptions, and a parade witnessed by 15,000 people. "The members of the press," observed the *Journal,* "were offered every facility by Secretary Chandler to witness the naval reception to Lieutenant Greely." After the expedition's survivors had recuperated at the Yard, the Arctic heroes received a tumultuous welcome in New York. Chandler's careful orchestration of these events meant the Navy received its most favorable publicity for peacetime, nonmilitary service since the Civil War.[74]

When Democrat Grover Cleveland was elected president in a

*Rescued by a naval expedition sent to the Canadian Arctic, the Greely party sur-
vivors arrived at the Yard amid great fanfare on August 1, 1884. Lieutenant
Adolphus W. Greely of the U.S. Army, leader of the ill-starred exploring party,
stands with his seated comrades during recuperation from their ordeal at Greely
Cottage. PNSY*

narrow election in November 1884, Portsmouth's hopes for a New
Hampshire successor to Chandler as Navy secretary centered on former congressman and local business tycoon Frank Jones. Responding
to a story that Cleveland had offered the post to Jones, the *Journal*
commented: "Mr. Jones would completely fill the bill, and we do not
doubt that . . . the interests of the Department would be sharply
looked after." As it turned out, however, William C. Whitney, a New
York banker, was appointed to the job. Like Chandler, Whitney naturally favored his home state for naval contracts, and he steered contracts toward the Brooklyn Navy Yard. Still, he perceived the overall
naval picture, remaining fully committed to carrying on Chandler's
work to create a steel navy and to completing his predecessor's half-
finished vessels. In July 1885, he invited naval officers to submit
plans to him for steel cruisers. "According to the Report of the Chief

Naval Constructor," the *Journal* reported on January 1, 1887, "ten years will wind up the life of every wooden vessel now in the Navy." During the late 1880s, the Chandler–Whitney steel cruisers *Chicago, Dolphin,* and *Atlanta* were completed and joined the fleet. Whitney also pursued newer and more efficient practices in his official duties. As the *Journal* reported on August 27, 1887, "Secretary Whitney arrived at Bar Harbor on Wednesday [August 24] evening by train from Boston. He said to a reporter, who asked him why he did not come on the *Despatch* from Portsmouth [Navy Yard], 'Life is too short for travel on that ship.'"[75]

Although Portsmouth did not build any of the new steel cruisers, these ships were frequent visitors to the Yard, prompting older sailors to feel nostalgic for the wooden-ship era. As the *Journal* reported on August 13, 1887, "The U.S.S. *Atlanta,* one of the new steel cruisers, arrived in the lower harbor Monday evening. She presents a wide departure in personal appearance from the old type of wooden sloop of war, and a still wider [divergence] in regard to fighting strength and usefulness. Sailors however will long continue to mourn the loss of beauty sustained in the effort to make these vessels simply 'fighting machines.'" Whitney had no sentiment for the past or American tradition, and he even purchased European plans and English ship designs. During his administration, the Navy laid down thirty ships of more than 100,000 tons, including the earliest battleships. In his annual report in 1888, Whitney admitted that, "in March, 1885 the Navy had no vessel of war which could have kept the seas for one week as against any first-rate naval power." By the time he left office in March 1889, he had kept his promise to revolutionize the United States Navy.[76]

It appears doubtful, however, that even the most modern American naval ship then afloat could have completely withstood the disaster that befell the United States naval vessels at Samoa on March 16, 1889. As the United States, Great Britain, and Germany were contending for sovereignty of the islands as coaling stations, a savage storm struck the area, wrecking ships and drowning crews—fifty Americans and ninety-six Germans. Almost a month after the event, Portsmouth citizens read American Admiral Lewis A. Kimberly's belated report, a cablegram sent from Auckland, New Zealand, mentioning the fate of the Portsmouth-built USS *Nipsic* and the USS *Vandalia,* the Yard's former receiving ship. "Hurricane at Apia [now

Notwithstanding the advent of the "Steel Navy," a photograph (ca. 1890) of the Yard waterfront provides a last nostalgic glimpse of two unidentified wooden vessels (extreme left and center foreground), with Shiphouses 4 and 5 in the background. UNH

Samoa], March 16. Every vessel in the harbor is on shore except the English man-of-war *Calliope,* which got out to sea. The *Trenton* and *Vandalia* are total losses. The *Nipsic* was beached, rudder gone, and may be towed, but the chances are against it. Will send her to Auckland, if possible. The *Vandalia* lost 4 officers and 39 men. . . . The *Nipsic* lost seven men." Assessing the impact of this natural calamity, the *Journal* editorialized: "This disaster is the most serious that the American Navy has encountered for many years."[77]

As it turned out, the *Nipsic* was refloated, her engines were repaired, and she was completely rebuilt in Hawaii. Otherwise, for the rest of 1889 and continuing well into the 1890s, the Portsmouth Yard limped along at best, with meager appropriations and few contracts, suffering with the rest of the nation from the Panic of 1893 and the ensuing depression. The Yard was adequately supplied by the York branch of the Boston & Maine Railroad and water transport communications as it waited for work. Some projects, moreover, were finished. A new three-story brick hospital was completed in 1891. In 1896, the Yard was ordered to build "one twenty-eight-foot steam cutter, two twenty-six-foot cutters, one twenty-eight-foot whale boat, one eighteen-foot dinghy, and one ten-foot punt, also all the spars, ditty boxes, blocks, fixtures, and furniture," for two United states gunboats being built at the Bath (Maine) Iron Works. For fittings on the new gunboats, Augustus Stevenson of Kittery, a former boatbuilder at the Yard, received a government contract to install his patented improved oarlocks. Stevenson reduced the noise "by the placing of a rubber guard in the oarlock so that the oars work on the rubber." The new oarlocks enabled boats to "move about at night without making a particle of noise, even though ten oars be worked to propel the boats."[78]

Whether or not contracts or inventions were forthcoming, changes in political administrations invariably meant upheavals in the Yard's workforce. In 1893, Secretary of the Navy Hilary A. Herbert of the second Cleveland administration dismissed (or, in Gilded Age parlance, "removed") eight Yard clerks because they were Republicans. Since the clerks' classification did not fall under the recent Civil Service Act, the *Journal* naturally was disappointed that Herbert did not honor the spirit of the Civil Reform Act and leave the unprotected clerks secure in their jobs. Instead, he acted as a spoilsman. "But it is understood," the *Journal* continued, "that the only charge which was preferred against them [the dismissed clerks] was that of being Republicans, and that every one of the men appointed to succeed them is a Democrat, or as the spoilsmen love to say, 'in sympathy with the administration.' It will be a bright day for the Portsmouth Navy Yard when it ceases altogether to be a football of politics." The next year, Herbert discharged fourteen Yard workers, all of whom received a form with a blank space or two filled in: "U.S. NAVY DEPARTMENT, Washington, June 20[,1894]. Sir: In view of the fact that your services are no longer required as———in the Department of———Navy Yard, Portsmouth, N.H. you are hereby discharged, to take effect upon the receipt of this communication. Very respectfully, H.A. HERBERT, Secretary of the Navy." The *Journal* angrily listed "the victims of this most summary decapitation."[79]

Deck view of the USS Constitution, *which served as a receiving ship, floating museum, and social function center between 1882 and 1897. Sailing to Boston on September 19, 1897, "Old Ironsides" remained in port there, becoming a prime tourist attraction. PA*

It is perhaps ironic that as the century drew to a close, local press interest in the Yard seemed relatively uninspired with the new steel navy, yet it was enamored with a symbol of the past, the wooden "Old Ironsides," which had been at the Yard since 1882. Decked over to serve as a receiving ship, the old relic created great local interest, frequently visited and photographed. Eventually she was converted into a floating museum and used for social functions. Over the years, rumors circulated that she would be towed to Washington, Annapolis, or elsewhere, while local politicians, especially former Congressman Frank Jones, fought to keep the old ship at the Yard. In 1888, the *Journal* minced no words when declaring why the *Constitution* should remain at the Yard in order to attract and train local and New England recruits: "There should be a receiving and recruiting vessel in commission and permanently stationed at this navy yard. The men shipped here in former years were much the best, on the whole, in the service, consisting as they largely did, of hardy fishermen, who took to naval life and discipline as naturally as they did to salt water. Although fewer men were shipped than on the 'guardos' [receiving ships for enlisted men who are to be drafted for seagoing vessels] stationed at the large cities of the country, they were mentally and morally much the superior of the class of men recruited at the other stations, most of whom have proved to be the veritable scum of the earth, a constant source of annoyance and disgrace, and of about as much use to a ship as the wake she leaves behind her."[80]

But the *Constitution*'s value as a receiving ship and museum at the Portsmouth Yard was outweighed and overruled by the Navy to accommodate the Boston Navy Yard, which planned a centennial celebration for the ship. In the autumn of 1897, the USS *Constitution* sailed away from Portsmouth, returning only for a brief port call thirty-four years later. The *Journal* described the departure: "The historic frigate *Constitution* left this navy yard at half-past one o'clock on Monday [September 19] afternoon in tow of the tugs *Leyden* and *Piscataqua*. Commander [Samuel W.] Very, U.S.N., was in charge of the vessel, which was bound to Boston to participate in the one hundredth anniversary of her launching [which occurred on October 21, 1797] at that port." The ship would become a leading Boston-area tourist attraction and a symbol of the United States Navy.[81]

Indeed, the country as a whole showed little initiative in 1897 to promote the United States Navy. John D. Long, the new secretary of the Navy in the William McKinley administration, was a typical political appointee for this cabinet position. A Maine native who became governor of Massachusetts, he had admitted to his chief that he had "no special attitude for the Navy." On an official visit to the Portsmouth Yard in the summer of 1897, Secretary Long and his party arrived aboard the USS *Dolphin* and traveled about the Yard on an inspection tour. "The secretary was much impressed by what he saw," commented the *Journal,* "and . . . he plainly showed his surprise at the capacity of the plant and the high state of efficiency in which he found everything, in spite of the fact that the yard had been practically shut down for a number of years." The relative weakness and status of the United States Navy among world powers was common knowledge. "Our navy on paper stands fifth in strength among the navies of the world," noted the *Journal*. "The order is: Great Britain, France, Russia, Italy, the United States, Germany, et al. . . . only six of our armored ships are still serviceable." Even such an astute observer as former Navy Secretary William E. Chandler, senator from New Hampshire since 1887, had succumbed to this lackadaisical attitude. In reacting to the impending American annexation of Hawaii and the advisability of enlarging the Navy, Chandler stated publicly during the summer of 1897: "The future power of the United States will not lie in the navy. . . . If we want a navy, we can get one. If a war came in which Italy, for instance, was not concerned, we could buy the whole Italian navy in 24 hours."[82]

During the fall of 1897, the Yard was still relying on antiquated communications, even utilizing carrier pigeons. Released from Admiral Montgomery Sicard's fleet in Boston, four birds traveled to their cote in the Yard at thirty-four miles per hour, giving the position of the fleet.

Portsmouth needed to look beyond Chandler, Long, and carrier pigeons for leadership and guidance into the twentieth century. "Teddy Roosevelt will be very popular [as the new assistant secretary of the Navy] with the navy and has apparently at least found his vocation," reported the *Journal* on September 18, 1897. "There is little doubt that he will have great influence in securing the increase of the naval establishment that is needed to hold our own with the great nations of the world and maintain our prestige and power in the affairs of the western hemisphere."[83]

War Jolts the Yard, 1898

A cataclysmic event in early 1898 shook the world. "Destruction of Battleship *Maine*," read the *Journal* headline in February 1898: "The whole country was thrilled [filled?] with horror on Wednesday [February 16, 1898] with the news that the U.S. battleship *Maine* was blown up and completely destroyed in Havana harbor on the night of Tuesday[,] Feb. 15th, at 10:45 P.M." This explosion, the cause of which has never been satisfactorily resolved, catapulted the nation into world-power status, with accompanying global commitments and responsibilities. The thirty-three-year era of peace was over. The United States, the Navy, and its shipyards awoke abruptly from its slumber.[84]

Within a few months, the Yard was bolstering its coastal defenses, sending its Marines to the Caribbean to confront the Spanish, and building a prison camp to accommodate Spanish naval prisoners of war. This "splendid little war," in Secretary of State John Hay's words, resulted in many American territorial annexations. By any measure, it was one of the most tumultuous events in American, even world, history. The philosophical underpinning of this mania for expansion—whether called imperialism, jingoism, Manifest Destiny, or the "white man's burden"—was articulated in the nation's popular literature in a craving for more territory, more coaling stations, and more economic and military power. Expounding such chauvinism in his poetry, Richard Hovey, an 1885 graduate of Dartmouth College, composed bombastic verses about the U.S. Navy, the *Maine* sinking, and the Battle of Manila Bay. In July 1898, *Harper's* magazine published Hovey's poem "Unmanifest Destiny" (for which he received $20), in which he predicted what he believed to be the inevitable future of the United States. The last stanza reads:

> I do not know beneath what sky
> Nor on what seas shall be thy fate;
> I only know it shall be high,
> I only know it shall be great.[85]

The Portsmouth Navy Yard and the country, inflamed by the *Maine* sinking, quickly sought revenge with the popular slogan, "Remember the *Maine*." Within days after the incident, the Kearsarge Association of Naval Veterans in Portsmouth passed a unanimous resolution offering its services to the president in the event of war. A copy was sent to President William McKinley. Toward the end of the month, a Sunday service was held at the Second Christian Church in Kittery in memory of the dead of the USS *Maine,* with many Yard officers and men in attendance.[86]

On April 25, 1898, Congress declared war on Spain. Even before the formal declaration of war was voted, though, preparations were underway at the Yard in case of a military emergency. On Monday, April 19, a detachment of thirty-nine of the Yard's Marines, commanded by Captain William F. Spicer and Second Lieutenant Melville J. Shaw, departed on the 2:38 P.M. train to report for duty at the Brooklyn Navy Yard. This stripped the Yard of most of the men in the Marine Barracks. A week later, a second contingent of twenty-eight Marines left the Portsmouth depot, bound for Key West, Florida. Several hundred citizens, including wives and sweethearts, cheered the men as they departed, with two buglers playing, "The Girl I Left Behind Me."[87]

A sense of war frenzy to avenge the *Maine,* coupled with a fear common to Americans along the Atlantic seaboard that the Spanish fleet would attack their seaport, gripped the populace. Governor George A. Ramsdell of New Hampshire telegraphed Navy Secretary Long: "The inhabitants of Portsmouth, our only seaport, and the people of New Hampshire, earnestly desire such protection as the navy only can afford. I earnestly recommend that a monitor or other war vessel be stationed there for the defense of the harbor." Senator Chandler contacted the Portsmouth mayor to reassure him: "The government is doing all in its power to protect our whole northeast coast from Spanish attack."[88]

The Yard responded quickly to dispel panic and to install adequate defenses. During May 3 and 4, the U.S. lightship *Lilac* set out buoys to mark proposed locations of underwater mines. The next day, various tugs and sloops laid twenty-one mines, each loaded with 101 pounds of gun-cotton and anchored with a 1,000-pound anchor. The buoys marked the channel for experienced river pilots in daytime, but "from eight o'clock in the evening until four in the morning the electric current is turned on in the hidden volcanoes," reported the *Chronicle* on May 6, "and the harbor is closed against all vessels." Shortly thereafter, the Lighthouse Board ordered that all lights and fog signals at Fort Constitution at the harbor entrance and at the Yard's Seavey's Island be discontinued at night. Finally, by early June, security measures underwent final tightening. "Visitors find much trouble getting into the navy yard just now," reported the *Journal* on June 11, "as a result of orders from Washington promulgated to the watchmen at the gates and ferry landing. All strangers are questioned as to the nature of their business and all suspicious-looking characters are refused entrance."[89]

While military preparations continued, momentous news arrived from the Far East indicating that the war probably would be over quickly. On May 1, with the hoisted signal, "Remember the *Maine,*" Commodore George Dewey and his Asiatic Squadron soundly defeated the Spanish fleet in the Battle of Manila Bay. "Commodore Dewey

The U.S. Navy caption reads: "Portsmouth, N.H., S.J. Shaw who fired first shot at Battle of Manila [Bay] on deck of USS Olympia." *Enlisted man Shaw poses next to the gun that ushered the United States into the modern age in 1898. The photo probably was taken in 1908, when the* Olympia *arrived at the Yard with a training squadron. PA*

ranged his fleet in column formation," reported the *Journal,* "the flagship *Olympia* leading, followed by the *Baltimore, Raleigh, Boston, Concord,* and Petrel . . . and . . . drove straight and hard at the centre of Spain's fleet, breaking it in two." In this one-sided firefight, the Spanish lost 400 of their men but the Americans suffered only seven wounded. One of the Americans, however, died soon afterward. Chief Engineer Frank B. Randall, of the dispatch boat *McCulloch,* succumbed to heat exhaustion and apoplexy. Randall, a Portsmouth native, was buried at sea. As a result of Dewey's victory, the United States controlled the Philippines and would soon shift the balance of naval power in the Pacific.

Many American naval personnel in the Battle of Manila Bay had Portsmouth ties. Dewey, who had been stationed at the Yard aboard the USS *Agawam* during the Civil War, had barely escaped court-martial in an assault-and-battery incident. He later married a Portsmouth woman, Susan Goodwin, daughter of former Governor Ichabod Goodwin. Commander Asa Walker, skipper of the *Concord*, and Lieutenant William Winder of the *Raleigh*, Dewey's nephew, were both Portsmouth natives. "The Reward of Heroism," as the *Journal* phrased its headline, was most favorable, including as much as $187,200 in prize money. Dewey received a bounty of $9,000, Walker got $2,000, and so forth. Each sailor received about $50. In addition to the purely financial aspects, Dewey received an additional bonus, becoming a national hero overnight and soon receiving from Congress a promotion to full admiral.[90]

Dewey's brilliant victory, however, did not end the war as the McKinley administration would have desired. Rather than surrender, the Spanish government reinforced her island possessions in the Caribbean—Cuba and Puerto Rico—and ordered Rear Admiral Pascual Cervera to cross the Atlantic with four cruisers and relieve the blockaded islands. In defense of the New England coast, the Yard continued its state of readiness. In late May, the steam yacht *Comanche* arrived at the Yard. Owned by Howard Melville Hanna, brother of Senator Mark Hanna of Ohio, the *Comanche* was quickly purchased by the Navy for $500,000 and refitted at the Yard for service as a combat vessel. It was believed initially that the *Comanche* would be assigned as the flagship of the commander of the fleet, including the monitors *Catskill* and *Lehigh,* to defend the New Hampshire and Massachusetts coastline. As it turned out, however, Hanna's yacht, renamed and commissioned as the USS *Frolic,* was not needed in New England waters. After her commissioning on July 6, the USS *Frolic* sailed for Cuba on July 23 with her full complement.[91]

Events were occurring so rapidly that as the *Frolic* was arriving at the Yard in late May, Spanish Admiral Cervera's evasive fleet had already slipped into its sanctuary within Santiago (Cuba) Harbor, where it was bottled up on May 28 by a loose blockade of the Flying Squadron of the American fleet. By the time the *Frolic* left the Yard in late July, two months after she had arrived, the war essentially was over. In the interim, the Yard Marines, commanded by Captain Spicer, comprised

Company D of the First Marine Battalion, one of six companies under battalion commander Lieutenant Colonel Robert W. Huntington. A thirty-seven-year veteran of Marine service (as of 1898), Huntington was the husband of a Portsmouth woman. After leaving its staging area at Tampa, Florida, Huntington's Battalion, totaling 646 men, was taken by the transport *Panther* to Cuban waters to prepare for invasion.

On June 11, 1898, at the mouth of Guantanamo Bay, Huntington's Marines waded ashore, the first Americans to land and see combat in the Cuban campaign. An Associated Press dispatch, dated the next day, described the fierce fighting: "[The Marines] on the hill guarding the abandoned cable station at the entrance of the outer harbor of Guantanamo, have been engaged in beating off a bush attack of Spanish guerrillas and regulars since three o'clock on Saturday [June 11] afternoon. The fighting was almost continuous for fifteen hours, until six o'clock this morning [June 12], when reinforcements were landed from the *Marblehead*. Four of the Americans were killed [among them, two Yard Marines] . . . Sergt. Charles H. Smith of Smallwood, N.J.; [and] Private William Dumphy of Gloucester, Mass. . . . The engagement began with desultory firing at the [American] pickets, one thousand yards distance [distant] from the camp. Capt. Spicer's company was doing guard duty and was driven in, finally rallying at the camp and repulsed the enemy at four o'clock. The bodies of [Privates James] McColgan and Dumphy were found. Both were shot in the head. The bodies were stripped of clothing, shoes, belts and cartridges and were brutally mutilated." In the following days, Huntington's Battalion, with the *Dolphin* offshore shelling the position in advance, captured Cuzco Well, thus depriving the Spanish troops of their water supply. Thereafter, the Marines tightened their grip and secured the Guantanamo Bay area against enemy counterattack. About twenty miles to the east on July 1, however, the most publicized military action of the Cuban campaign occurred when Rough Riders Lieutenant-Colonel Theodore Roosevelt, the recently resigned assistant secretary of the Navy, charged up San Juan Hill to reap the lion's share of glory and fame. Huntington's Battalion, as evaluated by the *Journal* with typical hometown pride, "has made the best record of any body of troops during the war."[92]

The military dénouement of the war came quickly. When Admiral Cervera sought to escape with his ships on July 3, the United States

Captain Mareau of the Spanish ship Colon *checks the names of the Spanish crew at the Seavey's Island prisoner-of-war compound in the summer of 1898. PNSMVC*

Navy took up the chase and sank or captured every vessel in the Spanish fleet. The main U.S. Army seized Santiago de Cuba, and a second separate force invaded Puerto Rico. The American government decided to utilize the Portsmouth Navy Yard as a temporary facility to house, feed, and care for the Spanish naval prisoners of war until the prisoners could be released and returned to Spain. On July 10, the USS *St. Louis* arrived at the Navy Yard with more than 600 prisoners; five days later, the USS *Harvard* docked, carrying an additional 962 POWs. After embarking at the eastern end of Seavey's Island, the detainees were escorted to nearby Camp Long, named for the Navy secretary. This detention facility was a recently constructed stockade of pitched tents and temporary wooden buildings. Guarding the prisoners was the responsibility of a contingent of American Marines from the Boston (Charlestown) Navy Yard, quartered in the Marine Barracks. Many prisoners were sick and wounded when they arrived, so they were treated by American military doctors, Spanish surgeons,

Panoramic view of Camp Long (present-day Naval Prison site), which housed 1,600 Spanish prisoners of war during the summer of 1898. On September 12, 1898, the POWs embarked on the liner City of Rome *to return to their homeland. PNSMVC*

and Red Cross nurses. Despite this care, thirty-one died during their confinement. The Yard issued clothing and fed the Spaniards with fresh rations. "Ten big cases, weighing four tons, containing trousers and jumpers for the prisoners, arrived here Friday [July 15] morning by express," reported the *Journal* the next day, "and 17 tons more of

During the summer of 1898, Spanish prisoners of war, incarcerated at Camp Long (later the site of the Naval Prison), wash their clothes in the Piscataqua River. PA

goods a day or so later. The government is contracting for their use for their stay here for 5100 loaves of bread, 6300 pounds of meat and 6300 pounds of vegetables, to be delivered three times a week."[93]

As the prisoners regained their health and awaited their release, Camp Long took on a festive air, with visits from Admiral Cervera and, on one occasion, a mock bullfight. On Sunday, August 21, "the Spanish prisoners held a burlesque bull fight at Camp Long Sunday afternoon," reported the *Portsmouth Herald* the next day, "and it was witnessed by crowds of people. The 1,600 Spaniards formed in a circle near the water front and there enjoyed their favorite pastime." William Dean Howells, the distinguished American novelist and critic, attended the spectacle, reporting the event for the *Atlantic Monthly:* "There were fifty or seventy-five spectators, who arrived by trolley near the island, and walked to the stockade which confined the captives. . . . The president of the bull-fight was first brought to the place of honor in a hand-cart, and then came the banderilleros, the picadores, and the espada [matador or swordsman]. The picador's pasteboard horse was attached to his middle, fore and aft. . . . The toro [bull] himself was composed of two prisoners, whose horizontal backs were covered with a brown blanket and his feet, sometimes bare and sometimes shod with india-rubber boots, were of the human pattern." After one particularly fierce "bull" was dispatched, Howells observed: "The espada . . . was showered with cigars and cigarettes from our side."[94]

With the peace negotiations to end the war already well underway, Colonel Robert W. Huntington's First Marine Battalion arrived at the Yard aboard the USS *Resolute* on August 25. Huntington's men were assigned guard duty to supplement the existing force, but, more important, they were in Portsmouth for much-needed rest and recuperation in a cooler climate after their campaign in the torrid Caribbean summer. Portsmouth citizens greeted the Marine heroes with heartfelt hospitality. "When they [the Marines] were on the *Resolute*," reported the *Journal,* "presents of cigarettes and eatables were sent on board, and since their arrival at the camp, pies, cakes and fruit have been generously donated." Huntington's Battalion quickly occupied quarters at Camp Heywood, another tent city in a grove of pine trees immediately north of Camp Long. Named for Marine Colonel Commandant Charles Heywood, a Waterville, Maine, native, Camp Heywood bustled with daily drills, guard duty, an inspection conducted by Heywood himself, and visits from streams of relatives and sightseers. The men enjoyed full rations, fresh water from a well, and—extremely important for morale—mail delivery of long-delayed items they should have received in Cuba. "The right mail for the battalion was anywhere from a month to six weeks old," commented the *Journal* on September 10. "Many of the officers received checks, which they should have received a month before."[95]

The excitement of the summer of 1898 ended abruptly. On September 12, aboard the *City of Rome,* 1,561 Spanish prisoners sailed for their homeland and freedom. Four days later, all Portsmouth turned out to observe the First Battalion parade through the streets of Portsmouth, with Huntington on his horse, "Old Tom," leading his men. With no prisoners to guard, the work of the Marine battalion was over. "Orders were received at Camp Heywood on Saturday [September 17] to break and disband the battalion," observed the *Journal,* "as soon as

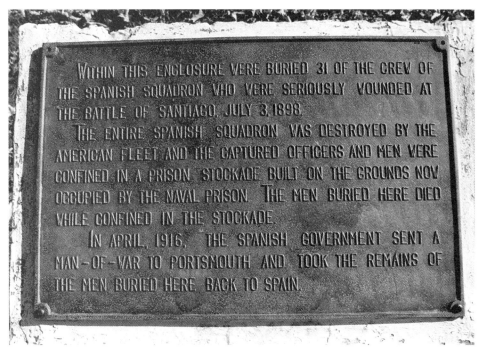

A mounted plaque on Seavey's Island marks the original gravesite of the thirty-one Spanish POWs who died at Camp Long in 1898 during the Spanish-American War. Of the approximately 1,600 prisoners—many of them sick and wounded from sea battles off Cuba—these casualties died in the camp hospital, despite the efforts of American and Spanish medical personnel. PNSY–Lashua Photo

transportation could be arranged." On September 21, most members of the battalion left by train for new duty posts. American commissioners met in Paris, and by February 6, 1899, the Senate had approved a treaty to end the war. At the Portsmouth Yard, tents were struck, and the temporary hospital, mess, and recreational facilities were dismantled; Camps Long and Heywood quickly passed into history. The "splendid little war" had vaulted the United States onto the world stage, and the United States Navy had come into its own as a global institution. Shortly thereafter, the Portsmouth Navy Yard expanded, with much new construction to support the Navy's responsibilities at bases and coaling stations around the seven seas.[96]

For some, however, the war brought no glory, opportunity, or

In memory of
Sergt. Smith,
and Pvt. Dumphy, Co. D.
1st Battalion, U.S.M.C.
Killed at
Guantanamo, Cuba.
June 11, 1898.

———

Erected by Comrades.

———

Unveiled June 11, 1907.

Affixed to the front wall of the Marine Barracks, a marble tablet honors the sacrifice of two Yard Marines who were killed in battle during the Spanish-American War. PNSY–Lashua Photo

advancement—only sacrifice. The thirty-one Spanish prisoners who died at the Yard were buried with full military honors outside the Camp Long stockade. But their graves received little respect. "Visitors to Camp Long, the late camp for the Spanish prisoners," noted the *Journal* on October 8, 1898, "report that relic hunters have carried away the card tablets which were placed on headboards of the graves. . . . Such desecrations show not only a mercenary but a morbid taste." Duplicate records, kept by both American and Spanish naval authorities, fortunately preserved the identification of each burial plot. In 1916, the Spanish naval transport *Almirante Lobo* arrived at the Yard to transport the exhumed remains of the dead for reburial in Spain.[97]

The Yard subsequently marked a solemn occasion for her heroes.

The United States Marines did not forget their comrades who fell on the field of battle. On June 11, 1907, nine years to the day after Sergeant Charles H. Smith and Private William Dumphy were killed in the war, impressive military ceremonies honored their memories at the Navy Yard's Marine Barracks. The entire Yard Marine Corps contingent, along with Civil War and Spanish-American War veterans groups, listened to a speech, a prayer, and military band music. Attached to the side wall of the Marine Barracks at the main entrance, a marble tablet, surmounted by the Marine Corps emblem, was unveiled:

In Memory of
Sergt. Smith,
and Pvt. Dumphy, Co. D
1st Battalion, U.S.M.C.
Killed at
Guantanamo, Cuba.
June 11, 1898.
———————————
Erected by Comrades
———————————
Unveiled June 11, 1907.[98]

"The America Since," and Submarines, 1898–1900

Winning the Spanish-American War for the United States brought new challenges and responsibilities as a world power. As an unnamed foreign diplomat commented in Washington three years after the conflict, "I have seen two Americas, the America before the Spanish-American War and the America since." For the Navy and the Yard, defense and administration of these newly acquired territories and related foreign-policy involvements required increased expenditures, new technology, and a versatile officer corps able to adjust to and carry out these obligations. No one grasped this new role better than Navy Secretary John Long, as he explained in an October 1898 letter to a volunteer officer: "The naval officer of today for permanent service must, on board ship, be acquainted not only with seamanship and the duties of navigation, but he must also have a thorough knowledge of the technicalities of steam engineering, electrical engineering, ordnance, and the many navy drills, and the practices of the navy in intercourse with foreign representatives, naval and diplomatic."[99]

As the United States became increasingly immersed in global matters, New Hampshire politicians found themselves battling anti-imperialists who opposed territorial expansion. The United States must remain strong and prepared, the Granite State politicians insisted, and for them that meant an adequate and bustling Portsmouth Navy Yard. In 1899, Senator William Chandler criticized tycoon Andrew Carnegie's anti-imperialist views, arguing: "If the president [William McKinley] were to follow the advice Mr. Carnegie has given, or advice of similar character from any one else, he would receive the execration of the friends of humanity the whole world over." New Hampshire First District Congressman Cyrus A. Sulloway was also eager to promote the Yard. "The Portsmouth navy yard," said Sulloway in 1900, "is beginning to get what belongs to it"—namely, a $2,500,000 congressional appropriation, of which $1 million was earmarked for a new dry dock. "When all is done we will be ready to build war ships at Portsmouth. The friends of the yard are not yet completely satisfied, but will keep on and get everything that they can. . . . We must continue our efforts in building up the yard."[100]

In the spring of 1900, McKinley appointed Portsmouth lawyer Frank W. Hackett as assistant secretary of the Navy. A familiar figure on the Portsmouth and Washington scenes, Hackett could be counted on to advance the Yard's interests and responsibilities. In June, a detachment of Yard Marines left to join a battalion being formed to go via train and ship to Cavite, the Philippines, in support of American troops already fighting to suppress the Philippine insurrection against American occupation.

At the Yard itself, various long-overdue projects finally were completed. In late November 1899, work commenced on a new dry dock. Included in the 1899 annual report for the Yards and Docks Department was an expenditure of $24,840.15 as the cost for the "Spanish camp," the temporary facility for the Spanish prisoners of war. New experimental technology at the Yard was implemented. "The plate furnace at the steel plant at the navy yard was given its first test," reported the *Journal* on February 10, 1900, "and the test was most successful. The furnace is different from any other in the country inasmuch as the heat is derived from crude petroleum, which takes but a few minutes to heat the furnace. A large steel plate was used and in five minutes it was red hot and ready to be bent. At the Cramp's shipyard [Cramp Shipyard, a private Philadelphia facility] the furnaces are heated with coal and it takes hours before enough heat is generated to work the plates."[101]

Other pending improvements at the Yard received prompt attention. To facilitate the arrival of supplies and "the old junk and other heavy articles that are being sent away," the Kittery Navy Yard station on the York Harbor and Beach Railroad branch was connected by a spur to the Yard itself to move freight efficiently. The spur was completed in 1900 with a $50,000 congressional appropriation.

The Yard had been in need of fresh water for some years, the reservoir on Seavey's Island being inadequate. In December 1900, the ever-opportunistic Frank Jones traveled to Washington on a lobbying trip to pursue this matter. The next year, he purchased Folly Pond at the base of Mount Agamenticus in York, Maine. Although the pond was fourteen miles from the Yard, Jones organized the Agamenticus Water Company and laid pipes. On January 12, 1902, his employees turned on the flow, and the Yard received its first water from the Folly Pond source. Jones died in the early fall of 1902, but shortly thereafter, the Navy Department purchased from his estate Jones's waterworks, assessed at $185,000, for $225,000. While Jones's estate realized a handsome profit from the sale, the Navy and the Yard had achieved their purpose, securing at last an ample freshwater supply.[102]

Along with these much-needed improvements, a concurrent development, virtually overlooked at the time, eventually took hold to become the decisive force in determining the Yard's subsequent history. A reluctantly accepted naval craft was destined to revolutionize America's sea power and, indeed, warfare itself. The submarine (or the submarine torpedo boat, as it was then usually called) had been long deemed too dangerous for use by the United States Navy. Such a strange craft was looked upon in many circles as little more than a Jules Verne visionary toy, rather than a practical military weapon. Only a very few grasped the submarine's potential.

Captain William H. Jaques, a world-renowned marine inventor who lived in Little Boar's Head, immediately south of Portsmouth, was

the president of the Holland Submarine Company and strongly promoted his vessel. The general public, however, was unaware, even indif-
ferent, to the submarine's capabilities. Finally, in 1900, the American
Navy decided to take a chance on this underwater mechanical whale.
The dawn of a new American naval age received the merest notice on
page four of the March 24, 1900, issue of the *Journal:* "Admiral
[George] Dewey has endorsed a favorable report made by Lieut [Harry
H.] Caldwell, his aid[e], on the recent test of the submarine torpedo
boat *Holland* in the Potomac River, just below Washington. Lieut. Caldwell was on the boat during the entire test, lasting nearly three hours,
and says in his report that a determined enemy, with a boat of the Holland type, could have made the occupation of Manila bay *[sic]* by Admiral Dewey's squadron impossible. Admiral Dewey sent Lieut.
Caldwell's report to the House Committee on Naval Affairs with a letter of his own, endorsing it strongly."[103]

The Navy purchased the *Holland* on April 11, 1900, the date subsequently observed as the official birthday of the Submarine Service.
Whereas Congress soon authorized the construction of five additional
submarines at private shipyards, it would be years before any were
built at public navy yards. In July 1900, the Navy's Bureau of Construction and Repair established a "department of submarine boats" in
order "to handle the work systematically. All information which per-
tains to submarine boat building and design will be submitted to the
new department." Later that summer, the Navy Department signed a
contract for the construction of these subs with the Holland Torpedo
Company, with "the contractors . . . allowed a number of trials of the
boats." Throughout the international naval world, especially in England and Germany, interest quickened in the submarine's vast potential. "The British admiralty has thoroughly wakened up," reported the
Portsmouth Herald in December 1900, "to the importance of submarine
and similar methods of warfare." The Portsmouth Navy Yard, following
this trend, would eventually become thoroughly involved in the "Age of
the Submarine."[104]

Centennial Day, June 12, 1900

While those developments were taking place in the first year of the twentieth century, the Yard reached a special anniversary on Tuesday, June 12, 1900—a century of service since its establishment in 1800. It might be logically expected that the centennial would have been celebrated with appropriate fanfare—with a parade, a band concert, a speech by a prominent New Hampshire politician such as Chandler or Sulloway, and even an official visit by the secretary of the Navy. It would have been an excellent time for the Portsmouth and Kittery civic and business groups to promote the Yard as one of the area's largest industrial entities. In fact, however, there was no official celebration on this day, a "nonevent" in today's parlance. June 12, 1900, passed quietly as a routine workday at the Yard.

The anniversary day centered on normal pursuits. Heads of the various Yard departments were requested to prepare their annual estimates and plans. Civil Service League members had arrived to investigate the Yard's Board of Labor. There were various arrivals and departures of naval officers and personnel. And there was a rumor (accurate, as it turned out) that the former Spanish vessel *Reina Mercedes,* captured in the recent war, might be sent to the Yard as a receiving ship to replace the *Constitution.* In lieu of a formal festive occasion on June 12, perhaps the best tribute to the Yard that day was the productivity of time and money intelligently spent on important naval matters. Its business-as-usual and get-the-job-done approach had served the Yard well during its long existence, while many less efficient or outmoded American military facilities had closed during the same timespan.[105]

What had the Portsmouth Navy Yard accomplished during its first hundred years? Considering its most modest beginnings in 1800, the Yard's achievements, by any assessment, were considerable, paralleling those of the United States during their mutual growth over the previous century. During that time, the Yard had delivered necessary prescribed services for its country: a strategically located naval base, effective warships, and technological advances.

In 1800, many European countries expected that the United States, a military and naval weakling, eventually would collapse. By 1900, this was no longer true—in fact, the situation was reversed. With the establishment of navy yards, bases, and coaling stations, the

United States had emerged as a world power with a formidable army and navy. The Yard contributed its share to this national common goal, aiding the country in its ascent to international leadership. The unobserved centennial on June 12, 1900, found the Portsmouth Navy Yard poised and well prepared to move forward into the twentieth century.

For 30 days in August and September 1905, the shipyard was the center of world attention when delegates from Russia and Japan met to negotiate a treaty to end their Far Eastern war. Here a steam launch transports the Japanese delegates to the shipyard dock from the USS Dolphin. PA

The Japanese delegation proceeding from the landing float with their naval escorts. PA

II 1900–1945

Big-Stick Diplomacy and a Presidential Visit, 1900–1912

WHILE THE FIRST HUNDRED YEARS of the Portsmouth Navy Yard were preoccupied with its establishment and growth, its second century, spanning the years 1900 to 2000, were involved with more costly and perilous foreign commitments and wars. The Yard, in short, became a part of the international scene.

When analyzing global demands of this new age, many historians consider Theodore Roosevelt as the first modern president. Ascending in under five years from assistant secretary of the Navy to Rough Rider colonel and then to vice president, Roosevelt became president upon the assassination of William McKinley in 1901. With his adopted motto, "Speak softly, but carry a big stick," Roosevelt aggressively expanded American interests worldwide, an expansion that necessitated a strong navy, bustling navy yards, and shipbuilding programs to support numerous interventions, mediations, treaties, and annexations. American involvement occurred in China, Puerto Rico, Panama, the Canal Zone, and the Russo–Japanese War.

The Portsmouth Navy Yard reflected this national commitment, riding the appropriations wave and receiving $1,085,000 in 1901, second highest after Boston among the twenty-two American navy yards and stations. Throughout this expansion, Senator Eugene Hale of Maine assured the Yard and his constituents that his home yard would not be forgotten. Known as the "Owner of the Navy," Hale was not only the chairman of the Senate Committee on Naval Affairs, but also near the top in the Senate Appropriations Committee.[106]

With the flow of congressional appropriations, the Yard pushed

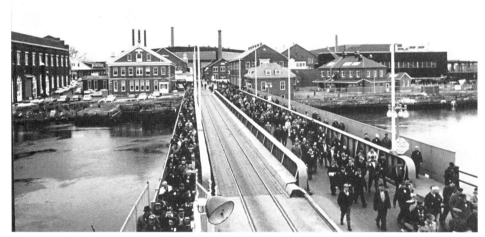

Before the automobile era, Yard employees at quitting time walked across the bridge over the Back Channel to Kittery. Note railroad tracks (center) in this vital transportation artery. UNH

ahead on long-overdue public-works projects. Between 1899 and 1906, workmen constructed a stone dry dock, utilizing the channel known as Jenkins's Gut between the Navy Yard and Seavey's Island. Built to accommodate larger ships, and more of them, the dry dock cost more than a million dollars. Stone and Portland cement arrived at the Yard either by sea or by the new railroad spur extending within the Yard, thus eliminating (in 1901) the need for oxen. Under the headline, "ANTEDILUVIAN TRANSPORTATION NEAR ITS END," the *Herald* noted on June 10, 1901: "The fat and formidable ox which has served as the means of hauling stores at that place will give way to the more alert and capable locomotive."[107]

The next project involved the removal of Henderson's Point, a 500-foot rock ledge extending from Seavey's Island into the main Piscataqua River navigational channel. The spur—since colonial times a hazard to ships entering or leaving Portsmouth's inner harbor and causing numerous accidents and groundings by swirling currents and tides—was long overdue for demolition. In February 1902, Senator

*Connected by a York branch spur of the Boston & Maine Railroad via Gate No.1
bridge across the Back Channel, the Yard has utilized rail transportation for more
than a century. U.S. Navy train engines deliver supplies to sites within the Yard.
PNSY–Lashua Photo*

Jacob Gallinger of New Hampshire introduced a $754,000 amend-
ment to the River and Harbor Bill to fund this project. The Massachusetts Contracting Company began work on July 24 that same year,
and demolition of the spur required almost three years of blasting,
construction of coffer dams, and rock removal. The final blast was
scheduled for Saturday, July 22, 1905. On the previous Monday, Yard
Commandant Rear Admiral William W. Mead posted General Order
No. 17, with many provisions to ensure the maximum degree of safety
for the Yard and the nearby communities. The Yard was closed to visitors. One paragraph specified: "The steam whistle at the power plant
will give . . . one long blast ten minutes before the explosion or at 3:50
P.M." Boats were not allowed on the river: "Two tugs will be detailed
to patrol the upper and lower portions of this part of the river to see
that this is carried into effect." Mead also issued a public letter,

directed to the citizens of New Castle, Portsmouth, and Kittery, outlining the many precautions. No detail was too small: "Bric-a-brac and all small articles that are liable to fall from sudden jar, should be secured."[108]

On July 22, 1905, a bright and sunny day, 18,000 people—including Navy Yard personnel, Senator Gallinger and many other politicians, and the general public—crammed onto wharves, islands, and wherever else they could find a vantage point to await the spectacle. It was slated to be the largest man-made explosion of all time, some thirty-six tons of dynamite calculated to dislodge and crumple a mass of solid rock with an estimated weight of 70,000 tons. If successful, the blast would widen the Piscataqua River channel by 400 feet at its narrowest point. After dredging, the water would be thirty-five feet deep where the promontory had jutted into the river. The *Herald* captured the dramatic moment with capital letters:

> AT EXACTLY ELEVEN MINUTES PAST FOUR O'CLOCK ON SATURDAY AFTERNOON MISS EDITH FOSTER TURNED THE SWITCH WHICH SENT THE ELECTRIC CURRENT THROUGH THE WIRES TO THE DYNAMITE EMBEDDED IN THE GIANT COFFERDAM AND BURIED BENEATH THE ROCKY WALLS OF THE POINT. ALMOST ON THE INSTANT AN IMMENSE BODY OF WATER LEAPED INTO THE AIR, TURNING INTO SPRAY AT A HEIGHT OF OVER 100 FEET. . . . THE GIGANTIC WATER SPROUT . . . WAS ELLIPTICAL IN SHAPE AND AT LEAST 300 FEET LONG AND 250 FEET WIDE. . . . THE PILES OF THE COFFERDAM SPRANG HEAVENWARD AS IF ENDOWED WITH LIFE, SOME OF THEM LEAPING A DISTANCE OF 150 FEET. WITH THEM WERE PIECES OF ROCK OF VARYING SIZE AND GREAT LUMPS OF HARDENED CLAY FROM THE SHATTERED COFFERDAM.[109]

The many safeguards proved successful. No property damage, injury, or loss of life resulted directly from the blast. Ironically, the only casualties of the explosion were people leaving the area. Two trolley cars left Portsmouth's Market Square shortly after five o'clock in the afternoon, less than an hour after the blast. On the outskirts of town, Trolley Car Special No. 181 of the Exeter, Hampton and Amesbury Street Railway, carrying more than a hundred sightseeing passengers, collided head-on

The dynamiting of 500-foot Henderson's Point on July 22, 1905, was, at the time, the world's largest manmade explosion. Removal of the spur ensured shipping-lane safety for the Yard and commercial traffic. PNSMVC

On July 22, 1905, sightseers on Peirce's Island and pleasure boats on the Piscataqua River view the aftermath of the great Henderson's Point blast. PNSMVC

with Car No. 41 of the Portsmouth Electric Railway. Ten people in Car No. 181 were injured, some with broken hips and legs. All ultimately recovered. "It is a rather sad coincidence that several of those injured," noted the *Herald,* "had left the city to escape possible danger from the Henderson's Point explosion and were returning to their homes."[110]

Two weeks after the reverberations of the blast had subsided, Russian and Japanese envoys began disembarking at the Yard to negotiate a peace treaty to end the war raging between their two empires halfway around the world. Following a meeting with President Roosevelt aboard a yacht off Oyster Bay, Long Island, New York, the plenipotentiaries arrived at the Yard via two separate vessels in early August 1905. Secret negotiations proceeded for nearly a month, with both delegations lodged free of charge at the nearby Wentworth Hotel seaside resort.

For a brief time, Portsmouth and its environs abounded with receptions, dinners, gala parties, and parades—all duly reported, photographed, and filmed by the international press corps. The publicity surrounding the conference quickly captured the world's attention. The *Herald,* seeing beyond the hoopla, grasped the crucial importance of the diplomatic proceedings, stating: "The men representing great empires of Asia and Europe will decide whether or not their countries will cease the war which has cost them both hundreds of thousands of lives, millions of dollars and has devastated the fair province of Manchuria."[111]

As host to the conference, the Portsmouth Navy Yard played a vital role in the day-to-day deliberations and their eventual result. The *Army and Navy Journal* fully understood the Yard's function in providing a suitable sanctuary for all parties involved: "President Roosevelt's selection of the navy yard at Portsmouth, N.H., as the place for the meeting of the peace plenipotentiaries of Russia and Japan is most appropriate. The new general store[s] building at that yard [now Building 86, the Yard's administrative headquarters], which has only recently been completed, will not only afford excellent quarters for the envoys and their attendants, but the yard itself is so located, being on an island, under the full control of naval authorities that the important negotiations in prospect can be conducted in absolute retirement and with no danger of annoyance from outsiders. Visitors can neither enter the island nor leave it without permission from the naval officers in

Greeted by a cannon salute upon their arrival at the Yard on August 8, 1905, the Japanese delegation marches to the Conference Building to negotiate a treaty to end the Russo–Japanese War. PA

On September 4, 1906, one year after the treaty of Portsmouth was signed, a ceremony was held to unveil the plaque naming Building 86 as the site where delegates of Russia and Japan affixed their signatures to the treaty documents. (See photo page 85.) PA

charge. . . . It is proper to add that the selection of Portsmouth is heartily approved by the Russian as well as by the Japanese representatives."[112]

Mead published detailed orders relative to the Yard's security and posted Marine sentinels to guard the General Stores Building day and night. Such vigilance achieved its purpose. In the General Store Building at 3:47 P.M. on Tuesday, September 5, 1905, the Russian and Japanese envoys signed the treaty, popularly known as the Peace of Portsmouth, ending the Russo–Japanese War. In a note published by the *Herald*, Jutaro Komura and Kogoro Takahira, the chief Japanese diplomats, thanked Rear Admiral Mead: "Before leaving Portsmouth, permit us to express to you our sincere thanks for many marks of courtesy and consideration that have been invariably shown to us by yourself and your officers during our stay here, which we appreciate very highly." Sergius Witte and Roman Rosen, their Russian counterparts, expressed similar thanks to Mead for "all the arrangements made, and the order maintained at this yard during [our] stay here." Commandant Mead, in turn, publicly thanked his officers and men "for their cordial cooperation in carrying out the orders relative to the meeting of the Peace Commission at this station, and knows of no incident in connection therewith which does not reflect credit upon all the officers and men of this command."[113]

In an editorial, "The Peace Conference," the *Herald* enthused: "Portsmouth has been made famous for all time. It was the scene of the crowning event of the latter day history and it will be remembered as long as books are printed and men read them." Russia and Japan, however, were dissatisfied with the terms of the treaty—both fretted over the territorial and indemnity settlements—but Russia's czar and Japan's Mikado ratified the document a month later. For Roosevelt, the treaty ended a war that threatened to upset the stability of the Far East. Assistant Secretary of the Navy Frank W. Hackett felt that the ringing of the church bells on September 5, 1905, when news of the peace was known in Portsmouth, should become an annual observance: "Why not then let the custom be instituted on Sept. 5, 1906, of ringing the bells for an hour, beginning at 3:47 in the afternoon? Thus 'Treaty day' ringing will become a local observance that shall keep alive memories across the sea as well as in our own favored land." On the first anniversary of the treaty, impressive ceremonies accompanied the

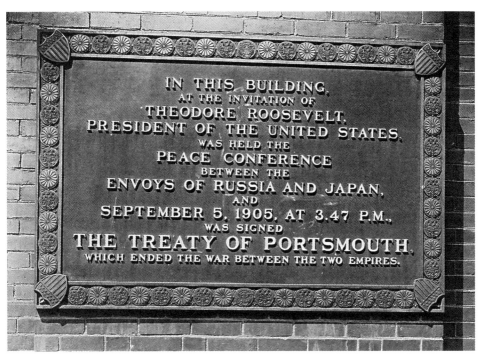

Dedicated in 1906, a year after the treaty signing, this plaque is affixed to the wall outside the main entrance of present-day Building 86. The marker has attracted many visitors, especially Japanese citizens, over the years. PNSMVC

attachment of a commemorative plaque to the wall near the entrance of the Peace Building.

With the passage of time, however, enthusiasm for an annual Treaty Day event has waned, and observances have been sporadic. The historical significance of this important treaty, however, is honored to this day. More than any ship, any commandant, or any invention, the Portsmouth Navy Yard has been best remembered worldwide as the site of the signing of the Russo–Japanese Peace Treaty, and many Japanese citizens still make the long pilgrimage to Portsmouth.[114]

Less than three years later, the Yard assumed another responsibility, the operation of a naval prison, ultimately the largest and most modern military penal facility in the country. In the planning since 1903, the United States Naval Prison, Portsmouth, was officially commissioned on April 11, 1908.

In July 1903, the USS *Southery* arrived at the Yard to serve on an

The Yard's Naval Prison, viewed from the Piscataqua River. The original elongated section (left) was begun in 1903 and commissioned in 1908; the distinctive castle-style tower (right) was added in 1912. PNSMVC

interim basis until the new prison was ready for occupancy. On January 28, 1908, the *Herald* reported, "The cost of completing the new Naval Prison at this yard will be very expensive. With the two additional wings planned, the officers quarters, the governor's house and the barracks for the men, will involve an expenditure of $680,000." At its opening on April 11, the prison was still unfinished. Fifty prisoners, taken from the *Southery,* formed the first detachment. "This number," reported the *Herald,* "are mostly mechanics and help who are to perform some work there in advance of the large number who are to follow."[115]

Within the prison's first month of operation, one issue was quickly resolved: the status of prison labor. When Yard workers learned that prisoners were removing machinery, boilers, and engines from the USS *Topeka,* then undergoing repair, they immediately sought to squelch this practice, expressing their grievance to New Hampshire's senators and congressmen in Washington. On April 30, Congressman Sulloway, Senator Gallinger, and others protested to the Secretary of the Navy:

An iron tablet, dedicated in 1908 to honor Admiral David Glasgow Farragut, is attached to the fence in front of Quarters A. PNSMVC

"As you are doubtless aware[,] work is very scarce at the Portsmouth Navy Yard, and we do not think it is either just or right that this or any other work of a similar character should be done by the prisoners to the exclusion of the men on the yard, who need the work for themselves and their families. . . . It seems to us that this great government should be the last to encourage convict labor, and [that] the order [permitting prison work on the *Topeka]* will be rescinded at once." The request was granted, and the Yard prisoners were assigned to more pressing work within the prison and the Yard itself—grading roads, lining sewers, removing snow, reinforcing the seawall, and performing general maintenance. In time, prison labor operated and maintained the bakery, garden, and laundry, as well as carpenter, blacksmith, paint, print, and shoe shops.[116]

By late July 1908, the naval prison had added 160 cells, doubling

its capacity. The emphasis of Navy officials in Washington was to rehabilitate the inmate and restore him to duty, not keep him behind bars
indefinitely. "From now on the policy of the navy will be to reform prisoners," reported the *Herald,* "rather than to punish them for offenses.
Certain privileges will be allowed prisoners of good record, schools will
be established and the prison made a place of training rather than of
punishment." The early prisoners still had a very stark and uncompro-
mising existence in "the Castle," or "Portsmouth University," as the
Yard prison was known locally. "During those days," according to the
Castle Courier, the prison newspaper, "the prisoners wore uniforms
with huge yellow numbers painted across the backs of their coats, the
fronts of their shirts, and on the knees of their trousers. The repeaters
wore red-legged pants with a red band around the bottom of their coats
giving rise to their nickname, 'red legs.' The food was plain, the work
long and hard, and entertainment scarce."[117]

The routine under the Marine guards and the work details at the
prison proceeded quietly over the years, and almost without incident.
Escapes were almost nonexistent, prison riots and massive breakouts
were unknown, and the few prisoners attempting escape usually were
captured within the Yard itself.

A year after the prison was established, an unexpected disaster
occurred. On Wednesday, August 11, 1909, the Portsmouth Navy Yard
tug, USS *Nezinscot,* en route from the Yard to Boston, sank in heavy
seas off Halibut Point, Cape Ann, Massachusetts. Of the thirteen aboard
(ten crew and three passengers), four naval personnel died. Two courts
of inquiry and a court-martial followed. At stake was the reputation and
career of Naval Constructor John G. Tawresey, who was officially held
responsible for the *Nezinscot*'s lack of seaworthiness.[118]

Tawresey's general court-martial began at the Yard on September
20, 1909, and testimony continued for several days. At this stage of his
career, Tawresey was a noted naval construction officer, an 1885
Annapolis graduate who had studied naval architecture at the Royal
Naval College in Greenwich, England. The court acquitted Tawresey
and blamed the captain of the *Nezinscot* for incompetent seamanship
that led to disaster. On the day the tug had loaded and sailed, Tawresey was in Bath, Maine, on special duty. Under the headline
"RESTORED TO DUTY," the *Herald* reported on September 29 that
the commandant of the Yard "immediately and personally returned

Naval Constructor Tawresey's sword to him and tendered his congrat-ulations." Not only acquitted but also fully exonerated of any connec-tion with the case, Tawresey continued to serve in the Navy with great distinction until his retirement as rear admiral in 1926.[119]

The *Nezinscot* sinking and the Tawresey court-martial occurred during the first year of President William Howard Taft's administra-tion. For the Navy and its Yards, the Taft presidency, in contrast to Roo-sevelt's, was not committed to naval matters. Congressional yard-district representatives and senators, not Taft, fought for appro-priations. American peace groups insisted that another war was unthinkable. This directly affected the Yard, and in the summer of 1912, there was even talk of abolishing the Portsmouth Yard. Congressman Sulloway, in his usual combative manner, prevailed upon Taft to ignore such talk; prodded by Sulloway, Taft squelched the idea. Sulloway, how-ever, wanted more than just assurances that the Yard would remain open. In late September 1912, Sulloway told the press, "I have written President Taft a letter urging the importance of keeping the men steadily employed at the navy. . . . I told the president . . . that these spasmodic and altogether too frequent layoffs of the men was demoral-izing to the force of splendid workmen at the local yard, and that the only way the government could keep and hold good men was to see that they are given constant employment." On October 3, Taft telegraphed Sulloway: "Repair work will be resumed at Portsmouth on the 16th or 17th of October, and continue as heretofore."[120]

On Wednesday, October 23, 1912, at 10:45 A.M., less than two weeks before the presidential election, President Taft and his official party, including the Navy secretary, arrived at the Navy Yard's main gate, greeted by Sulloway, Gallinger, former Assistant Navy Secretary Frank Hackett, and other politicians and dignitaries. Taft, facing an uphill battle to be reelected, needed every vote he could muster. At 11 o'clock, the Yard whistle sounded and workmen rushed from their shops to crowd in front of the Administration Building, which flew the president's flag. Taft and his entourage toured the historic rooms asso-ciated with the 1905 peace conference. Then Taft spoke briefly to the assembled crowd: "You have several ships for repairs but not as much money for the work as we need," Taft told the workmen. "I congratulate you on the beautiful and complete navy yard you have here." The pres-ident then left, after spending less than an hour at the Yard. But, brief as it was, Taft's appearance marked a significant occasion. He was the first incumbent president since James Monroe to appear at the Navy Yard. (Franklin Pierce had visited in 1857 as ex-president; President Chester A. Arthur had conferred with Yard officials in 1884 aboard a yacht anchored in Portsmouth Harbor.) Despite Taft's visit and his bid for the Yard workmen's votes during his last-minute campaigning, Taft lost his bid for reelection in early November, whereupon a new era, headed by Democratic President-elect Woodrow Wilson, was about to begin.[121]

Daniels, FDR, and "Preparedness," 1913–1917

The incoming Wilson administration quickly faced numerous foreign crises and entanglements, ones that affected not only the United States Navy but also the Portsmouth Navy Yard. Secretary of the Navy Josephus Daniels and Assistant Secretary Franklin D. Roosevelt stressed innovation in the Navy Department that would prove vital during the new age of the submarine, the world war spreading throughout Europe and Asia, and closer-to-home interventions in Mexico, Haiti, and the Dominican Republic. The Yard could not be satisfied with obsolete equipment and outmoded policies. The United States Navy and its Yards were compelled to maintain a high level of "preparedness," the buzzword of the times, to respond to any emergency.

Daniels, a North Carolina newspaper publisher and a Progressive, and Roosevelt, a wealthy yachtsman and New York politician, wasted no time in attempting to reform the U.S. Navy. Both visited the Yard on many occasions, spoke at luncheons and banquets, and granted interviews in their efforts to promote their programs. In June 1913, Daniels delivered a brilliant address before 150 Portsmouth businessmen at the downtown Rockingham Hotel. "If I had $20,000,000 invested in a great plant [the Portsmouth Navy Yard]," Daniels exclaimed, "I would use it." The Navy secretary had told his audience what it wanted to hear. "No Fear of Portsmouth Yard Being Abandoned," proclaimed the *Portsmouth Herald*. During another visit on August 27, 1915, Daniels spoke to Yard workers from the commandant's carriage at the rear of the Administration Building. "The day has passed when the patriot took off his civilian clothes and took his musket down from the wall and became an effective soldier," Daniels

On March 8, 1915, a work detail of inmates under U.S. Marine guard and super-vision leave the prison ship USS Southery *for a Yard project. UNH*

stated. "We now prepare for war in a different manner. The present fighting is done with machinery which is made by the skilled work-men of the navy yards."[122]

During an inspection of the Yard on July 10, 1915, Assistant Sec-retary Roosevelt echoed these sentiments, saying, "We want the men to have steady work and if we make this a manufacturing yard, we can provide against lay offs and discharges. We intend to have a lot of man-ufacturing so that when the ships are away the men can have other employment."[123]

This spirit of adaptation to changing custom and technology per-vaded the Wilson administration in naval matters from the outset. Regarding the presidential yacht *Mayflower,* Wilson declared his inten-

Standpipe and Wireless Telegraph Station - Portsmouth Navy Yard.

Standpipe and wireless telegraph station usher in the modern age of communication (ca. 1910) at the Yard. In the background (left center), across the Piscataqua River, stands the Wentworth Hotel in New Castle, New Hampshire. PNSMVC

tion in March 1913 to "use any ship of the navy when necessary for official occasions, but will not keep expressly for pleasure trips and entertaining purposes the *Mayflower* or any other craft of her type." The era of the onboard presidential tea party was over. That same month, naval officials announced their reliance on the Bertillion system of fingerprint records, a file of some 13,000 individual prints of those who had enlisted in the service. The Navy would thus be able to catch "repeaters"—deserters who had enlisted again or those who had been dishonorably discharged. Since the system was adopted in 1907, some 1,700 repeaters had been caught. The Yard also enforced rigid fire-safety precautions, ordering in mid-March 1913: "Under no circumstances will smoking be allowed on the Kittery bridge, or the magazine, Franklin ship house, store houses containing lumber, or paint shop."[124]

Daniels also stressed the need for instant communication. In April 1913, he issued an order, effective on April 15, authorizing officers and enlisted men to use the government wireless telegraph on land and sea when necessary. Shortly thereafter, beginning on May 1, all radiograms between naval ships and shore stations were to designate the exact time. By September, the Naval Radio Station at the Portsmouth Yard was instructed to "broadcast weather reports at 11 A.M. and 6 P.M. each day, on a wave length of 1,000 meters, for the benefit of shipping along the New England coast." The Navy's reliance on wireless telephone was subjected to a severe test on Saturday, May 6, 1916, as part of a four-hour preparedness exercise. Beginning at 4:00 P.M., Secretary Daniels, in his Washington naval headquarters with scores of high-ranking naval, army, and coast guard officials watching the experiment, talked by wireless with Captain Lloyd H. Chandler, commander of the battleship USS *New Hampshire* in Hampton Roads, Virginia. For the first time in world history, orders were transmitted directly from the office of the secretary of the Navy to a ship at sea. The exercise was conducted on a war footing. Chandler advised Daniels of the moment-to-moment progress of a search for a supposed foe. Daniels also spoke via long-distance telephone with naval stations in Norfolk, New York, Portsmouth, San Diego, and other points, "exchanging instantaneous messages and giving official orders by word of mouth over thousands of miles of territory for the transaction of naval business." During this test, there was, according to plan, virtually no written communication between Washington and the naval stations.[125]

Daniels wanted his department and the yards fully prepared, not only in communications but also in other categories. In 1913, he pushed the policy of "no more swivel chair admirals," those who were content to remain on shore stations. To be eligible for promotion, they, along with officers of lesser grade, would have to demonstrate their fitness for sea duty. That same year, he advocated shipbuilding of naval vessels at navy yards, not at private yards, despite the opposition of the civilian shipbuilding lobby. The policy served the Portsmouth Yard well. In early 1914, Daniels ordered—in his most unpopular and criticized action— the abolition of the officers' wine mess aboard ship, effective on July 1, to prevent inefficiency and drunkenness within the officer ranks. Late in 1915, when Annapolis was at full capacity, Daniels recommended the establishment of a second naval academy to be located on the Pacific coast, a plan never realized.[126]

The Portsmouth Yard reflected this era of expansion and readiness. In December 1913, the new naval hospital opened. Under con-

On April 12, 1916, at Yard ceremonies, the bodies of thirty-one Spanish prisoners of war, who had died and been interred on Seavey's Island in 1898, were taken aboard the Spanish naval transport Almirante Lobo *for reburial in Spain. Note American honor guard with flag (right center). PA*

During February 1915, aboard the USS Topeka, *auxiliary prison ship to the USS* Southery, *naval "detentioneers" limber up. UNH*

In an undated photograph (ca. 1913–18), Navy Secretary Josephus Daniels addresses Yard employees during one of his official World War I visits. A reformer and innovator in President Woodrow Wilson's cabinet, Daniels served with distinction in promoting the wartime Navy and its yards. PA

A peaceful scene, captured by a photographer on April 8, 1914, shows the Mall, Quarters A and B, and the bandstand. Just a few months later, the outbreak of World War I in Europe prompted an accelerated building program at the Yard to deliver submarines to the U.S. Navy. PNSMVC

struction since 1910, the facility cost $3,000,000. By January 1914, naval surgeons performed their first operations. In September 1915, a long-needed modern bridge opened to connect Kittery with the Yard, replacing the old wooden bridge that had been in use since the early nineteenth century. The 200-foot-long, 36-foot-wide bridge, built entirely of steel, provided a railroad bridge, a roadway, and a passenger walkway. With tungsten incandescent lights and cement walks, the $120,000 bridge was a long-overdue modern transportation link. Rumors circulated about a submarine base at the Isles of Shoals, but it never materialized. A new invention, however, planned by Charles Prince, a draftsman in the Yard's industrial division, proved successful and was adopted by the government for use in late 1915 throughout the Navy. This was an electrical device for the operation of life buoys on naval vessels. "In case a man falls from the ship into the water," explained the *Herald,* "this invention is so connected with the life buoys which are located on all parts of the ship that a life buoy can be released anywhere by the man on watch on the bridge by simply pushing a button. If a buoy is released at night it lights automatically as soon as it strikes the water." Before this time, the buoys were released by hand, and much valuable time was lost while men struggled in the water. The invention was tested by several trials on the battleship USS *Arkansas,* and after formal approval, the Navy ordered thirty-nine of the devices manufactured at the Portsmouth Yard.[127]

In the Navy's striving for modernization, some symbols of the Yard's shipbuilding past were sacrificed as unfit for modern service. Two historic ships, the USS *Portsmouth* and the USS *Franklin,* were torched, with no effort to retain them as museum relics in commemoration of their illustrious careers. The *Portsmouth* was the first to be fired. "Sixty years ago the *Portsmouth* was the pride of the U.S. Navy," commented the *Herald* on August 16, 1915. In addition to her role in attempting to curtail the slave trade and negotiating the Treaty of Ambrizette, she performed other historic duties. "She took possession of San Francisco Bay in the Mexican War," continued the *Herald,* "went with Commodore Perry when he negotiated a treaty with Japan . . . and assisted Farragut at New Orleans during the Civil War." Sold for $3,500 as junk, the *Portsmouth* was burned on the east side of Governor's Island in Boston on September 6, 1915, as the culmination of a South Boston carnival. A motion-picture company filmed the inferno as a sequel to a play about the ship. A year later, the *Franklin* went to her demise. Rebuilt and enlarged at the Portsmouth Yard in the Franklin Shiphouse, the *Franklin* had served as Admiral Farragut's flagship on his European cruise in 1867. The old vessel, which had cost the government $1,331,000, was sold to a salvage company for $16,766. Set afire along the beach in Eastport, Maine, on October 2, 1916, the *Franklin*'s ashes yielded a great quantity of copper and about $4,000 worth of gold that the salvage company extracted from the rivets.[128]

The scrap-metal industry found a ready customer in the Navy and the Portsmouth Yard. As early as the autumn of 1914, orders came down at the Yard not to sell scrap metals as had been the old policy, but instead to collect all brass, babbitt, and copper to be pigged at Yard foundries. The Portsmouth Yard was designated by the Navy to receive scrap from other yards. Some of the shipments from southern navy yards came from lots that had been lying around since the Civil War. In keeping with Assistant Secretary Roosevelt's suggestion that the Portsmouth Yard engage in manufacturing, the Yard's smelting operation was a decided financial success. In light of war conditions abroad, this program bordered on the essential, stockpiling such metals as copper, tin, zinc, aluminum, and lead. "From September, 1915, to May 1st, 1916," commented the *Herald* about the Portsmouth foundry, "about 2,000,000 pounds of scrap metal have been pigged and turned into the supply officer for issue to the manufacturing departments of the several yards representing a value of $480,000,000 with an outlay of less than $11,000,000."[129]

In the midst of the Yard's frenetic expansion, shipbuilding, and smelter production, a Washington dispatch brought the electrifying news that the Portsmouth Navy Yard would host another peace conference. Since 1914, American relations with Mexico had deteriorated, culminating on March 9, 1916, when Mexican bandit Pancho Villa raided Columbus, New Mexico. Six days later, General John J. Pershing led the American intervention, crossing the border with 12,000 troops. With great reluctance, Mexican President Venustiano Carranza permitted the invasion. American and Mexican officials subsequently agreed that a joint commission should be formed to withdraw the American troops and to prevent further bloodshed on both sides. "MEXICAN PEACE CONFERENCE AT PORTSMOUTH," read the large *Herald* headline on Saturday, August 26, 1916. "Delegates Will Come on Battleship," continued the subheadline, "and Hold Sessions in Navy Yard Peace Conference Building." For the next few days, Portsmouth and the Yard basked in the media publicity that the conference would be held in the historic rooms used by the Russian and Japanese delegations only eleven years earlier. "PORTSMOUTH OFFICIALLY NAMED FOR CONFERENCE, Delegates of Carranza Government and Representatives of United States to Come Here on Sept. 5," read another headline three days later, and in its September 1 issue: "COMMISSIONERS WILL ARRIVE ON SEPTEMBER 6."

Old stories of the "Peace City" were revived for 1916, with the expectation that a diplomatic settlement and treaty would again bring acclaim to the Yard. By September 2, doubts began to emerge, however, as to whether or not Portsmouth would actually host the conference. "The objection to Portsmouth," reported the *Herald,* "is that if the conference runs far into the fall, the climate may prove too severe for the delegates from Mexico. Several other cities, including New London [Connecticut], are under consideration." Shortly thereafter, New London was selected as the site for the conference, and the protracted proceedings later shifted to Atlantic City. Unable to resolve the crisis, the joint commission was dissolved on January 15, 1917. In lieu of the increasingly deteriorating American relations with Germany, which had embraced an open U-boat warfare policy, President Wilson concluded that America's best interests did not lie in dragging on the Mexican imbroglio indefinitely, but rather in addressing the more alarming situation on the other side of the Atlantic. The president accordingly decided to withdraw American troops from Mexico on January 28, 1917, and Pershing's men were back across the Rio Grande by February 5, 1917.[130]

Ship construction and repair, not hosting peace conferences, were always the chief responsibility of the Yard, and early in 1914, a new era began. After intense local lobbying, the Navy Department on March 11 announced that a submarine would be built in the Franklin Shiphouse at a cost of approximately $500,000. "This will be pleasing news to navy employe[e]s as well as our citizens in general," commented the *Herald.* Thus, from this relatively modest beginning emerged the Yard's chief role in the United States Navy. Since then, some eighty-six years ago, the Yard has been synonymous with submarines throughout the world. The local press gave Secretary Daniels the credit for directing the work to government, not private, yards. By the end of 1914, the Yard's hull division had laid the lines for the first submarine built in a government yard and was engaged in bending the keel. On February 24, 1915, the keel was laid for the *L-8,* as the submarine was named, with officials driving the symbolic first rivet into the midship frame. Work proceeded with relative secrecy and only limited press coverage. When the submarine *L-4* was launched at the private Fore River shipyard, Quincy, Massachusetts, on April 1, 1915, newspaper coverage provided the barest of details. "Under a new rule of the Navy Department," reported the *Herald,* "further details were not given out as the department has forbidden the giving out of any vital details of any boat under construction. So rigidly is this being enforced that no newspaper photographers were allowed to take pictures of the launching." With the Great War in Europe underway, announcements generally emanated from Washington, not from Portsmouth— from Secretary Daniels and not from local Yard commandants—in the best interests of security. Information released relative to the construction of the second Yard submarine, the *O-1,* was just as terse. The first rivet was driven into her hull on March 20, 1917, in the Franklin Shiphouse. "The work will be pushed with vigor," commented the *Herald.*[131]

Ever since 1913, increasing foreboding of impending U.S. involvement in foreign affairs affected the Navy and the Yard, and, as time went on, there was an increasing fatalistic resignation that the United States eventually would enter the Great War. Leave and liberty for naval personnel at the Yard were often canceled at short notice. The frequency of this during the Mexican crisis in 1914 caused the Yard Marines to withdraw their baseball team from the Sunset League, an amateur organization made up of local Portsmouth business and civic teams. The Yard baseball players instead formed teams within the confines of the Yard. In July 1914, a former Yard officer who was involved in the Vera Cruz (Mexico) occupation returned to his home in Brooklyn and declared, "Baseball will uplift Mexico and supplant brutal bullfighting." The Marines' restricted baseball schedule and leave policy reflected the nation's growing obsession with preparedness, increasing the number of war-related speeches, inspections, and sightings of mysterious vessels. On May 26, 1915, Yard Commandant Thomas Snowdon addressed the students at New Hampshire State Agricultural College (now the University of New Hampshire) in nearby Durham. "We need to be prepared," he said. "Our navy needs enlargement. We need 100 submarines and 48 battleships." The following February, Portsmouth citizens signed and sent a national defense preparedness petition to Congressman Cyrus Sulloway. In June 28, 1916, Captain William H. Jaques, the submarine expert and one-time president of Holland Submarine Company, delivered an inflammatory address in Hampton, New Hampshire, attacking the Wilson administration as the "peace party" and weak on preparedness. In early October of that year, Major General Leonard Wood, commander of the Department of the East and Theodore Roosevelt's longtime military associate, inspected Fort Constitution, guarding the entrance to

Portsmouth Harbor. In early December, he returned to New Hampshire and addressed the Durham college students, cautioning them against being lulled into a false sense of security. "Troops unquestionably can be landed here," said Wood, "if we lose sea control." Election Day, Tuesday, November 7, 1916, was a greatly anticipated event at the Yard. Virtually all the shops of the different departments were closed, because most Yard workers took a half-day leave of absence to vote. The election results were received at the Yard via the government radio station. In an upset victory in which he won New Hampshire by exactly fifty-six votes, Wilson eked out a second term. The preparedness issue, which the Republicans tried to exploit, was sufficiently deflected by Wilson, who, in fact, had been preparing the country for war. In its post-election analysis, the *Herald* insisted that Wilson would "guard our chief industry—the Portsmouth navy yard." Also, Secretary Daniels "kept his promises and has used the magnificent plant across the river for the purposes it was intended."[132]

The drift toward war could not be avoided. On January 31, 1917, Germany declared unrestricted open U-boat warfare against all merchant ships within a stipulated danger zone. A nervous public began to "see" nonexistent vessels coming up the Piscataqua. As early as October 1916, considerable excitement prevailed along the waterfront in the early evening as reports circulated that a German submarine was proceeding toward the Yard. The "submarine" proved to be the U.S. torpedo boat destroyer *Drayton*. Hysterical letters were printed in the *Herald*. One letter-writer, Mrs. C. Watt of Portsmouth, a student of mental telepathy, was convinced that the Yard was in imminent danger of being attacked. In her letter of February 12, 1917, she stated that she had received five telepathic messages in one day that U-boats would attack New York City, Philadelphia, Boston, Newport, and Portsmouth. Convinced that six large U-boats were waiting off the Isles of Shoals and would attack under cover of darkness, Mrs. Watt concluded, "As the forts [guarding Portsmouth Harbor] have no submarine nets or traps[,] it will only be the matter of a few minutes before the principal buildings of the navy yard are shelled."[133]

The reality of war was soon realized. After four unarmed American merchant ships were torpedoed in March 1917, Navy Secretary Daniels issued an announcement on March 25 that President Wilson had signed an executive order to increase the Navy to 87,000 men.

Daniels appealed for recruits. A few days later, the Navy Department, as if anticipating the inevitable, authorized a change in the minimum age limit—as low as fifteen years of age—in various categories for young men seeking work in the navy yards. On April 4, the first five women to enter into government service at the Portsmouth Yard were assigned as stenographers and typists. The women had been on the job only two days when, on Friday, April 6, 1917, the United States declared war on Germany. That evening, all Coast Guard stations and crews in the Portsmouth district were automatically transferred to the supervision of the U.S. Navy. War again had come to the Yard.[134]

Winning the Great War, 1917–1918

For the American Navy and its yards, entering World War I was vastly different from their involvement in the Spanish–American War almost twenty years earlier. The Navy had to make a total war effort on an international scale as the United States attempted not only to augment its armed forces but also to mobilize the civilian populace with effective propaganda, a draft, incorporation of women in the war industry, and Liberty Loan funding drives. The Yard geared every person, every hour, and every piece of equipment to one purpose: to win the war as quickly and efficiently as possible.

The day war was declared, the change at the Yard was instantaneous. On April 6, war orders governed every person on the Yard. Recruitment and enrollment accelerated. That same day, eighteen Dartmouth students on Easter vacation notified their enrolling officer that they were on the way to Portsmouth to join the Navy. By the end of the month, the first detachment of drilling officers arrived at the Yard to train recruits, and several hundred tents needed for the camp of seamen apprentices were shipped a day or so later by Boston tentmakers. Setting an example for his father and the Navy, Josephus Daniels, Jr., the eldest son of the secretary of the Navy, volunteered at a Marine recruiting station in Washington, passed the examinations, and was accepted for military service. The Yard Marines received special preparation and training. Each Marine assigned expeditionary duty was "supplied with a half pound tin case containing a two days' supply of food, consisting of chocolate and a condensed meat and veg-

Quartered at a tent-city camp on Seavey's Island in 1917, Naval Reserve officers and enlisted men underwent training during World War I. PNSMVC

etable compound that may be made into soup, or eaten raw if there is no opportunity to prepare it."[135]

The federal government in late July also made arrangements whereby Yard bluejackets and Marines would use the state rifle range at Lake Massabesic, near Manchester, New Hampshire, for sharp-shooter training. In September, seventy-three Yard Marines pitched their khaki tents at that facility and began target practice. After these Marines had departed to return to the Yard, two companies of Navy bluejackets arrived for their training, "and in a friendly competition [to] try to outshoot the marines." Prizes were awarded to the best snipers. By the end of the year, the Navy Department directed "that the names of all ships be taken from the caps of sailors and the same replaced by the words, 'U.S. Navy.'" This change was taken to avoid making the presence of naval ships known in ports and as a measure against German spies or other informers.[136]

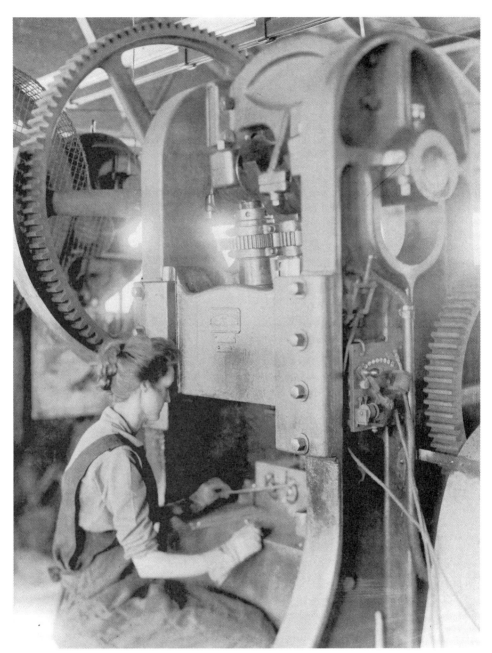

Of the 5,722 civilian Yard employees during the World War I employment peak, approximately one thousand women served capably in many job categories, including power press operator. PNSMVC

During World War I, female Yard workers prepare clothing, blankets, and linens for the Yard's war effort. PNSMVC

The hiring of women at the Navy Yard was a slower, more evolutionary process. In addition to the women stenographers hired on the eve of the war declaration, the United States Civil Service Commission announced on April 10 that there would be an open competitive examination at the Yard on May 2, for women only, for three telephone-operator vacancies. The pay was $2.24 per day. Applicants needed to be U.S. citizens and have one or two years of experience. These positions were filled with competent candidates, and by November, the Navy Department expanded women's job categories beyond clerical services. On November 14, the Yard was authorized "to hire females for duty in the electrical shops for assembly work." The maximum pay was $2.72 per day, the minimum $1.68. This call for women was a historic change in hiring policies in the Mechanical Department. The only other time in

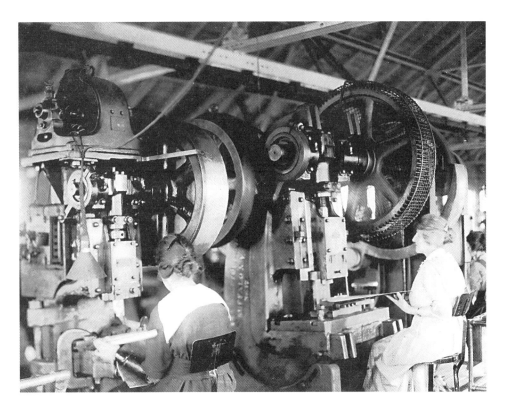

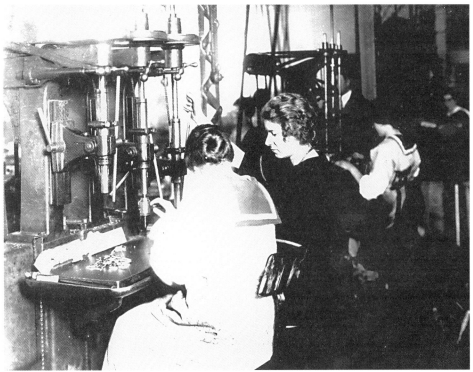

About a thousand women joined the Yard workforce during World War I, relieving able-bodied men for service in the armed forces. Women performed a variety of duties, including (clockwise) nailing wooden boat hulls, manufacturing bread pans, and operating various presses. PNSMVC

the Yard's history that women were employed had been when seam-
stresses were needed to work on flags and bunting.[137]

During the war years of 1917–18, the military exigencies of pro-
tecting the Yard from sabotage prompted many modifications of the
existing rules and regulations. On April 11, 1917, following President
Wilson's executive order, Army and Navy officials established a "dead
line" in Portsmouth Harbor. No ships were allowed to depart or
arrive between sunset and sunrise. The line extended in a 2 1/2-mile
arc from Whaleback Light, the territory covered by a patrol boat on
duty. Another directive, issued on June 25, required licensing for all
fishing vessels or pleasure yachts operating within the First Naval
District (comprising the Maine, New Hampshire, and Massachusetts
coastal waters). Failure to obey an order to stop, to heave to, or interference with mines or other defenses, would result in detention, and
even in prosecution. In September, a wild rumor originating in Dover
charged that fishing rights were being curtailed. The Yard commandant assured the fishermen that they would not be prevented from
fishing in the Piscataqua River or the harbor as long as the patrol
rules were not violated. In fact, they could "utilize as much of the
Atlantic ocean as they care to on Sunday or any other day when government regulations established since the war are complied with." A
further precaution to protect navy yards and naval stations origi-
nated in May 1918. By order of the Navy Department, there were
rigid restrictions on cameras and photography on government property. Furthermore, a pass to enter the Yard required permission from
Washington specifying the purpose for which the pass was intended.
As the holder left the yard, the pass would be collected by the guard
at the gate.[138]

The changing status of women in the Navy meant the adoption of
new directives to guarantee their rights and privileges as equals of
their male counterparts. By January 1918, there were 1,800 women
serving in the United States Navy. Secretary Daniels established dress
codes. The required clothes and shoes, costing $60, were furnished by
Uncle Sam. Called "yeowomen," the women wore blue uniforms in the
winter and white in the summer. In keeping with the war effort, plain
cotton stockings were issued instead of silk. In May 1918, while serving in these regulation uniforms, the yeowomen protested that they
were not saluted with proper military recognition. Their committee

Serving in the United States Navy in large numbers during World War I, women pose in their blue winter uniforms. Called "yeowomen," they filled essential Yard jobs. PNSMVC

During World War I, more than 1,800 women, called "yeowomen," served in the U.S. Navy to help alleviate the shortage of manpower. Rowing in the Piscataqua in 1918, a crew of Yard yeowomen practice for the Boston Regatta. UNH

Built between 1914 and 1917 in the Franklin Shiphouse, the L-8 was the Yard's first submarine for the United States Navy. PNSMVC

Following her launch in 1917, the Yard's L-8 underwent training exercises along the East Coast. In February 1918, she and two other subs were docked in New London, Connecticut, and locked in by eighteen inches of ice. PNSMVC

met with the admiral of the First Naval District, who was inclined to think that such a salute was unnecessary. The yeowomen pressed the issue, insisting that "as regular members of the naval forces they were required by the regulations to salute their superiors and that they were entitled to have the salutes returned." The admiral finally relented, ruling that the yeowomen were to be given the right of salute, both rendered and returned, in keeping with a restructured Navy.[139]

With the American entrance into the war, the Navy Department's firm commitment to the submarine's future was irreversible. On April 11, 1917, Secretary Daniels announced that contract bids were opened for twenty-eight submarines. Congress had authorized construction of thirty-eight subs, of which ten had already been assigned to the Portsmouth Yard. On April 23, at 1:15 P.M., the first of these submarines, the *L-8,* slipped into the waters of the Piscataqua from the Franklin Shiphouse. The launch went off without a hitch. In an ironic mishap, however, the submarine and the Navy tug *Penacook* collided shortly thereafter in the river [140]

Later that summer, on August 1, 1917, in another key development, Lieutenant Commander Thomas Mott Osborne reported for duty at the Portsmouth Navy Yard as the superintendent of the prison. A pioneering reformer in the American penal system, Osborne had served with distinction as warden at Auburn Prison, and subsequently at Sing Sing in New York state. There he developed the Mutual Welfare League system, with its motto, "Trust and Be Trusted." Its objective was to rehabilitate the prisoners with sympathetic guidance so they could achieve a degree of self-esteem and cooperation in a system of self-government. Osborne himself experienced actual prison conditions by posing as "Tom Brown" and living and working as an ordinary prisoner for a few days. His reputation came to the attention of Secretary Daniels, who appointed and commissioned him as commandant of the naval prison system, with the rank of lieutenant commander in the reserve corps. Daniels, it was said, gave Osborne a free hand in using his methods to reform the military prison system. At the time of his appointment, Osborne made his objectives clear. Stating that his work was to "save good sailors for the Navy," Osborne strove to restore prisoners with minor offenses to active duty, where their services were badly needed. "I found many confined to the prison," he stated, "for no real crime but merely misdemeanors against the navy regulations and they

Thomas Mott Osborne, noted penal reformer, was appointed Naval Prison superintendent during World War I. Osborne's lenient Mutual Welfare League system proved successful, restoring many naval prisoners to active duty and releasing them to fight the enemy, not to languish unproductively in cells. PNSY

are fully equipped valuable sailors that are badly needed. I hope to be able to repair them so that they will be able to return to the service fully equipped as is the wish of Secretary Daniels." Osborne's methods at the

Yard prison proved very successful. During November and December 1917, he ordered more than 200 men restored to active duty.[141]

As 1917 drew to an end, the accomplishments of the Yard and the Navy to further the war effort were impressive. "LARGEST NAVY IN HISTORY OF UNITED STATES," headlined a *Herald* article on December 31. "The Navy was ready when war began. . . . [I]t had only to go ahead with plans arranged in advance. It has not had to change its organization. It has simply increased in size at every point, and gone over the top." Statistics revealed unprecedented growth in the amount of ships, personnel, and congressional appropriations. "But the Navy has done more in the past year than merely expand," continued the *Herald*. "It has been engaged day after day for months in the actual business of naval warfare. It has sunk [German] submarines—how many, the Department is not telling. The first American forces to land in France for service against the Germans were units of the naval aeronautic corps. They were landed at a French port in early June."[142]

The German expectation and gamble that the U-boat offensive would cripple Allied shipping sufficiently to prevent American ship convoys from reaching England and Europe failed. Convoy-escorted ship losses were light.[143]

Even birds helped the United States Navy catch German submarines. A Massachusetts ornithologist, Edward H. Forbush, testified to a state legislative committee that gulls played an important role in detecting U-boats. "Gulls are the best submarine detectors in the world," said Forbush. "Gulls follow submarines in order to pick up garbage. Airplanes see the gulls and signal for destroyers to come up and take care of the submarines."[144]

Despite the fact that the gulls, the convoys, and the minefields were winning the war against the U-boats, New Hampshire and Maine coastal residents were always wary of apparent "sightings." On Sunday, June 2, 1918, during the late afternoon, summer residents of Rye claimed they sighted, through field glasses, several U-boats hovering off the Isles of Shoals. That same day, several motorboat parties claimed to have seen four U-boats near Boon Island. On Monday, July 22, 1918, one sighting turned out to be far from imaginary. A genuine U-boat stopped the Gloucester fishing schooner *Robert and Richard* sixty-five miles off Cape Porpoise, Maine, a short distance up the coast from the Portsmouth Navy Yard. After the fishermen were taken off

When Navy Yard Ferry 1048 was trapped in Piscataqua River ice on February 11,
1918, Yard commuters had to disembark and continue their journey to work over
boards laid across the ice. PA

and ordered into dories, the Germans placed a bomb aboard the
schooner, sending it to the bottom of the ocean. The dorymen reached
Kennebunkport the next evening.[145]

Despite these occasional incidents, U-boat activity off the New
England coast remained more of a nuisance and a scare, not posing
even the remotest possibility of curtailing American shipping. For its
part, the Yard worked hard to react to any enemy threat. In early
March, the Yard announced that jobs were available "for able-bodied,
intelligent men who are willing to learn the shipbuilding trade." Taken
on as helpers at $2.64 to $2.96 a day, the men were given the chance to
attend free night school twice a week within the Navy Yard in order to
become qualified mechanics. Promotion to mechanic's pay was assured
within a reasonable time. In the shipfitting force, riveting contests
were held. On May 23, riveter Michael Lynch and his crew—consisting
of a holder-on, a passer, and a heater—established a record by driving
1,931 rivets into a submarine in eight hours. Such motivation made it

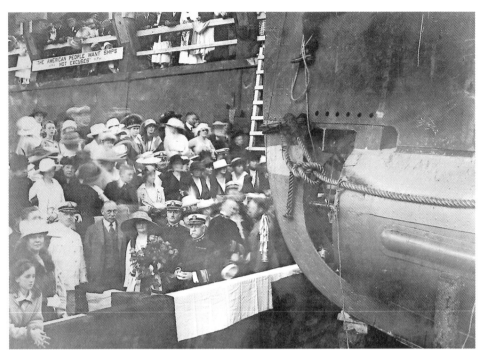

Scene at the O-1 *christening at the Yard's Franklin Shiphouse on July 9, 1918.
Note the World War I sense of spirit in the banner (top left) proclaiming, "THE
AMERICAN PEOPLE WANT SHIPS—NOT EXCUSES." PNSMVC*

possible to launch the *O-1,* the Yard's second submarine, on July 9.
With the vastly increased Yard workforce—which climbed to more than
5,500 men in 1918—the government, to ease the housing squeeze, took
over two local hotels in Kittery Point, the Hotel Champernowne and
the Pepperell. To give the men a chance to relax with physical exercise
after a hard day's work, the Navy Yard Baseball League was organized
in late July 1918; the season was scheduled from July 29 to October 21.
The games began at 4:45 P.M. and were called at 6 P.M., with five full
innings constituting a game (shortened to three innings when rain
threatened). The games were played on the prison grounds with nine
teams in the league: Shipfitters Shop, Boat Shop, Electrical Machine
Shop, Smith Shop, Foundry, Spar Shop, Pattern Shop, Building Trades,
and Trade School.[146]

Baseball, and sports in general, played a major role in Osborne's
administration of the naval prison to provide recreation for all the

Winning the Navy Yard Baseball League championship in 1918, the ten-member team poses for a group photograph. PNSMVC

inmates. In the Prison League during late August, the naval prison team was leading the three-team league, playing against the men of the auxiliary barracks and the USS *Southery* prison ship, the other league members. The Navy Commission on Training Camp Activities, headed by the renowned football coach Walter Camp, Navy commissioner of athletics, strove to provide athletic recreation for every inmate in Portsmouth's naval prison. According to Osborne's report, of the roughly 2,500 prisoners, with many participating in several sports, more than 7,350 were registered in some branch of athletic endeavor—football, soccer, basketball, volleyball, calisthenics, baseball, or playground ball.

A prison football league played until the snow began to fly. For holidays such as the Fourth of July or Thanksgiving, Osborne arranged boxing matches, track meets, football games, and evening entertainment. On an October Sunday, Chaplain Henry Van Dyke, the noted diplomat, minister, and author, gave an informal and well-received talk at the prison. Osborne himself frequently spoke at area churches and civic gatherings to articulate his objectives at the Yard prison. The rapport he developed with prisoners allowed them to be "trustees" working outside the walls "on their honor and without a guard." In time, "outside labor," as it was known, formed 102 working crews, busy at the Supply Department, Public Works, and Military Departments, performing labor essential to the war effort. Osborne also established a fund—supported in part by contributions earned at his lecture engagements—to aid needy prisoners. Among other compassionate purposes, the fund was used for "paying the expenses of prisoners who are called home by sickness or death in the family." Such humane rehabilitation produced satisfactory results for the Yard and the Navy, restoring hundreds of inmates to active duty. The newly released sailors were again on duty at various stations, working to defeat the enemy, not languishing unproductively behind walls.[147]

During the fall of 1918, with the Allies winning the war on sea and land, many military, industrial, and political dignitaries visited the Yard on inspection tours. On Wednesday, September 25, the U.S. Exports Commission arrived, along with the Shipping Board Commission, its chairman, and two of the most prominent American military leaders. General George W. Goethals, builder of the Panama Canal and quartermaster-general of the Army, and Admiral William S. Benson, chief of naval operations, toured the L.H. Shattuck Ship Yard, the Atlantic Corporation, the various Portsmouth breweries, and the Navy Yard itself. Everything ran like clockwork on a tight schedule until the distinguished party, forty in number, decided to go aboard a submarine (undoubtedly the *O-1)* at the Navy Yard. The shipkeeper on duty at the head of the gangway halted the group. "Pardon me," he said, "but you can't go aboard." The industrial manager of the Yard identified himself but had no regulation pass. The guard was unimpressed, saying, "I don't know anything about that." Admiral Clifford J. Boush was called and introduced as the shipyard commandant, but to no avail. "He may be the Commandant," responded the guard. "I don't deny it, but my orders are to allow no one to go aboard the submarine without the official pass." Benson and Goethals looked on helplessly. A master workman was sent for, and within a few minutes the crisis was

On October 31, 1918, Navy Secretary Josephus Daniels dedicated the new YMCA hut, located in front of the Castle. Built under the auspices of Lieutenant Commander Thomas M. Osborne, superintendent of the Naval Prison, the facility provided prisoners with a meeting place for religious services and recreation. PNSMVC

resolved, with Goethals and Benson allowed to go aboard with proper authority. Benson stepped up to the guard and said, "I am the senior officer of the Navy and want to shake your hand and compliment you for your proper performance of your duty."[148]

As Allied victory in the Great War neared, Secretary Daniels visited Portsmouth again—not only to dedicate the new YMCA hut at the Yard prison, but also, politician that he was, to address a Democratic Party rally at the Portsmouth Theatre in support of candidates in the 1918 congressional election. On October 31, with Lieutenant Commander Osborne as chairman of the dedication exercises, Daniels first inspected the Yard prison and then addressed 1,600 prisoners outside the YMCA hut. This facility, erected near the main prison building, provided a meeting place in its main room for religious services, musicals, and other entertainment. The club room was fitted with a fireplace, easy chairs, two pianos, and writing and reading tables. Afterward, Daniels addressed 5,000 workmen from in front of the commandant's residence. In his flag-waving speech, received with rousing cheers, Daniels concluded: "We shall look to carry on this great work until our Navy is so powerful that in a League of Nations we will furnish so many units that none of our children or children's children will ever see a king or emperor or autocrat dare to stir the peace of the world." Upon returning to Washington, Daniels issued an order on November 9, discontinuing all Sunday work in navy yards and other shore stations of the Navy. "The action is taken," Daniels said, "to save men from the strain of a seven day week now that production in most essentials is exceeding requirements.[149]

Notwithstanding Daniels's optimism as the Allies were approaching victory, a dangerous enemy invaded the United States—not in the form of bullets, shells, poison gas, or torpedoes. Spanish influenza struck the Atlantic seaboard, especially New England, in the late summer of 1918. Before the virulent sickness ran its course and ended approximately two months later, deaths in the United States totaled between 400,000 and 500,000. The Portsmouth Navy Yard, particularly the confined quarters of the naval prison, was hit especially hard. The "grippe," as it was called originally, spread northward from the Boston naval installations, first appearing at the Commonwealth Pier on August 28. "The symptoms are similar in each case," reported the *Herald*. "Pains in the bones, watery eyes, headache and high fever develop." Within a short time, the flu usually developed into pneumonia. Rest was prescribed. At its height at the Yard on October 1, the influenza crippled the war effort. Incoming prisoners communicated the germ to the workmen. Between 1,500 and 1,600 men, out of a total of 5,722 Yard employees, were away from work daily because of the epidemic. Four hundred Yard prisoners were ill. At least two inmates and one Yard workman died. Influenza-related fatalities for the Portsmouth area probably amounted to about ten people, a mercifully slight figure compared to the national and international toll. By early October, the number of cases lessened, and by the end of that month, the ban against enlisted men visiting Dover, which had been in effect during the epidemic, was lifted. At the same time, sailors were permitted to mingle in public places and enjoyed movies and other entertainment in theaters. The ordeal was over for the Yard, the area communities, and the nation.[150]

The news of the Armistice, ending the fighting, reached Portsmouth at 3:00 A.M. on November 11, 1918. Yard workers reported as usual to their jobs. At noon, the whistles on the ships, tugs, ferryboats, and other craft at the Yard filled the air with great noise for twenty minutes, while whistles on the Portsmouth side joined in the blow, accompanied by the ringing of bells. The excitement was so great that the Yard commandant suspended work in the early afternoon, and everyone went home to celebrate. The Great War was over.[151]

The heady excitement lasted but a short time, as the nation, the Navy, and the Yard faced the realities of a peacetime economy. The wartime budget was soon slashed, and appropriations, work projects, and the number of Yard personnel diminished. This process began before the month was out. On November 19, it was reported that the Navy could spare 50,000 men. By November 30, Secretary Daniels ordered that 70,000 men in the Navy be released as soon as possible. "The strength of the navy now is 500,000 men in round numbers," reported the *Herald* on November 30. "Under the demobilization plan of the navy, about 20 per cent of the duration of the war men and of the reserves will be released." Such reductions affected the Portsmouth Navy Yard immediately. With their idealism and patriotism to win the war ebbing since the Armistice, the Yard molders went out on strike on Friday, November 15. They protested the practice of allowing the prisoners to work in the shops. With the rush of war work during 1917 and most of 1918, when it was impossible to secure laborers and helpers, this arrangement had been permitted. Now that the war was over and overtime pay was cut, the union representing the molders fought to rescind the earlier agreement. The molders also sent telegrams to Secretary Daniels, citing the grounds for their protest. On Saturday, November 16, a committee of molders met with Yard authorities, and together they settled their dispute at a conference, agreeing that the prisoners would no longer be allowed in the shops. The molders returned to work on Monday. At the prison itself, a new mood set in. On Saturday, December 14, the prison released 200 men with a dishonorable discharge from the Navy and provided government funds for transportation to their homes. The prisoners were from almost every state in the Union, and some were from the Philippines. In view of the personnel reduction underway in the Navy, this decision offered a practical solution and reversed the earlier wartime practice of returning

As an escort guard in late 1918, Sailor Humphrey Bogart was assigned to accompany a prisoner to the Yard for internment at the Castle. A botched escape attempt left the future actor with facial injuries, resulting in a massive lip scar and a slight lisp. PNSY

prisoners to uniform. At the same time, however, Lieutenant Osborne restored 120 men to active duty, whereupon they returned to their ships and stations. During the same late-1918 time period (the exact date was not recorded), an unfortunate incident resulted in the Yard's dubious contribution to American theater and cinema. While escorting a prisoner to Portsmouth, a young Navy guard, Humphrey Bogart, was injured during an escape attempt, leaving the future actor with a massive lip scar and a slight lisp.[152]

On December 17, the Yard prepared to launch the submarine *S-3*. Two thousand or more spectators waited in the Franklin Shiphouse, on the bridges, and on the Kittery shore to watch the event. At 11:30 A.M., a chaplain gave his blessing, and shortly thereafter, the launching commenced. The sub moved down the ways about thirty-six inches, where she stuck hard and fast, and no amount of coaxing could budge the sub. Cold weather and a poor-quality grease were blamed. Four days later, a second attempt, with regreased ways, resulted in a successful launch. "The *S-3* is a credit to navy yard workmen," commented the *Herald*. "She is 800 tons displacement and one of the largest American submarines yet built." For the 4,688 Yard workmen (down by more than a thousand since October) and the American people, the four-day launch delay and the size of the submarine probably registered little concern in a time of peace. With Secretary Daniels's recent remarks and President Woodrow Wilson's devout belief that the Great War was "the war to end all wars," the American people basked in a temporary euphoria that the submarine launched that day might never be used in conflict, only for purposes of everlasting peace.

Concerning the future, the chaplain's blessing at the *S-3* launch undoubtedly seemed most appropriate, when the Reverend Edward D. Henry invoked, "May her errands on and under the deep sea be those which further the ends of peace and justice, humanity and Christian civilization. Through Jesus Christ, our Lord, Amen."[153]

"Our Ability to Make Good": Hard Times at the Yard, 1918–1933

The idealism embodied in Chaplain Henry's hope that submarines might thereafter be used only to advance peaceful aims prevailed for more than a decade. During the 1920s, politicians, diplomats, and

A riveting party at the Franklin Shiphouse on January 20, 1919, prepares to drive the first rivet into the keel of the submarine S-9. Along with two other Yard officers, Naval Prison Superintendent Thomas Mott Osborne (second from right) poses with two younger civilians, a rivet passer and a rivet heater. PNSY

pacifists, not naval officers, made the key decisions in determining the future of the United States Navy. After the Great War, the Yard languished with a smaller number of employees, fewer prisoners, and reduced budgets. During this sluggish period, the Yard workforce withered away from an all-time high of 5,500 employees in 1918 to fewer than 1,500 by the end of 1932.[154]

In January 1919, Yard Industrial Manager Laurence S. Adams articulated the challenge ahead. "Now that hostilities have ceased and emergency war work has been reduced," he wrote, "the question arises as to what the future prospects of the Yard are. Briefly, the answer to this is—it depends on us and our ability to make good."[155]

The Yard braced itself for a painful transitional period of downsizing. On January 2, 1919, the yeowomen were the first to leave, with eight from the Supply Department going onto the "inactive list." That same day, more than thirty women in the Industrial Department received their discharge notices. In April, according to the *Herald*, "Owing to lack of money, 25 female operators" were let go from the electrical shop. The Trades School, established during the war, was abolished. In May, Yard plumbers began working a three-day schedule due to a lack of appropriation. By September, the naval prison population dipped to 950 inmates, the smallest number since 1914, which led to the closing of several auxiliary barracks for housing prisoners. Amid severe cutbacks in virtually every category, rumors circulated that the Yard's very existence was in jeopardy.

"To Junk All Submarines," read a headline in the *Herald* on February 4, 1919. "The reported decision to the Peace Conference [then underway in Paris] to 'cut out' submarines and junk them caused a shiver to creep down the spine of some of the yard officials. . . . It appears to be a forgone conclusion that 'subs' must go."[156]

Despite this alarming rumor, the work of the Yard went on. In January 1919, the long-sought proposal to build a bridge across the Piscataqua was brought before the House Naval Affairs Committee in Washington. "The bridge is needed," declared Navy Secretary Josephus Daniels, "so that the 2,500 employees of the Navy Yard who live in Portsmouth can have better facilities getting back and forth to their work." The estimated cost of the bridge ranged from $1,750,000 to $2,750,000, with Maine and New Hampshire to pay half and the federal government to assume the other half. On June 30, the approved Naval Bill set the government's share at only $500,000, much lower than the figure originally proposed. But the bridge was built and ultimately opened to traffic on August 17, 1923.[157]

By providing this transportation artery for the Yard workers and for truckers conveying materials, the Navy was able to build its submarines more efficiently. During the 1918–33 period, the Yard completed seventeen submarines, nine of them S-boats. With the usual fanfare of a large crowd and a Navy band, the *S-5* was launched on November 10, 1919. "The *S-5* is 231 feet in length," reported the *Herald,* with "21 foot beam, 13 foot draught and surface displacement of 870 tons. She is capable of making 15 knots on the surface and 12 1/2 below."[158]

On March 15, 1920, news arrived that the Navy Department had awarded the Yard three submarine contracts, involving an outlay of $10 million, for the new V-class, to be the largest type of sub yet built by the United States Navy. With a displacement of 2,000 tons, double that of the S-class, the new submarine would be able to accompany the fleet anywhere. Commander H.S. Howard of the Yard was called to Washington to help perfect the design for the prototype. "This assures the retention," stated the *Herald,* "of the entire submarine organization that Captain [Laurence S.] Adams, the Industrial Manager, has perfected, and which has reached such a degree of efficiency that he was most anxious to retain it as a permanent organization."[159]

In the meantime, the remaining S-boats on the building ways continued to be launched—but with one change in the christening ceremonies. Because the Eighteenth Amendment prohibiting alcohol went into effect on January 17, 1920, the customary champagne bottle employed on such occasions was now banned. On April 21, the *S-8* launch from the historic Franklin Shiphouse found the woman sponsor using "Portsmouth ginger ale in naming the underwater sea fighter." On June 17 of the same year, at the launch of the *S-9,* the sponsor "used grape juice."[160]

The operation of the Yard prison also underwent postwar change. Lieutenant Commander Thomas Mott Osborne's era of prison reform ended with his resignation in February 1920. On March 10, Secretary Daniels accepted Osborne's resignation, commending him: "The policy of helpfulness and hope will be continued, for you have taught the navy and the country that prisons are to mend the prisoners and not to break them." Responding to Daniels, Osborne summed up his accomplishments: "During these two years and seven months there have been at the prison 6,844 men, as many as 2,500 at one time, and we have handled this enormous number with no riots, no strikes, no brutality, no excessive punishments." Before he left the prison in late March, Osborne reenacted the symbolic role he had assumed when he first began his service—as "Tom Brown," in prison grays sawing wood. The conciliatory spirit that Osborne had nurtured within the prison gave way to his successors' more restrictive and rigid policies.[161]

Events on the international scene were vital concerning the Yard's interests. On February 6, 1922, the world's leading naval powers—Great Britain, the United States, Japan, France, and Italy—signed the Five-Power Disarmament Treaty in Washington, D.C. The treaty mandated a ten-year naval holiday, assigning a 5–5–3–1.75–1.75 ratio to capital ship tonnage. Since capital ships

On February 7, 1921, ex-Assistant Secretary of the Navy Franklin D. Roosevelt (second from left), now a private citizen, appeared with his family at the launch of the S-11. *Anna Eleanor Roosevelt, his daughter, christened the boat with a bottle of sparkling cider, in accordance with the new Prohibition amendment. PA*

included battleships and battle cruisers but not submarines, the Yard escaped relatively unscathed from the direct effects of this treaty.

"Portsmouth has no such [capital] ships under contruction, not even under repair," commented the *Herald* on February 10. "The submarine work not being interfered with is the salvation of the Portsmouth yard." The resulting economic blow for other navy yards brought an immediate response from William H. Johnston, president of the International Association of Machinists. In a letter quoted in the "NAVY YARD NOTES" section of the *Herald*, Johnston wrote to President Warren G. Harding that any discharge of American navy-yard workers would be regarded as "extremely inconsiderate, heartless, and inhuman," as well as an act of "broken faith." Although the Portsmouth Yard was not a home port for ships being cut back, its workforce dipped from 2,200 employees in 1922 to 1,750 in 1923. It was estimated that

Commissioned at the Yard in 1924 as the first V-boat, the USS Barracuda *(SS 163) underwent dry-docking the following year to raise the tank top. During this work, a small fire broke out around the keel blocks on August 25, 1925, but caused no serious damage. PA*

the scrapping of old ships and unfinished ships on the building ways cost the United States Navy an estimated $500 million. On July 1, 1922, the United States Senate approved the disarmament treaty, authorizing the scrapping of fifteen battleships, among them the USS *New Hampshire,* pride of the Granite State.[162]

Later that year, the Navy League of the United States, realizing the value of public relations, promoted the first "Navy Day." Founded in 1902 as a civilian organization to support the Navy and national security, the Navy League designated Friday, October 27, Theodore Roosevelt's birthday, for its initial observance. On Navy Day, the Yard opened its gates to visitors. "NAVY YARD PROVED A BIG ATTRACTION," read the *Herald*'s first-page headline. "Throngs of School Children Received First Hand Information Regarding Our Sea Defenses."

Designed and manufactured for use on V-class submarines in the 1920s, an aluminum desk and other metal furniture were fire-resistant. This desk was installed inside the sub V-4, Argonaut. UNH

Thousands of people visited the Yard. With naval officers and personnel as guides, and with the workforce on the job building and repairing ships, Navy Day was a decided success. The general public enjoyed such attractions as a submarine dive at Pier Five, a deep-sea diving exhibition, band concerts, a football game between the Navy Yard team and the Portsmouth High School Alumni at the parade ground, tours of the prison, and Marine Corps exhibition drills. The Yard also provided a souvenir booklet for all visitors. During the 1920s and 1930s, Navy Day at the Yard was one of the most popular and well-attended events of the year.[163]

The launch of the *V-1,* or USS *Barracuda* on Thursday, July 17, 1924, brought 3,100 visitors and 600 automobiles to the Yard for the grape-juice christening, followed by a special luncheon for the launching party at the Commandant's Quarters. The *Barracuda* was not an ordinary submarine. According to the *Herald* headline, she was the "Largest Ever Constructed by United States Navy and Most Modern in

The submarine O-1 arrives at the Yard for repairs on April 30, 1927. Note three rail-road cars (including two tankers) on the track in back of the sub. PNSMVC

the World." Its designation as a "fleet submarine" derived from the sub's ability to match the speed of the surface fleet. As the *Herald* explained, "The *V-1* is designed primarily to accompany the fleet at sea in any weather and to maintain any speed of which the fleet itself is capable." The V-class submarine ushered in the era of the modern submarine. Its basic architectural plan was used during World War II.[164]

In engineering, design, and crew comfort, the *V-1* was superior to earlier subs. With a surface displacement of 2,164 tons, a surface speed of 21 knots, and a submerged speed of 9 knots, the *V-1* had berths in separate staterooms for seven officers and a comfortable berth and a locker for every member of the 80-person crew. Metal furniture of contemporary design was an effective precaution against fire. Improved galley facilities, ample cold storage, and sufficient medicine and surgical appliances within the *V-1* were nearly equal to standards maintained aboard surface vessels.[165]

Through the rest of the 1920s, the Yard continued a moderate pace

Driven ashore by a blinding northeaster blizzard on January 29, 1925, the battered and grounded sub S–48 awaits a cable tow and pull to the nearby Portsmouth Navy Yard. Finally arriving there a week later, the S–48 was reconditioned and recommissioned in late 1928. PA

of repair and submarine construction, launches, and commissionings. Perhaps the most dramatic event concerned the well-documented and-photographed saga of the *S-48* as she approached the entrance of Portsmouth Harbor. Caught in a blinding snowstorm, the *S-48* hit a ledge off Fort Stark, Jeffrey's Point, New Castle, and grounded on the mudflats off Frost Point. Although she was badly flooded, the officers and crew managed to escape. Salvage parties from the Yard arrived the next morning. A week later, the *S-48* was refloated and towed to the Yard. For two years, its status remained nebulous in the absence of funds for restoration and repair. Finally, on February 3, 1927, the sub was pulled to the Franklin Shiphouse by three Boston & Maine loco-

Battered and grounded in a January 29, 1925, northeaster snowstorm, the S-48 was towed to the Yard, rebuilt, and reconditioned. She rejoined the fleet in 1928. PNSMVC

motives. This engineering feat took twenty minutes. "Her reconditioning, amounting practically to a reconstruction," wrote a naval officer at the time, "was undertaken by the Yard." Extensively overhauled and altered, the *S-48* was lengthened by twenty-five feet. The sub was launched on September 4, 1928, and recommissioned. On January 9, 1929, after being out of commission for almost four years, she sailed on a shakedown cruise.[166]

After the Roaring Twenties reduced the strength of the Yard, the 1930s brought an even more difficult and critical phase. First the stock-market crash in October 1929 plunged the country into the Great Depression. The United States struggled with internal economic affairs and showed little interest in its Navy. President Herbert Hoover, burdened with a complete economic downturn, did not promote an increased naval budget, and the United States Senate approved the London Naval Treaty of 1930, which favored a reduction. According to the Navy League and other naval experts, the neglect of

Officers and crew of the S-4 *pose—probably at a Yard dock in the late 1920s—with one sailor peering through a sub life preserver (top center). The 1927 sinking of the* S-4 *during sea trials prompted major safety reforms. PNSMVC*

the United States Navy was at the point of jeopardizing national security. One of the few bright spots at the Yard during these fiscally pinched times was the observance of "Constitution Day" on July 4, 1931. On a goodwill tour, the USS *Constitution* attracted vast crowds, many coming aboard to tour the recently reconstructed historic vessel. Recalling the long association of the ship with the Yard, many citizens considered the *Constitution* "back home." In one of the speeches commemorating the event, Portsmouth Mayor F.W. Hartford related the significance of the ship to the current times. "That there may be no step backward in America. . . . The *Constitution* is our banner and the citizens are going to carry it to awaken the old-time spirit that the country so much needs today."[167]

As the Great Depression deepened, Navy Yards competed vigorously for work and contracts. In November 1932, President Hoover's secretary of the Navy, Charles F. Adams, decided to assign the repair of the destroyer *Patoka* to the Portsmouth Yard. The Charlestown (Boston) Yard felt slighted, compelling Adams to write to the mayor of Boston: "The matter of placing ships in our various yards for repairs, and providing a proper balance between navy needs of keeping a fair and equal work load at the various yards, is very complicated and difficult . . . it is all guess work. Under the circumstances. I believe the dispositions we have made to be as nearly as possible just."[168]

On Tuesday, November 8, 1932, Election Day dawned with President Hoover opposed by New York Governor Franklin D. Roosevelt. A number of Yard workmen were allowed as much as two hours without loss of pay to vote in towns where restricted hours would otherwise prevent them from casting their ballots. Roosevelt won handily. In his Annual Report issued in early December, outgoing Navy Secretary Adams openly articulated the glaring weakness of the United States Navy, which now trailed England and Japan in the number of fighting ships. "Curtailment of expenditures," he stated, "has been made principally at the expense of the fighting fleet."[169]

The national economic slump was reflected locally at the Yard, whose workers had been for some time on a system of "rotative leave," an alternative to discharge. The Yard's industrial manager, master workmen, and a delegation of the Navy Yard Improvement Society met on December 12, 1932, to assist the unemployed. Collections taken in the various shops were turned over to the Yard accounting officer for distribution to the jobless. By late 1932, the prison population had dropped to 291 inmates, the lowest number since the Great War.[170]

During January and February of 1933, as the Yard awaited the departure of the Hoover administration on March 4, 1933, nearly 200 men were out on the rotative furlough list, the naval prison population declined to 157 inmates, and the Yard workforce numbered only 1,488 civilians. In Washington, a proposed economic amendment included a provision requiring the Navy to cut expenditures by five percent. A Republican opponent of this amendment declared that such a program would "make it absolutely impossible for the United States to defend itself in case of war." The chairman of the House Naval Committee told reporters that such cuts, along with forcing the reduction of naval personnel and warship decommissionings, would result in "closing three navy yards on the Atlantic coast, those at Charleston, S.C., Boston, Mass., and Portsmouth, N.H." In this tense atmosphere, President Franklin D. Roosevelt, less than twenty-four hours after his inauguration, issued an executive order to close the banks to avert a national panic. Despite this "bank holiday," the Yard paid its workers on Friday, March 8. The Yard disbursing officer had made arrangements "with the First National Bank of this city [Portsmouth] and the Federal Reserve Bank of Boston for the necessary money to cover the regular payments.[171]

In 1933, a new administration offered some hope to the Yard that Commander-in-Chief Roosevelt, who had been assistant Navy Secretary a decade earlier, would return the Navy to its former prominence.

Roosevelt Galvanizes the Yard onto a War Footing, 1933–1941

When Franklin D. Roosevelt was inaugurated in March 1933, he responded at once to grave domestic and world conditions. Increasing foreign threats throughout the decade necessitated a large American Navy. Roosevelt's New Deal program put the Portsmouth Navy Yard back to work with numerous building contracts, expanded submarine construction, and a tripling of the Yard's workforce. The Works Progress Administration (WPA) created employment in Yard public-works projects. The president's visits to the Portsmouth area in 1933 and to the Yard itself in 1940 lifted morale. Despite accidents involving the subs *Squalus* in 1939 and *O-9* in 1941, the Navy and the Yard persevered to build a strong fleet, rated as the world's largest in 1940. Newfound pride was reflected in a naval officer's statement that the day of referring to Uncle Sam's men of war as "gobs" had passed. The unnamed officer further asserted that "the superiors throughout the service avoid using the word as it is considered a slur on the navy enlisted man, who is trained to maintain a clean cut, upstanding poise."[172]

On March 8, 1933, Roosevelt's choice for the post of secretary of the Navy, Claude A. Swanson, reflected his own desire for a strong U.S. Navy. In his first pronouncement as head, Swanson declared: "I think we should keep up a fleet adequate to protect our commerce and guard our rights and territory." Furthermore, "the fleet should go where

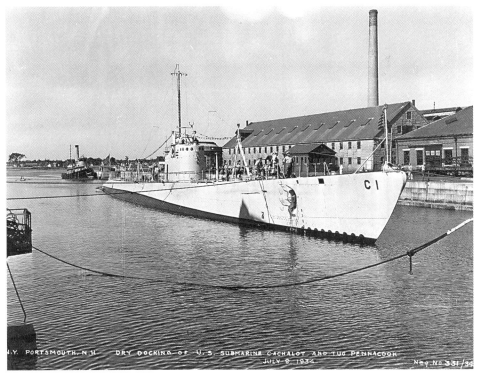

One of the last riveted-hull subs, the USS Cachalot *awaits dry-docking and repairs during the summer of 1934. Note the Navy tug* Penacook *in the left background. PNSMVC*

needed." Roosevelt and Swanson acted decisively. On August 4, 1933, Washington announced a naval building program costing nearly $300 million, with allotments for construction of two submarines at the Portsmouth Yard.[173]

President Roosevelt employed his first vacation from the White House on a yachting cruise along the New England coast in late June 1933. "The mere fact that he is President of the United States," commented the *Herald,* "has not lessened Franklin D. Roosevelt's interest in yachting." "Skipper" Roosevelt, or "America's sailor president," as the press called him, was reported to have donned oilskins during squally weather while handing the tiller. On the evening of June 21, his *Amberjack II,* a 45-foot schooner, docked at the Wentworth Hotel dock, Little Harbor, near Portsmouth. Upon receiving a radio order, the Yard's Supply Department loaded meat, bread, provisions, and fresh water aboard the Yard tug *Penacook* for delivery to the *Amberjack II.* The next morning, the *Penacook* returned with mail, messages, and various supplies for the presidential party.[174]

During the rest of 1933, the upgraded Yard marked the progress of the resurgent Navy. On October 19, the submarine USS *Cachalot* was launched from the Franklin Shiphouse building ways into the Piscataqua. A special distinction of the launch was that the sponsor used a bottle of real champagne, legal again with the repeal of Prohibition. (On December 1, the *Cachalot* went into commission, carrying a crew of five officers and forty-two men.) Only eight days after the launch of the *Cachalot,* on October 27, the Yard observed Navy Day with an open house, combined with the laying of the keel of the submarine *Porpoise,* the first keel put down in any of the government navy yards under Roosevelt's National Industrial Recovery Act. The *Porpoise* was the first of four cruiser submarines authorized by the Act. The others were the *Pike,* a forthcoming Yard project, as well as the *Shark* and the *Tarpon,* slated for construction at Electric Boat, Groton, Connecticut.[175]

In his 1933 Annual Report, Secretary Swanson urged the naval building program to make the United States "second to none" and further declared: "Our weakened position does not serve the cause of peace." As the holidays approached, Yard workers received more favorable news. An executive order from President Roosevelt granted all workers in navy yards two full Saturday holidays (December 23 and 30) before the Christmas and New Year holidays.[176]

As mentioned above, the Yard also benefited from projects of the Works Progress Administration (WPA), created by Roosevelt in 1935 to provide employment for useful public projects. Over a period of nine years, the WPA spent about $11 billion and gave jobs to nearly nine million people. The 135 WPA workers at the Yard during the 1930s undertook necessary projects and collected paychecks every two weeks. In 1937, part of the WPA crew was engaged in the operation of a stone crusher at Henderson's Point to prepare material for road repair work. Others sandblasted layers of excess paint from the discolored buildings of Officers' Row and the Marine barracks. That May, still another crew caulked the joints of the dry dock to prevent leakage, thus eliminating a problem that had existed for several years. By 1940, the number of WPA workers, under an allotment of $200,000, had increased to 500 men to continue construction and surfacing of railroad tracks, roads, and walks.[177]

After almost a century of service, the Franklin Shiphouse (Building 53) burned and collapsed in a predawn fire on March 10, 1936. Despite valiant efforts by the Yard's Fire Department, the structure was a total loss. UNH

The highly sought-after U.S. Civil Service jobs were snapped up quickly. In May 1937, for example, the list opened for apprentices at the Yard for ten days. Youths who passed the general examination could select from a number of trades: coppersmith, joiner, machinist, molder, patternmaker, pipefitter, plumber, sheet-metal worker, shipfitter, and shipwright. The pay started at $14.40 per week and increased to $28.80 upon completion of the four-year apprenticeship for the trade that they selected.[178]

The 1930s saw the end of several Yard institutions and traditions. For years, "Old Tom," the Marine Corps horse and personal mount of Colonel Robert W. Huntington during the Spanish-American War, had been the Yard mascot. After his death on April 23, 1933, Old Tom was buried with full military honors. His stone is located just to the rear of the present Portsmouth Naval Shipyard Museum. On March 10, 1936, a second link to the past ended. Just before 5 A.M., a sentry discovered that the historic Franklin Shiphouse was on fire, and he turned in an alarm from Box 35. Despite the heroic efforts of the Yard and the nearby Kittery Fire Department, the structure burned to the ground in less than an hour. Many historic ships had been launched from its ways, including six submarines. Another picturesque Yard tradition passed into history with the disappearance of "bum boaters," for years familiar waterfront figures. "These men moved about from one ship to another selling pies, candy, fruit, and other sweets," noted the *Herald* in June 1937. "They also sold articles of clothing. Since the modernization of ships, the ships' stores or commissaries take care of the selling of such articles, and the 'boaters' faded from the picture."[179]

A new modern Navy emerged at the Yard. When laying the keel of the submarine USS *Snapper* on July 23, 1936, workmen at first drove rivets into the hull, but tests revealed that an all-welded hull was much stronger, prompting a complete change in its construction. Launched on August 24, 1937, the *Snapper* was the Navy's first all-welded-hull submarine and became the prototype for all United States subs thereafter. After the sinking of the *S-4* off Provincetown, Massachusetts, in 1927, the Navy developed submarine safety devices to aid rescue in the event of accidents. The Submarine Escape Appliance, invented in 1929, is best known as the "Momsen Lung," after its inventor, Lieutenant Charles B. Momsen. This breathing devise supplies oxygen as its user ascends to the surface. In addition, the McCann Submarine Rescue Chamber, developed by Momsen, Lieutenant Commander Andrew I. McKee, and Lieutenant Commander Allan R. McCann, was a decided improvement over the earlier diving bell. These inventions and other safety features were incorporated on the *Snapper,* thus substantially increasing the chances of survival should disaster occur. At the Yard's Navy Day observances in 1937 and 1938, the Momsen Lung and a watertight door were on display.[180]

In 1939, Momsen's submarine safety devices and procedures were dramatically put to a test off the Isles of Shoals. On May 23, the USS *Squalus,* a Yard-built submarine on a practice dive, sank in 243 feet of water, trapping her crew. The twenty-six men in the aft compartment perished, while the thirty-three others in the forward compartment

After the sinking of the Squalus *off the Isles of Shoals on May 23, 1939, numerous attempts to raise the sub finally succeeded on September 13, and the boat was towed to the Yard. PNSMVC*

clung to survival in a cold torpedo room. Arriving from Washington, Momsen led the rescue attempt from aboard the *Falcon*. The McCann Rescue Chamber brought the survivors to the surface on May 25, whereupon they were quickly transferred to the Yard hospital. Less than a week later, the British submarine HMS *Thetis* sank off Birkenhead, England, in the Irish Sea. Using the British-developed Davis Lung, the British rescue team saved four men, although another ninety-seven perished. Analyzing the results of the two rescue operations, the *Herald* emphasized the superiority of the Momsen Lung to its British counterpart. "The British Navy had no such devise," continued the *Herald*, "as the American Navy's heaven-blessed [McCann Submarine] rescue bell that worked to near perfection in saving the lives of 33 men from the sunken *Squalus*."[181]

Diver Harold Ross prepares for a second attempt to raise the USS Squalus *off the Isles of Shoals during the summer of 1939. PA*

The Navy was determined to salvage the sunken $5 million *Squalus.* Some of the salvage equipment—in particular, a special curved airpipe—was developed by Momsen. After a number of attempts, the raised *Squalus* was towed into the Yard on September 13. Workmen began an extensive refitting and reconditioning job estimated at $1,400,000. On May 15, 1940, the decommissioned *Squalus* was recommissioned as the USS *Sailfish,* bearing no trace of its four-month stay on the ocean floor. "There will be no plates on the submarine," noted the *Herald,* "that will make any reference to its former name." Overcoming its jinxed image, the shiny new *Sailfish* later compiled a brilliant war record.[182]

The return of the *Squalus* (as the *Sailfish)* to the United States fleet characterized the energy of the Navy and the Yard in the late

A proud day for the Yard and the Navy occurred on May 16, 1940, with the commissioning of the USS Sailfish *(ex-*Squalus). *News media (left) cover the skipper's reading of his command orders to officers and crew. PNSMVC*

1930s. Alarmed by growing German, Italian, and Japanese aggression, the United States pressed its military buildup to counter potential enemies. As early as April 1937, the Navy conducted its annual war games in a two-week training exercise in the Pacific, engaging in Problem XVIII in an area of more than five million square miles. The Yard-built *Pike,* a new fleet boat, made its appearance in these exercises. When World War II broke out in Europe, with Germany's invasion of Poland on September 1, 1939, the United States remained militarily neutral but was determined not to be caught napping in case the war spread to engulf America. The year 1939 proved to be the busiest peacetime warship-building period in American naval history, with thirty cruisers, destroyers, and submarines completed and put in commission.

As shown in a 1940 photograph, the "Admiral's Motor Boat" (note two stars on the port-side hull) was available for the Shipyard commander or other high-ranking U.S. Navy personnel to pursue such official business as inspections, tours, and potential emergency situations. PNSMVC

The year 1940 saw an even more accelerated and determined effort within the Navy and at the Yard to elevate the United States to a level of war preparedness. This momentum was reflected with new leadership in the office of the secretary of the Navy. After Claude Swanson died in office in 1939, succeeded by Charles Edison (the inventor's son who was more interested in research and invention than policy), President Roosevelt, in a shrewd bipartisan move, nominated Frank Knox for the position in late June 1940. A Manchester, New Hampshire, resident for some years as a newspaper publisher, Knox later entered national politics as Republican Alfred Landon's vice-presidential running mate in 1936. In mid-July 1940, Knox was sworn in as Navy secretary in the White House study, with Roosevelt looking on. Knox thus became the third New Hampshire resident (after Levi Woodbury and William E. Chandler) to hold the crucial post of Navy secretary. Outspoken, effective, and vigorous, Knox proved to be an excellent choice to lead the Navy.

By the summer of 1940, the United States Navy was rated the world's largest, with construction proceeding at top speed to achieve "two-ocean" strength. In September 1940, Commander-in-Chief Roosevelt announced the largest naval defense contract in history, some $3.8 billion in allocations for 201 ships, including six subs to be built at the Yard. Throughout 1940, the Yard reflected this accelerated pace. Two important new buildings were completed during that year. In late January, the six-story brick Supply Building—costing $300,000, with two freight elevators, each with a six-ton capacity, along with an automatic passenger elevator—was placed in operation. "The building is considered," according to the *Herald,* "the best supply building on any navy reservation." Six months later (on July 18), another facility, the Outside Machine Shop, was completed. "With the exception of breaking a bottle of champagne over the front steps," noted the *Herald,* "the dedication exercises for the new $225,000 Outside Machine shop at the Portsmouth Navy Yard . . . were as complete as ceremonies launching one of the submarines for which the yard is famous." Utilizing these new buildings and equipment, the USS *Triton* was commissioned at the Yard on August 15, with the sub joining the fleet nearly six months ahead of its original schedule. Important naval personages began arriving in Portsmouth for consultation: Rear Admiral Chester W. Nimitz, chief of the Bureau of Navigation in Washington, visited the Yard. On Sunday, October 27, Portsmouth's first voluntary blackout was deemed a success. The Yard commandant applauded the effort and reported a 100 percent blackout, with warning flares at an excavation site even extinguished for the occasion.[183]

During 1940, Roosevelt personally dramatized the urgency of the nation's $10 billion preparedness drive. In mid-August 1940, he led an inspection team on a three-day tour of vital national defense units in New England. On Saturday, August 10, the president and his party arrived at the Yard, greeted by a 21-gun salute. The bustling installation showed positive results of the New Deal. One of the president's first inquiries concerned the number of WPA workers employed at the

Arriving at the Yard on August 10, 1940, Commander-in-Chief Franklin D. Roosevelt and his official party inspected sub construction and viewed the USS Sailfish *at her dock. After a thirty-minute tour, Roosevelt boarded the presidential yacht* Potomac, *bound for Boston. PA*

Yard. There were 300 on the payroll on that particular day. The official party viewed the *Sailfish* at her dock, back from recent reconditioning trials. The tour included the dry dock where the submarines *Bass* and *Barracuda* were being reconditioned. Three others—*Marlin, Grenadier,* and *Grayling*—were on the ways, with a total of $27 million allotted to submarine projects. More than $1.25 million was being expended on new buildings. With the completion of his inspection, the president and his entourage boarded the yacht *Potomac* for a cruise to the Boston Navy Yard. "The Navy yard which President Roosevelt inspected today," summarized the *Herald*, "is now at an all-time high for employment. . . . Today there are a little more than 6,000. About 4,800 of these are employed during the day, where there are 1,200 on night shifts. . . . Even more men are needed now, and officials are faced with a lack of experienced men."[184]

The president's three-day tour of New England's major military bases ended in Newport, Rhode Island, where he inspected a vital component associated with Portsmouth's submarines: the torpedoes to arm them. At the torpedo station, Roosevelt was shown the two-and-a-half-ton torpedoes. In an aside to a reporter, a sailor whispered, "They spent all night polishing them," and the Navy torpedomen made adjustments as the station commander explained the mechanisms of these weapons to the presidential party. The noses of the torpedoes on display—called "fish" in naval lingo—were painted yellow to show that they were unarmed "duds."[185]

In 1941, the wartime pace accelerated, especially at the Yard—more building, more submarine production, and more secrecy. On January 24, an official order was posted in the Yard shops to notify the employees that the Yard had gone on a six-day, forty-eight-hour week. Time-and-a-half overtime pay was authorized for engineers, draftsmen, and other specialists. Four days later, the Yard commandant predicted the possibility of a seven-day work week. On January 29, the USS *Marlin*, a light scout-type submarine, slid down the ways with bare formalities, all details classified as official Navy secrets. Only the regular crew and Navy officials witnessed the launch. In late May, the Arctic schooner *Bowdoin* arrived at the Yard, a new acquisition for government service. World War I–vintage submarines were also reactivated. The *O-9*, built in 1918, had only recently been recommissioned for use as a training sub. On June 20, 1941, with thirty-three men aboard, she left the Portsmouth Yard on a routine training mission, but she failed to surface from a dive. The *O-9* sank in more than 400 feet of water, almost certainly with a crushed hull, just north of the Isles of Shoals—a short distance from the site of the *Squalus* incident just two years earlier. This time, however, the men in the stricken submarine could not be saved. Rescue attempts to reach the sub in such a great depth failed, even with the availability of a McCann Rescue Chamber.[186]

Despite this tragic event, the work of the Navy and the Yard had to go on. The city of Portsmouth shared in this undertaking. In mid-September, the huge Frank Jones brewery complex was partly demolished and carried away. Wreckers toppled the huge clock and bell

The Free French submarine Surcouf *underwent repairs and overhaul in the Yard between July and October 1941. The largest sub of her time, the* Surcouf *sailed on October 29, 1941, and sank under mysterious circumstances in the Caribbean in early 1942. PNSMVC*

tower (a local landmark for generations), as well as other buildings, to salvage 15 million bricks and 2,000 tons of cast iron, the latter needed for national defense. By the following month, 10,000 men were working at the Yard in three shifts.

For its 1941 observance of the traditional Navy Day on October 27, the occasion was renamed "Navy and Total Defense Day." The Yard was not open for public inspection as it had been in years past, responding to the realities of a national emergency with stepped-up production and armament secrecy. In its place, the Yard commemorated the occasion with officers speaking at public dinners off the base.[187]

On November 5, Harry E. Yarnell arrived at the Yard as a civilian consultant on an inspection tour for the Navy Department. As the commander of the Asiatic Fleet during the 1937 *Panay* incident, and retired since 1939 by the compulsory naval age limit, Yarnell was a leading expert on Japanese foreign and military intentions. "I believe that Japan will not stop," Yarnell told Yard officials, "until she has eliminated all foreign powers from their holdings in the East." He added: "They [the Japanese] are fully determined to carry out their 'New Order' in the East." The Yard launched its sixth sub within the year, on Wednesday, December 3, 1941, with the USS *Halibut* sliding down the ways. Four days after the launch, Yarnell's speculations proved true when the Japanese bombed Pearl Harbor on December 7. With the arrival of the news, Navy officials immediately sealed the Yard to secure the base.[188]

Delivery of Seventy-Nine Submarines, 1941–1945

No single undertaking in the Yard's 200-year history was more tumultuous than the four-year effort of every officer, sailor, and worker to win World War II. By every yardstick, production, employment, and overall activity soared to all-time peak capacity. The Yard built seventy-nine submarines during this frenzied period, surpassing Electric Boat's total by one, with roughly 22,000 employees on a three-shift, around-the-clock work schedule. Local housing developments, such as Wentworth Acres and Pannaway Manor, were constructed during this rush period to accommodate the influx of the constantly expanding workforce. Many hundreds of workers commuted from communities as distant as Amesbury and Haverhill, Massachusetts; Concord and Manchester, New Hampshire; and Biddeford and Portland, Maine. This epic effort materially helped to win World War II.[189]

On December 7, 1941, the Yard immediately swung into action. By evening, the most rigid military security had gone into effect. The Yard doubled its guard force and all leaves were canceled as sailors and Marines hurried back to their stations. Trunk telephone lines connecting all key military and naval positions were hooked up. All merchant-marine ships were ordered out of the lower harbor. Plans were completed for boarding and examining all shipping entering the harbor.[190]

On Monday, December 15, a war rally, the first held since the trying days of 1917–18, galvanized the Yard. Admiral John D. Wainwright, the Yard commandant, addressed the 8,000 workers: "When you men go back to your machines today, make them do double work.

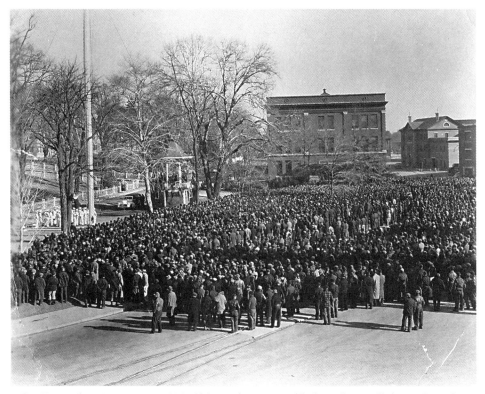

On December 15, 1941, 8,000 Shipyarders assembled at the Mall (now Squalus Memorial Park) *to hear Yard Commandant Rear Admiral John D. Wainwright deliver a wartime rallying call. PNSMVC*

We need it. You need it. In 1836 the war cry was, 'Remember the Alamo'; now, the war cry is, 'Remember Pearl Harbor.'" That same day, J. A. Perkins, a molder in the foundry, called Wainwright ro announce that he and 350 of his fellow employees had decided to work the following Sunday (December 15) to "give the President a 'lift,'" and the idea spread to the other shops. Wainwright gave approval to the suggestion at a conference of Yard officers. Such a "gift day," would have been unprecedented in Yard history. However well-intended this idealism may have been, Secretary of the Navy Frank Knox wired Wainwright: "This expression of patriotism is highly commendable and deeply appreciated. However, such gratuitous service cannot be accepted under existing statutes." Reflecting the urgency of the stepped-up workforce effort, Wainwright conveyed a dispatch that all

Gate No. 2 leads to Whipple Road, Kittery, Maine. When the Marine Guard gate service ended in June 1984, a civilian security force was contracted to assume that responsibility. PNSY–Lashua Photo

A bridge over the Back Channel connects the Yard (left) to Gate No. 2 and the town of Kittery, Maine (right). World War II expansion, rising to more than 20,000 employees at its peak, necessitated the creation of this second entrance to relieve the congestion at Gate No. 1. PNSY–Lashua Photo

*Shot Park cannon-
balls in a railroad
car await shipping
on February 2,
1942, to become
scrap-iron salvage
for the nation's war
effort. PNSMVC*

Yard workers, contrary to usual custom, were expected to be at their
machines and posts on New Year's Day.[191]

Two weeks later, unwavering Yard commitment to work production was realized with the launch of the submarine USS *Herring*, the
first undersea craft to be launched since the United States declared
war on the Axis powers. Only essential personnel, the smallest group
since World War I, witnessed the event; the others remained at their
work stations. "Latest Japanese Headache," read the *Herald*'s caption
for the photograph of the *Herring* sliding down the ways into the Piscataqua.[192]

During 1942, the Yard underwent a vast mobilization. The Works
Progress Administration (WPA) continued to augment the Yard's workforce. From an average of 235 persons during December 1941, the WPA

shifted 300 additional workers from nondefense projects in Manchester directly to the Yard in late January 1942. Occupations represented in the Manchester contingent were skilled carpenters, painters, jack-hammer operators, transit men, dynamite men, supervisors, as well as laborers. The men commuted daily by Boston and Maine train between Manchester and Portsmouth, with the transportation costs covered by the government. The train left Manchester at 5:40 A.M. and arrived in Portsmouth at 7:20 A.M. The return train departed Portsmouth at 4:15 P.M., with arrival in Manchester at 5:48 P.M. The work was conducted on a six-day basis, eight hours a day.[193]

Regular Yard workers' value to the defense effort prompted special orders from the War Department. In late January, all federal workers in all departments of the government who were members of the New Hampshire State Guard were given an honorable discharge. The Portsmouth Navy Yard men in the State Guard numbered several people. Yard workers were also entitled to special transportation accommodations as the result of tire and gasoline rationing. The Navy Department provided inexpensive transportation to workers within a fifty-mile radius of the Yard. Hundreds of buses, traveling 40,000 miles a day, fanned out to cities and towns across Maine, New Hampshire, and Massachusetts. The 14,000 men then at the Yard were insufficient to handle the enormous undertaking at hand. The Civil Service Commission recruited more qualified workmen for Yard service. Appointments were made thirty to ninety days after the application date. Positions included electrical engineers with pay of $2,000 to $2,600 a year; inspector of ships with electrical submarine experience at $2,600 annually; radio mechanics, $1,440 to $2,600 a year; and electricians at $1.06 per hour.[194]

The transition to a feverish wartime economy at defense areas brought a *New York Times* reporter to Portsmouth. In a major article, a reporter gauged the impact experienced by many Americans whose lives were "turned topsy-turvy by the war." Among others, he interviewed George and Margaret McKee, natives of Nebraska, where they had lived previously in a modest cottage on a ranch with little disposable income. In their new life, they were paying $27.50 a month for a federally built three-room cottage at Wentworth Acres. McKee was working at the Yard, "which dominates Portsmouth's economy to a heretofore unprecedented degree." At fifty-four years old, McKee drew

Taken fourteen years apart, two aerial views of the Yard demonstrate the rapid expansion stimulated by World War II. The earlier (1929, above) photograph shows a great deal of open space compared to the 1943 panorama with the enlarged prison (left), cranes, a second bridge to Kittery, and Jamaica Island development. NA–College Park, Maryland

The USS Crevalle, *built at the Yard in 236 days in 1943, compiled an outstanding patrol record, sinking the* Nisshin Maru, *the largest Japanese tanker during the war. PNSMVC*

$68 a week as a molder, which he heartily confirmed was "more damn money than I've made in my life." McKee also was certain that his high wage compensation was the same with "ninety-nine and forty-four hundredths per cent" of the yard personnel.[195]

Joining the Yard's effort in June 1942 was Rear Admiral Thomas Withers, the new Yard commandant. The kindly, hard-working commandant set an example for the Navy as well as for Yard employees. On September 1, Secretary Knox in a public letter congratulated the Yard's war effort with a Navy "E" pennant waving from a flagpole and individual buttons for the 16,000 workers. Withers started the Yard newspaper, the *Portsmouth Periscope* (with continuous publication to the present time), with its first issue on September 16, 1942. With patriotic articles, war-bond appeals, cartoons, Navy Department releases, announcements, messages from Withers, and a "Riders and Rides Wanted by the Following" column, the *Periscope* kept every Yard person thoroughly informed. A mock "reprinted" letter from the Japan-

In the first double launching of American submarines on July 20, 1942, the USS Scamp (left) and the USS Scorpion, built on parallel ways, await christening. Both boats were lost in the Pacific during World War II. PA

ese emperor in the first issue warned: "Honorable Portsmouth Worker: If you do less than your best, it will help me win the war. Thanks, Please. HIROHITO.[196]

In the meantime, Portsmouth-built submarines carried the war to the enemy in the South Pacific. Launched and commissioned at the Yard in 1939, the USS *Seawolf* operated off Java and Christmas Island, sinking a freighter-transport and a cruiser and heavily damaging two other cruisers. After each attack, the submarine was the target of prolonged depth-charge counterattacks, but the *Seawolf* escaped unscathed. "Portsmouth Navy Yard's emissary to the reaches of the China Sea, the USS *Seawolf*," reported the *Herald* in April, "has been ripping the Japanese navy to pieces."[197]

At the Yard itself during 1942, new records were set for submarine production. A double launch of the USS *Scorpion* and the USS *Scamp*

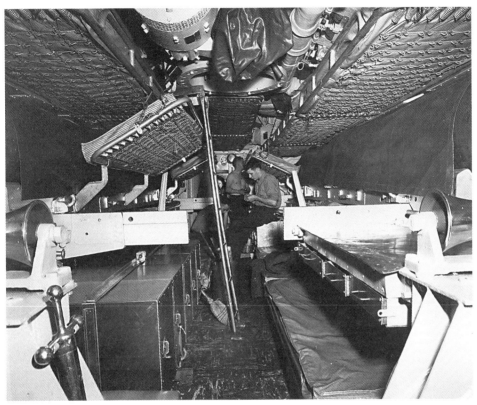

Life aboard a World War II–vintage submarine meant cramped quarters. Fold-up bed racks on the USS Sea Leopard *served as "hot bunks," with sailors sleeping in shifts to conserve precious space. PNSMVC*

on July 20, 1942, marked the first time that two submarines had been launched at one navy yard on the same day. The feat was duplicated on December 24, when the Yard achieved another double launch of the USS *Cisco* and the USS *Cabrilla*. "Yard Sends 2 Subs, 13th and 14th of 42," reported the *Herald,* "as Yule Gifts to [the] Axis." Moreover, construction of the *Cisco* was accomplished in record time for any American submarine—from keel-laying to launching—just fifty-six days. To honor the occasion, Admiral Withers relaxed the usual procedures. Many of the Yard employees who had not witnessed a launch in months were allowed to attend the festivities. Furthermore, Withers issued an announcement "that all three shifts would have tomorrow [Christmas Day] as a real holiday."[198]

Opened in April 1943, the Navy Chapel has a seating capacity of 200. Renamed the Thresher Memorial Chapel in 1963, the newly installed carillon—named the Thresher Bells—rings out daily in memory of the crew lost at sea. PNSMVC

During 1943, the Portsmouth Navy Yard received news of the first sinking of a Yard sub in combat since Pearl Harbor in 1941. On February 21, the Navy Department announced that the USS *Argonaut* was overdue and presumably lost. The sixth American sub lost, the *Argonaut* was the largest active submarine at the time—a 2,710-ton, 381-foot-long, mine-laying leviathan. She carried sixty mines. Her last patrol was off the southeast coast of New Guinea, an area where she was "prowling the Pacific where the hunting is best." Months passed, and in June 1943, the Navy Department confirmed that the *Argonaut* had been sunk in a heroic engagement. "On a war patrol conducted by the USS *Argonaut* in heavily patrolled waters," the Navy citation read, "that vessel is known to have closed and delivered a successful attack against an enemy destroyer. As a result of a severe counter-attack the *Argonaut* was forced to break surface but with no regard to personal safety and in the face of imminent death, the officers and men accepted destruction rather than surrender.[199]

To provide for the spiritual and religious needs of the Portsmouth naval community, the Yard built a new chapel on a knoll near the Submarine Barracks. Opened in early April 1943, the main chapel had a seating capacity of 200 persons, together with a small prayer room, office space for two chaplains, and a Sunday-school room.[200]

The year 1944 saw the Yard's busiest wartime production, with the delivery of thirty-two submarines. On January 24, the Yard launched four submarines—the *Redfish, Ronquil, Razorback,* and *Scabbardfish*—to establish a one-day record that still holds. The launch of the USS *Spikefish* on April 24 honored the Portsmouth equivalent of "Rosie the Riveter," symbolizing all women workers who labored for the World War II effort. Mrs. Harvey W. Moore, Jr., wife of a submarine lieutenant missing in action and a student at the Yard's welding school, welded the angle iron to the bow of the sub, fastening the nameplate that would bear the brunt of a champagne bottle used in the christening. Two days later, on Wednesday, April 26, Mrs. Moore wielded the bottle with her trusty right arm shortly before the *Spikefish* slid down the building ways.[201]

The man who sparked this gigantic construction program, Secretary of the Navy Frank Knox, died at age seventy on April 28, 1944, at his home in Washington. Under his leadership, Knox had given the United States the mightiest navy in world history. "Well done, Frank Knox," said Admiral Ernest King, naval commander-in-chief. "We dedicate ourselves, one and all, to what would surely have been his last order—carry on." New Hampshire grieved her own. "I am sure that New Hampshire," said one federal official, "will rank Frank Knox with Josiah Bartlett and Levi Woodbury, as one of her patriots." On May 1, at 2:00 P.M., the United States Navy held memorial services throughout the world, including the Yard's impressive rites conducted on the parade ground in front of the Marine barracks. The only exceptions to this observance were Navy ships in actual battle with the enemy or carrying out emergency missions. Replacing Knox as secretary of the Navy was James V. Forrestal, who had served as undersecretary for four years.[202]

An unexpected event that reflected Knox's sense of purpose occurred the following month, as Marine guards, firemen, and Yard prison inmates reacted jointly in fighting a common enemy. World War II had activated the prison to an all-time high population. As recently as May 1940, the inmate headcount had been only 85 prisoners, the

On August 9, 1944, Mrs. William B. Sieglaff, sponsor, and Mrs. George L. Street III, matron of honor, wives of two of the most successful World War II skippers, participate in launching ceremonies for USS Tirante, which Street commanded. PNSMVC

lowest in its history. During World War II, however, the building of the south annex in 1943 brought the command's potential capacity to 3,000 prisoners. On Thursday, June 8, 1944, at 4:50 A.M., with nearly 2,500 inmates in the facility, a major fire swept through two buildings and damaged a third in the sprawling complex.

Starting in what was a converted World War I mess hall used for storing camouflage nets made at the prison, the blaze spread to an adjoining carpenter shop. The third building, a Quonset hut under construction, was heavily damaged. Twenty-four prisoners and Marines were overcome by smoke; one man was seriously injured. During the conflagration, there was no sign of disorder as prisoners joined firemen in fighting the flames. It was believed the fire was started by sponta-

As one of the most successful submarines in the destruction of Japanese shipping during World War II, the USS Tirante *(SS 420) was memorialized at the Yard in 1975 with the naming of the Tirante Tavern, a popular gathering place in the Officers Club. PNSMVC*

neous combustion, with no evidence of sabotage. The total loss amounted to $100,000.[203]

Just two months later, on Wednesday, August 9, 1944, the Yard launched its twenty-first submarine of the year as the USS *Tirante* slid down the ways. For the first time in many years, a Navy chaplain did not offer a prayer for the ship before she was launched. Despite the lack of a religious blessing, though, the *Tirante* achieved a brilliant record. On her two war patrols, conducted in the spring of 1945, the *Tirante*'s exploits became part of American submarine legend. The first of these exploits won her skipper, Lieutenant Commander George L. Street III, the Presidential Unit Citation, which reads:

> For extraordinary heroism in action during the first war patrol against enemy Japanese surface forces in the harbor of Quelpart

Island off the coast of Korea on April 14, 1945. With the crew at surface battle stations, the USS *Tirante* approached the hostile anchorage from the south within 1,200 yards of the coast to complete a reconnoitering circuit of the island. Leaving the ten-fathom curve far behind, she penetrated the mine and shoal obstructed waters of the restricted harbor despite numerous patrolling vessels, and in defiance of the five shore-based radar stations and menacing aircraft, prepared to fight her way out on the surface if attacked, she went into action, sending two torpedoes with deadly accuracy into a large Japanese ammunition ship and exploding the target in a mountainous and blinding glare of white flame. Instantly spotted by the enemy as she stood out plainly in the flame of light, she quickly set up the torpedo data computer while retiring and fired her last two torpedoes to disintegrate in quick succession the leading frigate and a similar flanking vessel. With emergency full speed ahead, the *Tirante* cleared the gutted harbor and slipped undetected along the shoreline diving deep as a pursuing patrol dropped a pattern of depth charges at point of submergence. This illustrious record of daring combat achievement during her first war patrol characterized the *Tirante* as an aggressive and skilled fighter and reflected the splendid seamanship, the effective teamwork and the courage of her officers and men.[204]

With ultimate victory in sight during the spring of 1945, the nation and the Yard received the sad news that Commander-in-Chief Roosevelt had died suddenly on April 12. During his twelve years in office, the sailor–president had proved to be a loyal friend of the Yard through his visits and his continual support during its vast expansion. Praising Roosevelt, Commandant Withers eulogized: "He [Roosevelt] would wish no greater tribute than the final victory for which he has built. The navy will continue to move toward that goal."[205]

Three weeks later, this goal was partially achieved with the surrender of Nazi Germany on May 7. U-boats still at sea were either towed or escorted into the Yard for their surrender. During May, four German submarines arrived peaceably. The biggest prize was the giant 1,600-ton *U-234*, which nosed meekly into the Piscataqua and docked with her secret and grandiose mission aborted. Carrying war plans, the *U-234* had been en route to Japan with matériel hidden in her hull. Now, as prisoners-of-war, the German crew obeyed the orders of their U.S. guards to keep their arms folded. When the *U-234* skipper protested to the U.S. Coast Guard lieutenant that "your men treated us

At the end of the war with Germany in 1945, four U-boats surrendered at sea in mid-May and were escorted to the Yard, including the U-805 (left to center), fol-lowed by an American naval vessel (right). At the Yard, U-805 crew members (cen-ter) aboard the USS Argo (GPC 100) were guarded by U.S. Navy personnel (foreground). NA–College Park, Maryland

From 1945 to 1951, the captured German submarine U-3008 was studied, analyzed, and tested at the Yard to incorporate its advanced technical features in American subs. PNSMVC

like gangsters," the American captor growled, "That's what you are! Get off!" Missing from the boat were the bodies of two Japanese who committed suicide when the surrender was announced. The German submarine crew had tossed their bodies overboard. The German POWs were immediately taken to the Yard prison for housing until arrangements could be made for their removal by the Army. Some of the German prisoners remained to work on the U-boats, removing equipment and instructing Yard officials about the operation of their vessels. During this time, the Yard prison population peaked with 3,088 inmates.[206]

With the announcement of V-E Day on May 7, Admiral Withers issued a statement that the job was but half done. "Here at the navy yard, there will be no stoppage of work to celebrate," he noted. Only when Japan was defeated, Withers concluded, "the Portsmouth navy yard will rightfully rate the navy, 'Well done.'"[207]

With President Harry Truman as the new chief executive, the United States steeled to accomplish this goal. The Yard made an overseas contribution as Captain Andrew G. Bisset, its former public-works officer, was assigned to Okinawa in late May to take charge of construction troops developing the island, south of the Japanese homeland, into a powerful advance base. Bisset's crew reconstructed existing airfields and built new ones.[208]

After the dropping of two atomic bombs in August 1945, the United States was poised to invade the Japanese homeland. The enemy elected instead to seek peace. On August 14, despite rumors that Japan's acceptance of surrender terms was imminent, the Yard announced that its employees would report to work as usual on V-J Day. The following day, with the surrender officially confirmed, Admiral Withers hailed the momentous achievement with praise for the Yard's workers and the submarine force. "The Portsmouth Navy Yard with its military and civilian personnel has made a major contribution toward victory," he said. "The submarines from Portsmouth inflicted vital damage on the enemy and paved the way for the surface and air supremacy that carried the war to the homeland of the enemy."[209]

This accomplishment marked the Yard's finest hour in its long history. The delivery of seventy-nine submarines to the fleet earned the well-deserved "Well Done" salute from the United States Navy.

Dedicated on Armistice Day, November 11, 1946, the Squalus *plaque on the* Squalus/Sailfish *superstructure honors "all men of the U.S. Submarine Force." PNSYMVC*

III 1945–2000

The End of the Submarine Construction Era, 1945–1969

AFTER WORLD WAR II, the United States defined a new mission for the Portsmouth Navy Yard. Adjustment to the postwar realities was reflected in numerous ways: a small workforce, stricter economy measures, new technology with nuclear-powered submarines, missiles replacing torpedoes, and revolutionary designs for submarine construction for deeper, faster, and longer underwater cruises. Notwithstanding the exigencies brought on by the Cold War with the Soviet Union, and by brushfire wars in Korea and Vietnam, the Yard found itself struggling to remain open, and, in fact, it faced a closure order. In keeping with the then-current military saying, "More bang for the buck," during this quarter-century period, the Yard was called upon to produce more sophisticated submarines with reduced appropriations.[209]

After being known as the Portsmouth Navy Yard since its inception in 1800, the facility was given a different name designation—"the Portsmouth Naval Shipyard"—in accordance with the Navy's postwar reshaping. The official date of the change was November 30, 1945. The Navy itself decided on this change in articulating a new role for the nation's government yards. A reorganization of such facilities at war's end was spelled out six weeks earlier in General Order No. 223 of September 14, 1945, to become effective on or before December 1, stipulating that the Navy Yards in Portsmouth, Boston, Brooklyn, Philadelphia, Norfolk, Charleston, Bremerton, Mare Island, and Pearl Harbor would be "U.S. Naval Bases." The directive established within each yard a component known as the "U.S. Naval Shipyard," with its commandant first and foremost responsible for production and logistic support to the

165

The superstructure of the USS Squalus/Sailfish *was placed in the Mall (later renamed* Squalus *Memorial Park) in 1946. A popular gathering place, the memorial and its grounds have been the site of numerous official ceremonies as well as "Moe's on the Mall" outdoor picnic lunches on Thursdays during the summer months. PNSY–Lashua Photo*

fleet. In turn, the Naval Hospital, Marine Barracks, and Disciplinary Barracks became additional components within this new administrative structure. In its drive for streamlined efficiency, the Navy Department acted quickly, classifying in mid-November 1945 five Portsmouth-built submarines as obsolete and ordering the 1935–41 vintage *Porpoise*, *Pike*, *Plunger*, *Marlin*, and *Snapper* to be decommissioned and scrapped.[210]

The historic *Squalus/Sailfish* submarine, however, was partially rescued. After a local "Save *Sailfish*" campaign, with New Hampshire political backing, the old naval warrior's superstructure—the bridge and conning tower—was dedicated as a memorial at the Yard Mall on Armistice Day in 1946. On May 3, 1948, the rest of the gallant *Sailfish* was sold at auction—as junk—for $43,167.[211]

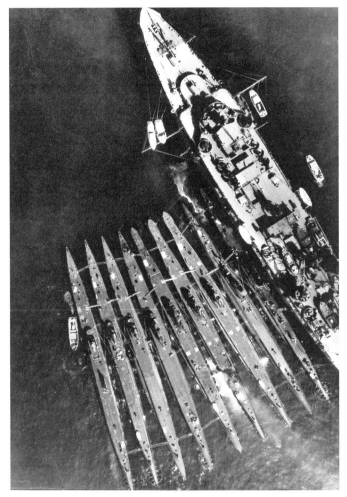

From the sub tender
USS Sperry, *the*
attached submarines
receive every imagin-
able type of supply
and assistance to
enable them to serve
the Navy at sea.
PNSMVC

While paying homage to the past with the *Squalus/Sailfish* Memorial, the Yard forged ahead technologically in the late 1940s by converting World War II–vintage submarines in its pioneering GUPPY program. An acronym derived from "Greater Underwater Propulsive Power," with the Y added for euphony, the GUPPY conversions—starting in 1947 with streamlined hulls and more powerful batteries— extended the working lives of fleet submarines into the 1970s. At about the same time, the adaptation of the snorkel, taken from German World War II U-boats, was incorporated in the GUPPY II design for the *Volador*, launched at the Yard in May 1948. Later that year, Yard work-

In 1946, at an undisclosed location, the sub tender USS Orion *(A518) lies at anchor with submarines alongside. PNSMVC*

men converted the USS *Tigrone* for radar picket duty. This modernization gave the first American submarine the capability of cruising into Arctic waters "impassable for surface craft and take station on radar watch for strange aircraft." The "picket" submarine *Tigrone* was commissioned on November 1, with a complement of eight officers and a crew of thirty-five men. Its commander charged his men with the responsibility of operating the submarine faithfully so that "we can continue to maintain the leadership which our navy has enjoyed."[212]

Less than a week later, the Navy reported the positive results of its recent and extensive North Atlantic Maneuvers in Canada. The mock invasion of Argentia, Newfoundland, with its heavily defended airbase, was delayed by eight snorkel subs. At the same time, the "Guppies" were credited with "sinking" or "crippling" an undisclosed number of the invading force. The Portsmouth Yard contributed half of the submarines—the exact number was listed as classified—which temporarily halted the mock invasion. Climaxing the war games, the

The legendary Archerfish *(SS 311), which sank the Japanese aircraft carrier* Shinano *in 1944, was refitted after the war with electronic equipment for scientific work. PNSMVC*

Second Marine Brigade, wearing special Arctic equipment, swam ashore on the beaches.[213]

Charged by the *Portsmouth Periscope*'s masthead motto, "WE BUILD THE BEST—WE SERVICE THE REST," the Yard's innovations ranged from the practical to the ingenious. In July 1952, the urgent need for dock work due to the heavy workload spurred more efficient sand blasting. The old method of wet sand blasting, begun in 1946, had represented a vast improvement over the previous procedure of hand scraping and wire brushes. Yet wet sand blasting proved difficult in freezing weather. In commercial as well as navy yards, the new technique of dry blasting was demonstrated to be considerably faster, more effective, and less expensive.

Thus, at eighty percent faster efficiency, the Yard was able to provide a cleaner surface for all protective coating. Less technical but just as practical, the Yard tackled the problem of high grass at the Naval Fuel Annex on Long Island, Casco Bay, Maine—at that time a component of the Portsmouth Yard. Rather than relying on manpower as they

SILHOUETTE	NAME	SS NO.	YEAR
	HOLLAND	I	1900
	K-I	32	1914
	GATO	212	1940
	AMBERJACK (GUPPY II)	522	1947
	TANG	563	1952
	ALBACORE	569	1954
	NAUTILUS	571	1955
	BARBEL	580	1959
	SKIPJACK	585	1959
	THRESHER	593	1961
	GEO. WASHINGTON	598	1960

Evolution of the submarine's shape from the Holland's *bulbous design to the* Albacore's *whale-shaped hull (half a century later) has ensured maximum underwater speed and maneuverability for today's subs. PNSMVC*

had in the past, the Yard Supply Department purchased five goats to graze on the island, consume the grass, and thereby reduce fire hazards. Dubbed "automatic lawnmowers," the goats eliminated grass-cutting details.[214]

The spic-and-span, up-to-date aspect of the Yard and its environs served the Navy well when Commander-in-Chief Harry S. Truman visited the Portsmouth Naval Shipyard in ideal fall weather on Friday, October 17, 1952. On a campaign swing to stump for Democratic candidates, the president found time in his tight schedule to come to the Yard—the first presidential visit since Roosevelt's inspection tour in 1940. After Truman's motorcade stopped at the Yard Mall, he climbed the steps of the *Squalus / Sailfish* Memorial to receive a twenty-one-gun salute.[215]

While Truman was at the Yard, he was doubtlessly briefed about the work underway on the USS *Albacore,* featuring a revolutionary design. The laying of the keel of the *Albacore*, the 120th sub built at the Portsmouth Yard, had taken place on Saturday, March 15, 1952. From the start, the *Albacore*'s objectives were clear. "The *Albacore* is to be an experimental submarine of extremely advanced design," stated the shipbuilding superintendent, "intended to give the ship high speed when submerged." It was estimated that it would require 300,000 mandays of shipyard labor to build the ship. After a year and a half of intensive work, the *Albacore* was commissioned on Saturday, December 5, 1953. The principal speaker, Rear Admiral Charles Momsen, had devoted five years to shepherding his idea toward reality. "Up to now submarine design had become a compromise with the various bureaus all exerting their influence," said Momsen. "The *Albacore* was designed by the Bureau of Ships from the point of view of submerged performance only." Stubbier than previous submarines, the *Albacore* was designed with a whale-shaped hull, enabling her, in Momsen's words, to "be able to make more than 50 knots while submerged." For years, through numerous conversions, adjustments, and sea trials, the *Albacore* was a mainstay at the Yard—until her decommissioning in 1972. As Momsen had properly envisioned, the *Albacore* was the fastest submarine of her day, providing a prototype not only for United States Navy submarines but also for other navies.[216]

Aiding the work on the *Albacore* at the Yard in the 1950s were two improvements—one relatively simple, the other a major breakthrough. In the spring of 1953, an outside contractor constructed a footbridge on the east side of Gate No. 1. The addition of the footbridge speeded up pedestrian traffic entering and leaving the Yard at starting and quitting times, besides reducing the chances of accidents and injuries. That same year, a special submarine test tank proved successful. Climaxing five years of research in conjunction with the David Taylor Model Basin

On July 6, 1983, a bronze likeness of Admiral Hyman G. Rickover was dedicated at the Mall. During his long naval career, Rickover frequently appeared at the Yard to supervise construction and to go on sea trials of nuclear-powered submarines. PNSY–Lashua Photo

in Maryland, the test tank was another Portsmouth "first" invention. The purpose of the Portsmouth tank, a hulking, all-welded cylindrical steel structure—30 feet in diameter and 75 feet long—was to establish the collapse depths of submarine hulls underwater. Previously, the margin of safety was unknown, making it foolhardy for sub commanders to take their ships beyond specified operating depths. This new invention could simulate strain depths and check them with gauges on land, saving money and possibly lives. The test tank meant construction of stronger and better submarine hulls.[217]

The adoption of nuclear power for submarine propulsion ushered

The USS Swordfish *(SSN 579), launched in 1957, was the first nuclear-powered submarine built in a government-owned yard. PNSMVC*

in a new age for the more sophisticated steel hulls. After its rival Electric Boat built the first nuclear submarines in the early 1950s, the Portsmouth Yard was the next to join the exclusive nuclear club, laying the keel of the *Swordfish* on January 24, 1956. The first nuclear component fabricated at the Yard was a practice pipe loop of stainless steel in late September of that year. On Monday, January 7, 1957, shipyard workers conducted the first welding on nuclear plant piping. The demands of the nuclear-age workplace meant utmost caution at the Yard—where safety in any event had always been a major concern. On March 14, 1957, the Yard attained sixty-five days without a disabling lost-time accident, setting a new record that lasted another ten days until a worker fractured two fingers. The next year, the safety record reached 133 days—until a pipefitter fell from a ladder and broke two ribs. The Yard emphasized "clean room procedures" for all nuclear-power work, making every effort to keep foreign matter from contaminating the workers themselves as well as their product. With regard to the *Swordfish* reactor department, strict rules were in effect, with workers wearing white nylon, lint-free coveralls, plastic boots, taped collars and cuffs, filtered air supplies, glasses taped to their heads, and lanyards on all tools.[218]

Such meticulous attention to safety and performance was incorporated in the *Swordfish*, launched on August 27, 1959, a clear summer day. The addition of Portsmouth's first nuclear boat was described by Rear Admiral Chester C. Smith, the principal speaker at the launch, as a "new symbol of power in the preservation of peace and our capability to wage a successful war should it be forced upon us." Despite this positive note, the Yard was at the time of the launch losing employees. The shipyard commander announced that the current 7,100-employee level would "not exceed 7,000 on December 31 [1957]." All hiring at the Yard had been suspended except for "the filling of particularly critical positions."[219]

As it turned out, the employment level in 1958 stabilized, even increased to 7,500, demonstrating that the Yard, operating at less than half the all-time-high World War II workforce, could still produce superior ships. The Yard's second nuclear submarine, the USS *Seadragon,* made nautical history in 1960 with her underwater transit in the practically uncharted Arctic Basin, a feat that had evaded five previous submarine attempts. A proven route through the Northwest Passage was strategically needed by the Navy as a connecting link between the Atlantic and Pacific Oceans, providing an alternative to the Panama Canal. Commissioned in 1959 and carrying the latest navigational systems, the *Seadragon* sailed from the Yard on August 1, 1960, with a chaplain's blessing. Her mission was not only to pioneer a new Arctic underwater route but also to enable the top civilian scientists aboard to collect data on ice structures and temperatures. Cruising on the surface as well as submerged during her voyage, the *Seadragon* was also slated to crash through the ice during maneuvers. "We will be able to see," said the *Seadragon*'s skipper, Lieutenant Commander George P. Steele II, "what the ice suit of the Arctic is really like." With the motto, "Under the Ice to Paradise [Hawaii]," the *Seadragon*'s ultimate destination, Commander Steele proceeded up the Greenland–Labrador slot, avoiding or diving below icebergs and then turning westward through Canadian Arctic waters and through the Parry Channel in a bid to reach the North Pole. If the *Seadragon* had been forced to turn back at this point

Prior to a voyage to the Arctic and a Northwest Passage exploration similar to that of the Seadragon *expedition, Yard personnel were fitted out with heavy-duty thermal clothing tested to withstand the harsh elements. PA*

because of block ice in the Parry Channel, Commander Steele could have pursued an alternate route, mapped out in advance, to the North Pole via the channel through Ellesmere Island and Greenland. No such detour was necessary, however, as the *Seadragon* successfully navigated the various shallow and narrow sounds and straits of Parry Channel to surface at the North Pole on August 25. The surprise appearance of Santa Claus, and even a celebratory baseball game, marked the event. Thus, this first east–west transit of the Arctic Basin proved the route entirely feasible for military as well as scientific purposes.[220]

The official Navy caption reads: "[On August 25, 1960] Santa Claus, the Mayor of the North Pole, extends a hearty welcome to his frozen domain to [USS] Sea Dragon [sic] frogman Lt. G.M. Brewer, USN. Despite the helping hand and warm greeting, Lt. Brewer seems a little chilled although it may be he is simply awed by the surprise greeting from the North Pole executive." PNSMVC

The submarine *Thresher*, on which the Department of Defense and the Navy had placed high hopes, was expected to advance even further the advent of underwater technology. From its keel-laying in 1958 through the early 1960s, the *Thresher* marked many new innovations in submarine design: the most advanced underwater sound system to reduce noise, a deep-diving capacity, and the location of torpedo tubes in the middle portion of the ship. The *Thresher* was the first nuclear-powered sub to incorporate a built-in, bow-to-stern, anti-detection sound system. With the motto, "Silent Strength" (a major concern in the submarine service), the *Thresher* was slated to become the quietest sub in the United States Navy. At the launching on July 9, 1960, this optimism was articulated in many congratulatory speeches. "Revolutionary submarines such as the *Thresher*," said Rear Admiral Carl F. Espe, "are well on the way to becoming the undersea counterpart of the wartime fighter aircraft." Speaking for the Yard on this historic launch, Captain Henry P. Rumble declared, "The launching of *Thresher* here today is a great milestone for the Portsmouth Naval Shipyard."[221]

For the next two-and-a-half years, the *Thresher* lived up to her name as the world's quietest, most advanced attack submarine. But on Wednesday, April 10, 1963, the *Thresher* disappeared in the Atlantic east of Cape Cod during routine diving trials with 129 men on board. Leading the nation in mourning as commander-in-chief, President John F. Kennedy announced: "The courage and dedication of these men of the sea pushing ahead into depths to advance our knowledge and capabilities is no less than that of their forefathers who led the advance on the frontiers of our civilization." On Saturday, April 13, *The New York Times,* in an editorial widely reprinted, proclaimed, "The *Thresher* is gone, but *Thresher* lives." On the following Monday, the largest memorial service of its kind was held at the Yard Mall, concluding with "Taps" by a Navy bugler.[222]

Shaken by the *Thresher* tragedy, the Yard's status looked precarious the following year. On Friday, April 17, 1964, Secretary of Defense Robert S. McNamara and his official party arrived by helicopter at the Marine Corps Parade Ground. In his press conference and official statement, McNamara contended that the Portsmouth Yard was "one of our highest-cost yards." Furthermore: "It has been our experience in the past that whenever costs are high, it's a management responsibility. . . . We propose to reduce those costs." On November 19 of that year, McNamara announced that he would shut down ninety-five obsolete and surplus military bases. On his list was the Portsmouth Naval Shipyard, then carrying 7,274 on the work rolls. The yard was given ten years to phase out. The next day, Shipyard Commander William C. Hushing told the Yard workers assembled on the Mall that, despite the closure announcement, he anticipated no layoffs or reductions in force for the following three months. "The effective producer with a good public image," Hushing said, "always survives." The only way out of this predicament, Hushing emphasized, was top performance from every Yard worker: "Our product must be of such high quality, such timeliness and at such a cost that the customer will clamor for what we have to offer."[223]

A plaque to the right of the main entrance door of the Thresher Memorial Chapel commemorates the lost submarine and her crew. Memorial Day services are held annually for the Thresher *at nearby Albacore Park. PNSY–Lashua Photo*

The eagerly anticipated event at the Yard during 1964 — in fact, the biggest in the shipyard's history — was completely preempted by the impact of the McNamara visit and its aftermath. During their inspection tour on April 24, the McNamara party stopped at the waterfront to view the fleet ballistic missile sub *John Adams,* known as "Big John," and proceeded on to see the Polaris submarine *Nathanael Greene* on the building ways. These two subs were the heaviest and largest ever built at the Yard. Less than a month later, on Tuesday, May 12, 1964, a capacity crowd gathered to attend the "Triple Header," in which Big John would be placed in commission, the keel would be laid for the nuclear-powered submarine *Grayling,* and the *Nathanael Greene* would be launched. A tragedy intervened, however, to mar this historically significant day. Three hours before the *Greene* was to be sliding down the building ways, as a work crew was readying the boat for launch, one shipyard employee was accidentally

Polaris missile firing from an unidentified submarine. Having built and commissioned two Polaris subs, John Adams *and* Nathanael Greene *in 1964, the Yard has also repaired and overhauled many Polaris subs over the years.* PNSYMVC

electrocuted and five others were hurt while working under the bunting-draped bow of the sub.[224]

Despite these unfortunate setbacks in the early 1960s, the Yard remained undaunted. Extensive testing and pioneering safety devices for all submarine construction fostered a watchdog attitude throughout the Yard. As the common phrase asserted, "Every sub is now safer because of *Thresher*." A new public-relations attitude also emerged. Just four days after the *Nathanael Greene* launch, the nation sponsored the fifteenth annual Armed Forces Day, and almost 6,000 visitors attended an open house at the Yard. Many toured the Naval Reserve training submarine *Crevalle* and the cable ship *Aeolus*. That summer, from July 28 to August 1, the Norwegian windjammer *Staatsraad*

An employee of the Yard Foundry (ca. 1960s) carefully tends a crucible of molten iron. PNSYMVC

Lehmkuhl docked at the Yard and was open to the public. A Navy bus was stationed at Gate No. 1 for transporting visitors to the ship. The windjammer was a training bark, one of the world's last tall training ships visiting the United States as part of Operation Sail. The Navy Chapel, soon renamed the Thresher Memorial Chapel, was located atop a forested knoll on Seavey's Island. The "Thresher Bells" carillon rang "out loud and clear over the sea every day in memory of the men lost on the submarine *Thresher*." Finally, on October 16, 1964, Captain Hushing signed a historic employee–management agreement with the Yard's Metal Trades Council. The first such agreement ever negotiated and signed at the Yard covered more than 5,000 nonsupervisory employees, addressing such matters as working hours, leave, safety, training, and grievances. "I hope that the agreement," said Hushing at the signing ceremony, "will contribute to improving morale of employees, improving efficiency and building a better image of the Portsmouth Naval Shipyard by reducing costs."[225]

In 1965, the Yard further expanded its horizons to benefit the workforce. Under the president's Youth Opportunity Campaign (also known as the Federal Summer Employment Program), the Yard employed young men and women as summer aides. They were known as "YOCs," derived from the acronym of the federal agency funding their service. Designed to provide summer employment within both public and private industry for youngsters between the ages of sixteen and twenty-one, the program paid them $1.60 per hour. The jobs—maintenance work, painting, cleaning, clerical duties, and related assignments—helped the students pay for their college tuition, books, clothes, and related expenses. In 1968, the Yard provided jobs for 234 YOCs, expanding to 292 summer hires the following year. Many students worked under the guidance and supervision of seasoned Yard employees, who reported their work performance as outstanding. The student contribution, in fact, was so outstanding that regular Yard supervisors expressed the hope that "the same youngsters would be assigned to them again next year." In many cases, college engineering students, with their education nearing completion, were given job offers upon graduation, and some accepted the Yard's employment offers.[226]

With the enthusiasm and idealism of the "summer hires," coupled with the professionalism of the regular shipyarders and Navy officers and men, the Yard forged ahead in the late 1960s, determined to build the best submarines whether or not there was a closure order. On December 19, 1964, the keel of the *Dolphin* was laid. An experimental submarine in the tradition of the *Albacore*, the *Dolphin* was a small, deep-diving submarine with a complement of twenty-one submariners plus space for four scientists. Construction proceeded for three years. In the fall of 1967, Shipyard Commander Hushing (now Rear Admiral) established the *Dolphin* Project Team, selected from the various Yard departments. Among the aims of team members, assigned to the job from start to finish, were "minimizing the turn-around time between discovering the problem and resolving the problem." Each team member became identified with the job, worked more efficiently, and wore a white button with twin gold dolphins and the words, "Dolphin Project Team." Commissioned on August 17, 1968, the *Dolphin* sailed on sea trials the following February. All her tests were entirely successful, including descending to a test depth (classified as secret by the Navy) beyond what had been done by any other Navy submarine then operational. "The Triple Nickel" (her nickname was derived from her number) more than paid for herself in military and scientific research.[227]

On November 11, 1969, the Yard's fifty-five-year submarine construction era ended with the launch of the USS Sand Lance *(SSN 660). The Yard's 134th and last submarine was deactivated on January 15, 1998, in Groton, Connecticut. PNSMVC*

The submarine whose keel was laid shortly after that of the *Dolphin* was the yet-unnamed nuclear attack submarine SS (N) 660. On January 15, 1965, Shipyard Commander Hushing was the first of six men to weld the lettering on the 660. "[There are] three essentials for Portsmouth's product," emphasized Hushing. "First is quality—second is timeliness—then the cost factor." With the closure order hovering overhead, the Yard was determined to deliver one last great submarine—soon to be named the *Sand Lance*—to the fleet. After four years of construction, that day came on Armistice Day, November 11, 1969, at the Yard building ways. "*Sand Lance* Launch May Mark End of Era," read the *Herald*'s headline. Referring to the "last new vessel on the order books," the reporter noted that "the band music and screeching klaxons may have been the swan song for launching at the 170-

year-old shipyard but helped to give a rousing send-off for the 4,600-ton submarine." As the principal speaker at the ceremony, New Hampshire Senator Tom McIntyre, a member of the Senate Armed Forces Committee, expressed his dismay about the closure order. Despite the prevailing uncertainty about the Yard's future, McIntire expressed his conviction, nevertheless, that the *Sand Lance* would play a dominant role against any potential enemy aggression. "I believe very strongly that our most effective, least vulnerable deterrent to enemy attack," McIntire said, "is not our land-based ICBM [intercontinental ballistic missile] system, not our long-range bombers, but our nuclear submarines." Furthermore, he pointed out that nuclear-powered submarines could cruise 400 miles in a day and remain submerged for months at a time. "They will be thousands of miles closer to the enemy than land-based missiles."[228]

The widespread local speculation that the *Sand Lance* was to be the last Portsmouth-built submarine proved to be true, thus ending a proud and distinguished tradition of fifty-five years of submarine construction.

"Semper Fidelis!": The Marines Depart, 1969–1987

With the submarine construction era over, the Portsmouth Naval Shipyard adjusted to its new status as an overhaul-and-repair facility. This transition was not easy. During the next two decades, virtually every aspect of the Yard's operation—whether the U.S. Marine Corps barracks, the hospital, or the prison—was analyzed, evaluated, and acted upon, all in connection with the Navy's changing priorities in the 1970s and 1980s. Some components survived intact, while others were greatly modified, reduced, or shut down. Unlike other eastern-seaboard government yards—Boston, New York, and Philadelphia—which were closed during these difficult times, the Portsmouth Yard remained open.

With the closure order lingering ominously over the Yard, every effort was made to rescind that directive. In June 1970, the *Portsmouth Periscope* argued: "Portsmouth Naval Shipyard, a leading designer and builder of submarines, is 170 years old today. The first of all naval shipyards, Portsmouth is one of the largest industries north of Boston and south of Montreal. From an investment of $5,500, the

Shipyard, in 170 years of service to the Fleet, has expanded to a major submarine facility valued at $85,500,000—$1 million in land; $30,600,000 in plant equipment; and $53,900,000 in buildings and other facilities. The phrase, 'Sails to Atoms,' symbolizes the evolution of shipbuilding at the Portsmouth Naval Shipyard." To abandon such a well-established and proven facility, it was implied, would be utterly foolhardy. In January 1971, Captain Donald H. Kern, the shipyard commander, spoke out in response to the order to abolish 777 positions to reduce the workforce to 6,000 employees by the end of the fiscal year (June 30, 1971). "It is imperative that this Shipyard make every effort," he emphasized, "to increase its productivity to a point where we will become competitive with any shipyard, be it public or private." During that same month, Kern assigned responsibilities to members of the newly formed Environmental Control Board. He also granted permission to the officers and stewards of the various unions to place insignias on their hard hats, identifying the wearer as a member of a specific union. Such pride and determination to save the Yard—not easily measured but certainly felt—was soon rewarded. In a March 24, 1971, letter to Maine and New Hampshire congressmen and senators, President Richard Nixon stated: "I am pleased to inform you that the McNamara order closing the yard in 1974 will be rescinded."[229]

Great local rejoicing and relief reverberated for days. "SHIP-YARD WILL STAY OPEN," announced a giant *Portsmouth Herald* headline. But, as everyone knew, this reprieve was no excuse for complacency; it meant the Yard had to work harder than ever to secure what remained. Work rolls dropped during the next two years—from 5,991 employees in 1971 to 5,582 in 1972, and finally to 5,511 in 1973. Two ceremonial events brightened this period of transition. On Friday, September 1, 1972, the *Albacore* was decommissioned at the Yard with traditional naval ceremonies. Rear Admiral J. Edward Snyder, Jr., oceanographer of the Navy, was the principal speaker, and he gave a stirring address. [The submarine *Albacore*'s] "contributions will be long remembered," said Snyder, "and are forever reflected in the design of the operating units of our submarine force." The *Albacore* was ultimately towed to Philadelphia and became a member of the Ship Inactivation and Maintenance Facility. The next year, on August 18, 1973, in honor of the 350th Anniversary of the City of Portsmouth, the Yard held an open house for the public. A special feature included

Outside the most modern section of the Yard prison, opened in August 1943, a watchtower housing a Marine guard (in a 1964 photograph) provides tight security against possible escape. UNH

a deck tour of the HMS *Minerva,* a British frigate docked at the Yard's Berth 7. Among the ship's personnel was Lieutenant Charles Windsor, the Prince of Wales, serving as deputy missile and gunnery officer.[230]

The Yard braced for the next change in its long history. Ever since 1968, the Naval Disciplinary Command, or "the Castle," had been slated for phaseout. The prison population was down to 847 inmates in 1966. After several extensions, the prison was decommissioned at the end of the fiscal year, June 30, 1974. The remaining 210 inmates were immediately reassigned to other government detention facilities. More than 86,000 prisoners had passed through the Castle during its seventy-six-year history. During the prison's final years, it was known for its liberal treatment. The last prison commander, Marine Colonel Walter Domina, stressed ongoing reform and rehabilitation with on-the-job training and furlough and work-release programs. "We were the only prison in the United States," said Domina, "that sold beer." Despite this progressive approach to penology, the Navy decided to shut down the aging prison—a facility built to handle a few thousand inmates—as economically unfeasible.[231]

Although the prisoners permanently left the Castle in 1974, the prison has nevertheless remained in the news for many years. Maine prison officials have sought to utilize the vacant Yard buildings as a solution for overcrowding in their other facilities. In 1983, Domina believed otherwise. "The building just isn't conducive," he said, "to today's theories of penology." Modeled after the nineteenth-century European prisons, the Castle was, in Domina's words, "an architectural monolithic monster. It is like a warehouse, and you can't administer modern rehabilitation in an old warehouse." In addition, Domina emphasized: "the deterioration has just been phenomenal." Over the years, successive shipyard commanders and editorial writers have echoed Domina's sentiments in regard to both economic and security considerations, emphasizing the impracticality of rehabilitating the old prison to accommodate civilian convicts. "The location of The Castle is such that any access routes must go through the shipyard," editorialized the *Herald*. "The shipyard's primary purpose is to repair submarines, and no other purpose should remotely interfere with this." Furthermore, the shipyard commanders have emphasized that the empty structure constitutes little more than a shell, built decades earlier with health-threatening asbestos materials. "In fact, most engineers who have viewed the structure," wrote Captain Joseph F. Yurso as shipyard commander in 1982, "consider demolition to be the only realistic alternative." The Castle remains standing today, totally unsuitable as a modern prison and too costly to demolish.[232]

Another mainstay at the Portsmouth Yard underwent a reorganization in 1974. On October 4, the Naval Hospital, first established in 1834, was officially designated as a Naval Regional Medical Clinic. In its heyday during World War II, the hospital had the capability of caring for as many as 350 inpatients. With the new realignment, the old hospital wards were converted into clinic spaces, and several buildings in the hospital compound were demolished for a parking lot. No longer concerned with long-term hospitalization, the emphasis at the clinic became outpatient treatment.[233]

While changes at the Yard went on, the Navy and the Submarine Service continued to honor traditional celebrations. On April 18, 1975, retired Navy Captain George L. Street III, the wartime commanding officer of the legendary *Tirante*, returned to the Yard for the 75th anniversary commemoration of the Submarine Service. Street was the main speaker and guest of honor at the Submarine Ball held at the Officers Club. Recalling the World War II exploits of the *Tirante*, Street proclaimed that she "was the best ship of all combat-types—the meatball—and performed extremely well." Just four years later, the Yard's close association with the *Tirante* was further publicized with the ded-

The U.S. Naval Hospital, viewed from the Piscataqua River in 1965, was opened on this site in 1913. Treating as many as 350 in-patients at a time during World War II, the facility has now become a Naval Regional Medical Clinic for outpatient care. PNSMVC

The main entrance to the Yard Naval Hospital, reorganized in 1974 as a Regional Medical Clinic specializing in outpatient care. The fence railing on the second floor (left center) encloses the patio that was used by Fleet Admiral Ernest J. King (USN Ret.) to enjoy the ocean breezes. A plaque on the door inside the building denotes the room where King died on June 25, 1956. PNSY–Lashua Photo

Originally built as the Ordnance Building in 1857, and later used as the Officers Club, this building houses the Yard Recreation Center. Located across from Building 86, the facility contains a library, barbershop, game room, meeting rooms, movie theater/auditorium, and dining rooms for Navy and civilian personnel. PNSY–Lashua Photo

ication of the Tirante Tavern in the Officers Club. For this ceremony, Captain Street headed the delegation of veteran submariners who had commanded and served on Portsmouth-built submarines during World War II. The various *Tirante* patrol reports, photos, Street's Congressional Medal of Honor, and other memorabilia are permanently displayed in a glass case on a wall outside the tavern. Since then, the Tirante Tavern has continued to be a popular gathering place for officers, enlisted personnel, Yard workers, and their guests.[234]

During 1976, when the United States celebrated its bicentennial, the Yard reached out to the public in grand style. During the Yard's three-day open house, Saturday through Monday, July 3–5, 1976, an estimated 125,000 visitors thronged to the Yard to participate in and witness the many events—horse show, gymkhana, tugboat rides, militia performances, stage show, religious observances, block dance, prison tour, outdoor band concert, softball games, tour of Quarters A, diving demonstration, drill team, antique auto show, square dance, helicopter hovering techniques, and medevac drill—capped off with a twenty-one-gun salute and fireworks. A bicentennial queen officiated at numerous events. Some 10,000 cans of soft drinks and 60,000 hot dogs were consumed by the visitors. "Let's have a repeat of the whole deal," many commented long after the event, "for the Nation's 201 birthday [July 4, 1977]."[235]

The euphoria of the bicentennial seemed to have generated a newfound spirit at the Portsmouth Naval Shipyard. At a Yard that appeared to be on the verge of closing a few years earlier, major construction projects were underway, thus ensuring the prospect of a bright future. On June 6, 1977, a groundbreaking ceremony for the new Machine Shop/Central Tool Shop prompted the appearance of many naval and political figures. The $3.1 million building, the first major new structure at the Yard in twenty years, was assigned the crucial mission of speeding the time to repair and overhaul submarines. "What this means is that both the Navy and the Department of Defense," said New Hampshire Senator Thomas J. McIntyre at the event, "have real confidence in the ability of this Shipyard to continue contributing in a significant way to the security of our nation." In a letter the following day, conveyed to the shipyard commander, McIntyre wrote, "I think this is a real turning point for the Shipyard." Within the same month, on June 16, the Captain C. Douglass Fletcher Recreational Complex was dedicated in memory of the Yard's late administrative officer, who had died that spring. The complex, a $250,000 project awarded under the Minority Contracting Program of the Small Business Administration, included a gymnasium, handball and squash courts, an indoor tennis court, and an outdoor swimming pool—available to all military personnel and their dependents. Fletcher's devotion to this facility was articulated in a plaque, stating, "He [Fletcher] was highly instrumental in the start of this complex. Terminally ill during his last year, he nonetheless carried out all of his duties in his usual exemplary manner. His resolute dedication to duty was in the finest tradition of the United States Navy and the Submarine Service." Other inspiring news followed. It was announced that the projected 1977 annual payroll for the Yard would be over $130 million. In turn, the aggregate work on all submarine projects at the Yard

The great blizzard of February 6–7, 1978, dumped twenty-three inches of snow, with winds gusting to fifty mph, on the seacoast area. In line with the Yard's policy to keep the facility open, the workforce managed to overcome the elements. PNSMVC

SUBMEPP Chief Engineer's Office including the first employees, located in Building 79, 1967. SUBMEPP (Submarine Maintainence, Engineering, Planning, and Procurement), then called PERA(SS), grew out of Portsmouth Naval Shipyard and is now a separate NAVSEA tenant activity, at the shipyard, with over 200 employees who centrally perform submarine maintenance engineering, planning, and procurement for submarine repair activities worldwide.

Providing essential and convenient services for its employees, Building 15 in 1976 houses a bank, post office, and safety office. PNSMVC

Day's end (ca. 1960s) sees the exodus of a work shift across the bridge to Gate No. 1. Note the U.S. Marine sentry (center of bridge) directing traffic flow. PNSMVC

represented an expenditure in excess of $264,800,000. After a long ordeal of uncertainty, the Yard was busy again.[236]

In addition to carrying out its military work, the Yard found the time to participate in an unusual assignment in June 1977. Hollywood sought out the Yard as a locale for filming a movie, *The Defection of Simas Kudirka,* with scenes shot on location at Quarters A, Building 86, the former naval prison, and Berth 7. The two-hour made-for-TV film was based on the actual defection attempt of a Lithuanian seaman in 1970 from the Soviet refrigerated factory ship *Sovetskaya Litva* off Martha's Vineyard, Massachusetts, during an at-sea conference on foreign fishing rights and American territorial waters. Kudirka jumped ship onto the Coast Guard Cutter *Vigilant* while both ships were moored together. Returned to the Soviet ship, Kudirka was taken back to the USSR and imprisoned for treason. He was later released when it was discovered he was legally an American citizen, as his mother had been born in the United States. Allowed to return to the United States, Kudirka took up residence in New Jersey. Paramount Films of California operated with minimum interference with the Yard's regular activities. The film crew and cast put in twelve-hour days, and many Yard employees served as extras. There were some startled looks when the Maine Maritime Academy training ship tied up at Berth 7, had her name changed to *Sovetskaya Litva,* and raised the hammer-and-sickle flag to replace the Stars and Stripes. On the last day of filming, according to the *Periscope,* "the real Simas Kudirka paid a visit to the set" at the naval prison, and "met the 'reel' Simas Kudirka, Alan Arkin." The film was aired on Tuesday, January 24, 1978, on CBS, and many viewers recognized fellow workers in their roles as extras. Unconfirmed and obviously exaggerated rumors held that some extras had been offered acting contracts, and one individual was reported to have been considered for his own TV series. The entire experience was most enjoyable for all parties and provided favorable publicity for the Yard.[237]

One of the major events at the Yard in 1978 concerned the force of nature itself. On February 6 and 7, 1978, a storm struck with such fury that many compared the winter gale to the March 10-12, 1888, blizzard that paralyzed the Northeast for days. The 1978 storm walloped the New England seacoast, which was officially designated a major disaster area. During that time, twenty-three inches of snow fell at the Yard, with winds gusting at more than fifty miles an hour and tides reaching almost fifteen feet, five feet above normal. In keeping with Yard policy never to close the facility, shipyard civilians, military, and ship's forces battled the blizzard for two days. Some worked twenty hours and stayed for thirty. Despite the terrible conditions, the Yard managed to stay open. Adequate preparation, no major breakdowns of snow-removal equipment, and pride contributed to keep the Yard operational. Referring to the plowing crews, Kenneth S. Abuddell, transportation superintendent, said, "Absenteeism was minimal. Several employees walked to work but they were here. A large percentage of them worked 16 hours, 8 hours off and came right back and put in another 16 hours." Power outages, and flooding around dry docks, were overcome. The Navy also responded to emergencies beyond the Yard, sending two 12-foot boats to Hampton, at the request of the New Hampshire Civil Defense. Shipyarders worked alongside the National Guard. Overcoming the storm prompted the shipyard commander to send a message to the entire Yard family, describing their efforts as "a can-do spirit of cooperation."[238]

While the Yard had defeated the storm, everyone realized it was mandatory to continue to maintain the facility's credibility and fine reputation. In the eyes of the Navy, the Portsmouth Yard—indeed, every government yard—had to excel in the increasingly cost-efficient world. In this regard, the Yard received a pat-on-the-back concerning one of her subs. In March 1978, the Portsmouth-built sub *Abraham Lincoln* docked in Apia Harbor, Guam. Since her commissioning seventeen years earlier, the sub had performed magnificently. The *Abraham Lincoln* became the first ballistic-missile sub to complete fifty patrols, spending more time underwater—eight and one-half years—than on the surface. "Throughout her lifetime," reported the *Periscope,* "she has met every operational commitment and passed every readiness inspection."[239]

A commitment to excellence, both in the final product and in the attitude of everyone associated with the Yard, was the goal of the shipyard commander, Captain William D. McDonough. After reading Elbert Hubbard's famous inspirational work-ethic essay, "A Message to Garcia," originally published in 1898 during the Spanish–American War, McDonough decided to have the article reprinted, together with his commentary, "Is Your Name Rowan?" in the *Periscope* in 1979. In this

Observed by more than 2,000 invitees, the USS Portsmouth, *named for cities in New Hampshire and Ohio, was commissioned at the Yard on October 1, 1983. PNSMVC*

essay, an American named Rowan, facing almost impossible odds and without questioning his orders, delivered an important message to Garcia in Cuba. "I thought to myself that if we had more Rowans in the Shipyard family," McDonough wrote in his accompanying remarks, "we would improve our performance manyfold. Such improvement would make us far better than we are, far more efficient and economical for our customers and, most importantly, insure a continuing in-flow of work for years into the future."[240]

Recognition of the many Rowans in the Yard's history was realized in the naming of a Los Angeles–class submarine as the USS *Portsmouth*. Named jointly for the cities in New Hampshire and Virginia, the 360-foot nuclear attack submarine was built at Electric Boat in Groton, Connecticut. The 6,900-ton submarine was the most advanced vessel of its type in the world—equipped with highly accurate sensors, weapons control systems, and central computer com-

Nearly 1,500 military and civilian guests at the commissioning of the USS Augusta on Saturday, January 19, 1985, endured the rigors of a frigid, snowy day. Maine Senator William S. Cohen read a poem, "A Tribute to Augusta", which he had composed for the occasion. PNSMVC

plexes. Her sea trials, including the Navy's final acceptance trial, were outstanding. It was a proud day when the *Portsmouth* was commissioned at the Yard on October 1, 1983, with more than 2,000 invited guests, whereupon she assumed her place in the Atlantic fleet. "The heart of a ship is her men," read a sign in sub skipper Donald M. Olson's stateroom, "and her greatness is similarly determined." Olson and his sub lived up to that pledge.[241]

Having honored New Hampshire, the Navy extended its recognition of the area to name another Electric Boat submarine for the capital of the state of Maine. On Saturday, January 19, 1985, nearly 1,500 military and civilian guests attended the commissioning of the USS *Augusta*. The event occurred in true New England fashion, with frigid temperatures and falling snow, as the guests bundled up with blankets, gloves, and scarves. Under a heated shelter, the Navy Band played the National Anthem. Maine Senator William S. Cohen delivered the principal address and then read his own poem, "A Tribute to *Augusta*," written for the occasion. Yard Commander Captain Lennis L. Lammers offered his invitation for the *Augusta* to return. "Portsmouth Naval Shipyard is a Shipyard on the move," he told the audience. "When you return to PNS for your first overhaul, we will not only be ready, but you will be returning to the finest nuclear submarine overhaul facility in the world."[242]

Although the Yard's submarine overhaul-and-repair responsibility has been discharged with utmost attention to safety, accidents cannot be entirely eliminated. On Monday morning, April 6, 1987, the overhauled submarine USS *Ulysses S. Grant* left for routine sea trials prior to returning to her home port of Groton, Connecticut. Still on the surface, the sub was underway about two miles outside Portsmouth Harbor. Lieutenant David Jimenez and enlisted man Larry Thompson were on deck, both wearing lifejackets and tethered with submarine lifelines. The two men were swept overboard, with the seas running at about ten to twelve feet. Ninety minutes later, Coast Guard rescuers plucked Jimenez from the cold, storm-swept waters and rushed him to the mainland, attempting to resuscitate him during the trip. These efforts failed, and Jimenez was declared dead at Portsmouth Regional Hospital. Despite an extensive several-day air search, hampered by bad weather and limited visibility, Thompson's body was never found. An investigation probed the circumstances of the accident, which claimed two men on official duty during peacetime.[243]

Notwithstanding this unfortunate accident, in this case during sea trials, the Yard's repair-and-overhaul safety record has been noted for its meticulous attention to safety standards. As early as 1966, Commander Raymond P. Jones, commanding officer of the submarine USS *Blueback,* emphasized in his article, "Submarine Repair Is Different," the Yard's unrelenting effort to ensure quality and safety. "Submarining is hazardous," he wrote. "We use a system of rig and rig check. One man does his job and another checks him. Not that we don't trust him; we can't afford to let a mistake sneak through. In this shipyard, this method is quality control." To make certain that the subs were operating with the most reliable replacement parts and the most updated service standards, the Yard in 1967 developed the PERA (Planning and Engineering for the Repairs and Alterations) System for submarines. It ensured that every precaution was taken before breakdowns could occur. "Essentially PERA defines what should be done, how often, and by whom, for every piece of equipment or component in the ship, just like General Motors does for a car," explained a *Periscope* reporter in 1983. "You always get a User's or Maintenance Manual with your new car. This manual tells you how often you should change your oil, spark plugs, air filter, check your brakes, and so forth. PERA does something similar for components installed in . . . submarines. The biggest difference is that submarines have literally thousands of components to be maintained, where a car probably has less than 100." During the 1980s, overhaul costs ranged upward from $60 million per overhaul, with the sub unavailable to the fleet for eighteen months to two years. Furthermore, no two overhauls were exactly the same. "Engineers here today work mainly on submarine maintenance and modernization," observed Kenneth Lanzillo, former chief engineer of PERA and special assistant to the shipyard commander in 1984. "In many cases submarine maintenance technology is more difficult and challenging than new design. It's more challenging because of the many unknowns associated with the degradation—the wear and tear of submarines in service. These unknowns have to be investigated, and in some cases it's very difficult to provide answers as to why things happen as they do.[244]

The PERA program extended far beyond the Yard boundaries, as the Navy prepared a work package, called Extended Refit Period (ERP), for use wherever needed, but in particular at the U.S.–controlled base at Holy Loch, Scotland. Designed as a major tuneup of a SSBN sub and administered through PERA directions and procedures, the ERP work at Holy Loch, an arm of the Firth of Clyde, was designed to keep subs in top operating condition between overhauls. The Portsmouth Naval Shipyard contributed replacement parts, and work crews to conduct these critical repairs for Polaris submarines at a facility thousands of miles closer to Soviet waters. The Holy Loch arrangement made sense fiscally and strategically to accomplish the Navy's purpose. Over a thirty-year period, the Yard sent to Scotland handpicked crews known as "Tiger Teams," with the motto, "Have Tools, Will Travel," to tackle the jobs. Accommodated at local hotels, the workers looked forward to the challenge, and many returned for repeat assignments. The teams were transported by shuttle boats to the worksite, a floating dry dock named the USS *Los Alamos*, and a submarine tender, either the USS *Proteus* or the USS *Hunley* on a two-year rotation. Tugs, barges, and motor launches made up the rest of the flotilla, all controlled by U.S. Navy crews. The sub tender, with a 600-man crew complement, had its own shops as well as a Navy Exchange, post office, and banking facilities available to Yard workers. In 1984, Dick Sanborn was the Yard's ERP on-site manager, and he coordinated the many aspects of this united effort. "The cooperation among all concerned has been outstanding," Sanborn said. "We had a difficult assignment, and thanks to a tremendous team effort, we did it successfully and on time."[245]

Not only at Holy Loch, but also throughout the entire Navy, the United States government during the 1980s increasingly provided recreational outlets for off-the-job and off-duty hours. Family services also were available. These programs and benefits served to make the Yard a more attractive place to work and live. In October 1980, the Yard opened a $900,000 eight-lane ten-pin bowling alley constructed with non-appropriated funds from Navy Exchange profits and recreation fees. In 1983, the Yard renovated a building to provide a day-care center, available to military as well as civilian personnel, for forty-four children between the ages of six months and eight years. With a full-time assistant and ten child-care aides, the center included a playground, baby and toddler rooms, and a large activity room; according to the recreational services director, it offered "a well rounded program tailored to meet individual needs." In September 1983, the Yard recreational facilities, originally intended for the use of Navy and Marine Corps personnel and their families, were opened up to civilian employ-

In 1983, the Yard opened the Child Development Center to provide day care for both military and civilian personnel. Located near Meade Pond in Bowman Park, the center is staffed with a full-time director and a number of child-care aides. PNSY–Lashua Photo

ees. In return for a small membership fee, participants could enjoy their free time at the bowling center, wood hobby shop, auto hobby shop, marina area, indoor tennis and racquetball courts, gym, and ceramic studio. At the outdoor rental gear center, they could hire out boats, motors, canoes, and ski gear.[246]

In May 1985, the Portsmouth Naval Shipyard History Foundation, founded by volunteers, was established. It sought to safeguard the Yard's historic past by preserving the oral, written, pictorial, and artifact traditions that had been accumulating during its 185-year history. Largely through the incentive of Bea Lammers, wife of Shipyard Commander Captain Lennis L. Lammers, the volunteer group met on a regular basis, gathered artifacts on walking tours, and made plans to start a museum. This last dream was realized in April 1987 with the official opening of the display area, housed in Building 35, a former storage facility constructed in 1851. The display includes Navy diving suits, foundry patterns, photographs, submarine scale models, and launching tags. After a ribbon-cutting ceremony and a tour of the museum, Captain and Mrs. Lammers hosted a reception at Quarters A. Since then,

(Above) Decked out with bunting and flags, Quarters A is noted for receptions and hospitality. Under the arch is the main entrance to the Shipyard commander's residence. PNSMVC

(Left) The family and informal guest door (center) of Quarters A leads to the stairway and the main reception room. Over the years, the Shipyard Commander has hosted numerous Yard and Navy functions here. PNSMVC

under the leadership of Director James Dolph and the assistance of
many dedicated volunteers, the museum has continued to expand and
thrive, moving into successively more commodious quarters to house
the collection and to serve an increasing number of visitors from within
the Yard and from the general public.[247]

As the 1980s came to a close, an almost indivisible component of
the Yard's long saga itself became history. In September 1987, the barracks for the Yard detachment of the United States Marine Corps was
decommissioned, and the men were reassigned elsewhere. Just as with
the Yard's hospital and prison, the day had come when the Marines,
after more than 170 years of service, were deemed no longer economically feasible to guard the facility. In 1986, the Marine Corps had
announced the reorganization of its security forces around the nation,
deciding to close the Portsmouth detachment. A systematic shutdown
at the Marine Barracks followed—a downsizing that had been long in
the making. After World War II, the Yard's Marine force had been
reduced to a peacetime level of four officers and seventy-three men. In
addition, Corporal Chesty V, USMC, the mascot boxer dog, also faithfully served during the 1980s. Named after the person whom every
Marine tries to emulate, Lieutenant General Lewis B. "Chesty" Puller,
the mascot wore his custom-tailored uniform cloak decorated with his
rank, good-conduct medal, and meritorious unit citation.

Throughout their illustrious history, the Yard Marines did much
more than checking IDs. They were trained as part of a drill to be ready
to respond to an emergency in less than five minutes. When submarine
crews arrived, the Marines provided orientation and security briefings.
During the winter, they participated in cold-weather exercises in the
White Mountains. In addition to providing perimeter security for the
Yard, the Marines served as public-relations personnel in giving directions and other information to visitors. Finally, they performed in sixty
parades annually, various civic ceremonies, charitable activities, and
funeral details. The month of June 1984 marked the last time the
Marines served as sentries at the two Yard entrances, their duties subsequently taken over by contracted civilian police. For their last three
years at the Yard, the Marines had the role of guarding specific areas
inside the Controlled Industrial Area.[248]

On July 29, 1987, emotional ceremonies were conducted at the
Portsmouth High School football field, as thousands of spectators bid

Maintaining top physical fitness, U.S. Marine guards engage in running exercises around the Yard. Winter training in the White Mountains also ensured that the Yard's Marine detachment would be ready for all contingencies. UNH

farewell to the Marines of the Portsmouth Barracks. Although the Marine Barracks would not officially close until September, the event provided local residents the opportunity to honor the innumerable contributions of the Marine Corps during their 173 years of service to the area. The sixty-five-member red-jacketed Drum and Bugle Corps from the Washington, DC, Barracks and the Silent Drill Platoon provided impressive and precise demonstrations. A message was read from the commandant of the Marines, General A.M. Gray. "The closing of this Barracks is in many ways a sad event because it marks the end of an era in our Corps history," Gray wrote. "For all the Marines present today, please accept my congratulations for a job well done. . . . Semper Fidelis!"[249]

Under damp and dreary skies on Friday, September 18, 1987, as the Yard clock struck eight bells, the Marines raised the flag for the final time—a ceremony conducted thereafter by naval personnel. Ship-

The historic Marine Barracks served as the home of the Yard's security force from its construction in 1828 until the decommissioning of the Marine detachment in 1987. During a three-year period (1987–90), the museum was housed in two first-floor rooms of the building. PNSY–Lashua Photo

yard workers gathered at the Mall to observe the flag-raising and to bid farewell to the seventy-seven Marines standing on the conning tower of the *Squalus / Sailfish* Memorial. Captain Peter Bowman, shipyard commander, noted that through the years, "the sharp uniform, the professional attitude, the crisp salute, have created an aura of strength and security which we have come to take for granted." In summary, Bowman said, "Marines on parade in dress blues, Marines running in formation in their red sweatsuits. Marines on guard duty, Marines at morning and evening colors on the Mall—these are all images that will remain in our minds and hearts long after today's ceremony. Although they won't be far away, and we will still have their presence here whenever needed, it just won't be the same."[250]

After the ceremony, the Marines marched back to their barracks and soon departed. Along with the prison and the hospital, they passed into Yard history. Only the deceased Marine mascot dogs still remain, buried beneath memorial plaques, with an American flag flying, at the base of a hill below the barracks.

BRAC Blocked, 1987–1995

In contrast to the rigid atmosphere of World War II and the restrictions of the Cold War, the Portsmouth Naval Shipyard—indeed, the entire Department of Defense—during the late 1980s and early 1990s faced up to and adjusted responsibly to the new social issues of the day affecting the United States. With the advent of a more liberal era, a spirit of reform pervaded women's rights, community involvement, and environmental issues both within and beyond the Yard's two gates. Major changes followed.

Simultaneously with these developments, the Yard, along with other defense installations across the country, faced the scrutiny of the Base Realignment and Closure (BRAC) Commission, charged with deciding which government defense properties would remain open and which would close. Twice—during 1993 and 1995—Portsmouth anxiously awaited the BRAC Commission's decision. Unlike in times past, the upfront stakes were not to win a war but to save the Yard. A negative BRAC vote would constitute a devastating blow to the seacoast region.

With a change in Navy policy during the 1980s, allowing women to go to sea aboard a submarine during sea trials, four women participated in this critical phase of a submarine's overhaul. In the fall of 1987, the four engineers undertook their professional duties aboard the USS *Simon Bolivar*. "The type of testing we do at sea can't be duplicated dockside," said Pam Celli, a mechanical field engineer technician in the Planning Department's Ship Silencing Branch. "Going on sea trials gives us a better understanding of our objectives—of the type of information we need to do our analysis. What we learn on sea trials affects how we accomplish our dockside testing in the future." All the women agreed that the entire experience was very valuable professionally, and they endured minimal problems while at sea. "Any complaints I had," said Kathleen Walsh, a navigation system civilian field engineer, "were the same as anyone else's—short shower time and small bunks."[251]

Other significant changes reflected the Yard's up-to-date adaptation to national trends. In 1987, the active-duty Navy women established a chapter of WAVES National, Maine Unit 41, at the Yard. On

January 14, 1992, the Yard's medical clinic signed a Partners-in-Education agreement with the Kittery (Maine) School District. Dr. Joanne P. Newcombe, superintendent of the district, and Commander David Wheeler of the clinic arranged that the resources of the clinic, with a staff of more than a hundred military and civilian personnel, would be available on a volunteer basis to the four schools in the district. In May of that year, the Yard enforced the Department of Defense policy of guaranteeing "the right to work in an environment free from any type of discrimination, including freedom from sexual harassment." Every supervisor and manager (military and civilian) had the responsibility to deal with any violation "immediately and appropriately."[252]

Sensible innovations in turn made the Yard a more open institution. On Thursday, April 28, 1994, the Yard sponsored the second annual "Take Our Daughters to Work Day," a nationwide program created by the Ms. Foundation for Women. The event was "designed to boost girls' self-esteem and introduce them to possible future careers as well as help girls realize all the options available to them in the work place." Girls between the ages of nine and fifteen came to the Yard with a parent, friend, or relative to view demonstrations, watch videos, and take bus tours. The shipyard commander greeted them during their visit, and the Yard provided a box lunch. Feedback on the evaluation forms was most enthusiastic, and the day was judged as a resounding success.

The PNSY Restaurant Board, in turn, inaugurated "lunch on the Mall," in which the Yard workers consumed Moe's Italian sandwiches on the park benches or under the trees. A brass ensemble provided music. "This is a great way to get people to socialize at lunch time—a great morale booster," commented one Yard employee.[253]

In addition to providing a more relaxed atmosphere in the workplace, the Yard was committed to adhere to strict environmental standards during the 1980s. Through the 1984 Resource Conservation and Recovery Act (RCRA), the federal government mandated the cleanup of all hazardous solid-waste releases. Following this directive, the Environmental Protection Agency (EPA) sought to eliminate hazardous waste sites all across the country. The Yard was required to submit information to the government to ensure that all legal requirements had been met. As early as 1982, the Yard purchased a twenty-six-foot boat skimmer with onboard equipment for cleaning up potential oil spills on the Piscataqua River and other waterways. Following the directives of various federal and state agencies in 1989, a team of six professionals performed below-ground studies on Jamaica Island, the part of the Yard that included a landfill. Workmen drilled holes to recover soil samples for analysis. The Portsmouth Shipyard adopted color-coded dumpsters to segregate different categories of waste at the Hazardous Waste Storage Facility. Air-monitoring sites checked the quality of the air. Offshore studies determined the water quality of the river and gauged the integrity of the habitat of the biological resources, such as mussels, lobsters, fish, eelgrass, and other organisms.[254]

A Hazardous Material Response Team at the Yard undertook to enforce the federal standards, since violations could jeopardize, even shut down, its operation. "It is imperative to make every effort possible to ensure the oil or chemical products we use are not released into the environment," warned a *Periscope* editorial in 1991. "An incident as seemingly harmless as spilling a gallon of hydraulic oil on the ground could violate several state and federal laws. If the oil reaches a storm drain and is released to the river, even more federal laws come into play. The willful discharge of materials, or failure to report spills, could make you as an individual liable to criminal prosecution that could result in jail sentences or huge fines." In 1992, thirteen sites were deemed potentially hazardous and were to be corrected by cleanup and future control measures by 1994. These sites included the Jamaica Island landfill, mercury burial sites, battery-acid tanks, waste-oil tanks, four rinse tanks, and a number of pipes that—prior to 1976—discharged industrial wastes directly into the Piscataqua River. The Navy's commitment to its cleanup program was reflected in its funding—$157 million in 1990, increasing to $250 million in 1992 at naval and marine bases across the country.[255]

On Earth Day, April 22, 1992, the Yard joined with seacoast communities and business leaders to promote the use of recycled materials. The Environment Action Report was distributed and posted in all the Yard's shop stores. The purpose of the report was "to identify, document, and correct poor environmental work practices and deficiencies." To emphasize the link to the past, the *Periscope* featured short biographies of Henry David Thoreau, Theodore Roosevelt, and Rachel Carson, with mentions of their pioneering writings and work in preserving the earth.

"Like these Americans," concluded the *Periscope,* "we too can have an impact this Earth Day by practicing the three R's, 'Reduce–Reuse–Recycle.'" The Yard fulfilled its pledge. After launching its first recycling program in 1991, the Shipyard by 1993 was recycling 60 percent of its solid waste, and sending less than 10 percent to off-Yard landfills. These figures compared most favorably with a national average of 17 percent recycling and 70 percent landfill. A new waste-handling facility was built on Jamaica Island in 1993. That same year, the Shipyard issued its first solid-waste operations manual. The Yard became nationally recognized as a leader in the field of solid-waste management, and Yard employees addressed national conferences on this topic. One example of environmental protection concerned the previous policy of dumping apparently "clean" snow into salt water during the winter. The ban on such a practice, following the passage of a Maine law in 1988, stopped the filling-in of wetlands with snow containing gravel and sand. It was discovered that the snow, in addition to carrying gravel and sand, was also picking up salt, de-icing chemicals, and other polluting materials. The Yard then piled up the snow, creating an ugly brown mountain after every storm, at a special site on Jamaica Island, where it was allowed to melt on land. It was eventually determined that the snow also contained such other pollutants as pieces of wood, metal, plastic, glass, and other foreign materials—all of which, before the ban, would have ended up in the Piscataqua River. A Yard employee monitored the shrinking brown mountain as summer approached, and on the Fourth of July 1993, he determined that there was still one small frozen chunk of ice left under the dirty debris![256]

While remedying social and environmental shortcomings, the Yard did not neglect its primary role of providing for the national defense. Technological and construction projects moved forward. Advancing into a modern age of communications, the Yard in early 1985 received its own zip code, 03804-5000, and a new telephone-system prefix of 438. To house such an expanding communications system, to streamline and consolidate functions, and to improve efficiency, the Yard undertook to build a major addition to Building 86, the Yard's administrative headquarters. Inheriting the space then currently occupied by three outmoded and obsolete structures, the proposed PNSY Engineering/Management Facility would involve a six-story, 114,000-square-foot addition on the east side of Building 86. Upon completion,

The new $9.5-million Engineering/Management Facility—a six-story, 114,000-square-foot addition to the east of Building 86—was opened in 1989, thus streamlining the Yard's efficiency in competing with other yards. PNSMVC

the new building would provide space for functions previously scattered among several separate buildings. In addition to an atrium or a connector from Building 86, the new structure would provide five computer rooms and six conference rooms. On August 27, 1987, at the groundbreaking ceremony, Shipyard Commander Captain Peter Bowman pointed out that this building marked a new beginning after years of trying to play "catch-up" from the 1964–71 closure threats, when modernization was held to a standstill. "This military construction project," Bowman said, "represents another step forward in upgrading our facilities, relieving the crunch of too little appropriate space for technical and administrative work." After Bowman's remarks, the assembled naval and civilian dignitaries broke ground with their golden shovels. Less than two years later, on May 25, 1989, the Engineering/Management Facility was officially opened in ribbon-cutting ceremonies. The building actually cost $9.5 million, more than $1 million lower than the

Located near a picnic shelter in a spacious open setting, a sign honors the beautification efforts of Shipyard Commander Captain Peter B. Bowman (1987 to 1990). To set an example for others and to publicize his crusade, Bowman often carried a plastic bag to pick up litter as he made his rounds about the Yard. PNSY–Lashua Photo

original estimate. It was observed by U.S. Senator Gordon Humphrey that the new facility, through increased efficiency, would pay for itself within a few years. That prediction proved true.[257]

On January 28, 1988, an individual interested in the Yard's industrial progress appeared in his black limousine. Vice President George Bush toured the Yard, accompanied by Shipyard Commander Peter Bowman, who explained the Yard's mission and current efforts. Bush went below decks on the USS *Groton,* a submarine undergoing overhaul. Disappearing down the hatch for a quick tour and wearing his new *Groton* cap, the vice president soon reappeared, minus his cap, probably the upshot of a tall man negotiating low bulkheads. At the Yard's Galley Hatch Restaurant, Bush greeted several hundred Yard workers at lunch. After commenting that he was glad to be in the region he loved, near his summer home in Kennebunkport, Maine, Bush complimented the workforce. "It's a great yard," Bush said, "and if you ever need somebody to witness to it, speak to the Vice President." A little more than a year later, in April 1989, the Portsmouth Naval Shipyard was asked to provide support to its recent visitor and one of its most famous neighbors—President George Bush, who had been elected to that office the previous November. The White House Special Programs Office requested the construction of special facilities in Kennebunkport for use by the president and his staff. Although the initial request was for "just a little assistance," "Operation Kennebunkport," as it was informally known, ultimately involved virtually every division of the Yard's Supply Department. The Naval Mobile Construction Battalion Seven performed the actual work. Completed in early 1990, the new facilities at Walker's Point at the Bush Compound included quarters for the presidential military aide and medical officer, helicopter pads, and a hangar for Marine One.[258]

The new Portsmouth Naval Shipyard motto, "When we work as a team, we are unbeatable," fostered progress in public relations. The Shipyard Museum and Visitor Center, as it was renamed, forged ahead with the joint effort of volunteers, community groups, and military personnel. From its one-room genesis in Building 22, the museum moved into successively larger quarters—first into a renovated garage stall in Building 35, then to the Marine Barracks, and finally to Building 156, the barracks for the enlisted submarine crews. Occupying half of the barracks, the new museum opened on December 7, 1991, with a hundred dignitaries and special guests in attendance. Aptly referring to the museum as a naval "time tunnel," Director Jim Dolph had assembled a vast collection of memorabilia in various displays. A library with shelves of books and files of archives provided many opportunities for research. Volunteers also interpreted and presented the Yard's history in an outreach program of lectures, slide slows, and seminars for the area's schools, civic organizations, and community groups. A major gift to the museum was a model of the USS *Thresher*, donated by craftsman Jim Roushey, who devoted a year and a half of work to the project.[259]

As a living link to the past, Herbert ("Herbie") Grimes was frequently featured in *Periscope* articles in the late 1980s. Beginning as a laborer in the Rigger Shop in 1940, Herbie marked his fortieth anniversary of government service in 1988. Other than being caught in two RIFs (reductions in force) and doing one stint as a commercial fisherman, Herbie, at the age of eighty and burdened with illness, retired in

June 1989 with forty-one-and-a-half years of service. Herbie received an affectionate farewell from his co-workers at a retirement ceremony. "A lot of knowledge and skill are leaving this shop," said many fellow workers. "He could teach things to apprentices or to anyone, skills that aren't remembered anymore." As the retirement party wound down for the "oldest Shipyarder," Herbie remarked, "I hate to go." A voice called out from the crowd: "Any last words of advice?" "Yeah," Herbie responded. "Do your job!" Four months later, Herbie Grimes was dead, and his funeral was attended by many Yard friends. In a moving *Periscope* article, "Farewell, Herbie," the veteran's advice about doing one's job was recalled. "You've done yours, Herbie," the *Periscope* eulogized. "Rest in peace."[260]

For the Shipyard, however, the hard economic realities overshadowed the excellent progress the Yard was making. The Base Realignment and Closure (BRAC) Commission in Washington analyzed the effectiveness of more than 4,200 military properties. On December 29, 1988, the BRAC Commission recommended to the Defense Department and to Congress the closure of eighty-six installations, among them nearby Pease Air Force Base in Newington, New Hampshire. Rumors flew that other closings were bound to occur—among them the Yard itself. In this tense setting, Captain Lewis A. Felton assumed command of the Yard on August 17, 1990. His remarks at the change-of-command ceremonies reflected his full awareness of the Yard's vulnerability in an era of smaller defense budgets. Felton, however, threw out a challenge. "We're the Portsmouth Naval Shipyard," he said. "Catch us if you can!"[261]

For the next five years, the Maine and New Hampshire congressmen and senators once again sought to prevent further erosion of the Yard's dwindling workforce and to enhance its chances of survival. In their minds was the recent fate of two other New England bases, Fort Devens in Massachusetts and Loring Air Force Base in Maine, both casualties at the BRAC Commission's next meeting in 1990. By the end of 1991 at the Portsmouth Shipyard, a cutback of 380 employees brought the employment level to 7,000. In response, the Maine/New Hampshire delegation sent a letter to the Navy Department, urging that the Yard be designated as a home port for research-and-development submarines. The plan included reassigning two submarines—one from New London, Connecticut, and the other from Norfolk, Virginia—

to the Portsmouth Yard to provide ample work. In response to this proposal, the Navy was reported to have taken the position that this submarine transfer "would involve a duplication of services, and would make the ships less accessible to their operations commander."[262]

Aiding in the fight to save the Yard was the Seacoast Shipyard Association (SSA), founded back in 1964 during the first closure order. In 1992, Russell Van Billiard, a retired PNSY engineer and SSA member, articulated the concerns of the Yard and the interests of the seacoast region. Estimating the economic impact on the region should the Yard close, Van Billiard calculated that, in goods and services as well as the military and civilian salaries, the Yard contributed about $1 billion to the local economy, compared to the $329 million represented by Pease, which ultimately was phased out. Looking ahead to the next round of BRAC Commission recommendations in 1993, Van Billiard urged citizens to lobby their elected officials in making the government aware of the Yard's importance in Naval Sea Systems Command. "It [the Yard] has three very important things going for it," Van Billiard said. "First, the work we do is still going to be done—although there won't be as much of it. Second, the Shipyard's facilities have been kept completely up to date," as exemplified by its new $26 million dry-dock facility. "And third, our production and efficiency are excellent."[263]

For the next eighteen months, rumors circulated about layoffs and the threat of a new closure order. On June 12, 1993, more than 600 Portsmouth Shipyard supporters attended a one-hour public hearing in Boston before the BRAC Commission. The auditorium was crammed with PNSY banners proclaiming, "Save Our Shipyard," and " The Navy Knows Best." On Friday, June 26, 1993, the BRAC Commission unanimously voted to remove the Yard from the 1993 base-closure list. By late afternoon, Senate Majority Leader George Mitchell and Senator William Cohen, both of Maine, triumphantly displayed an "Extra" edition of the *Portsmouth Herald* at a packed council chamber in the Kittery Town Hall. "Shipyard survives!" read the banner headline. The battle to save the Yard in 1993 had been won, but the next round of BRAC Commission decisions would be coming up only two years later. No one was foolhardy enough to take anything for granted. Mitchell declared, "The effort for 1995 . . . begins tomorrow [Saturday], Monday, Tuesday." In a public statement, Captain Felton observed: "When Senator Mitchell talks about that [the finest teamwork] being the key to the Yard for the future, it clearly is."[264]

During Admiral Jeremy Michael ("Mike") Boorda's first visit to the Yard in October 1994, the Chief of Naval Operations addressed Yard military personnel in the auditorium, stressing quality-of-life issues. PNSY

On the hard road ahead, the Yard was fortunate in gaining a valued friend. On April 23, 1994, Admiral Jeremy Michael "Mike" Boorda became the twenty-fifth Chief of Naval Operations (CNO). In his close-to-forty-year naval career, Boorda had risen from the ranks as a sailor. As a "Mustang" (Navy slang for an officer who had received his commission from enlisted status), Mike Boorda thoroughly sympathized with the common sailor and average yard worker. In October 1994, he visited the Portsmouth Naval Shipyard, stressing quality-of-life issues during a question-and-answer session for military personnel in the Yard auditorium, where every seat was taken. Boorda's dynamic, persuasive personality impressed the audience—not only because of his handling of military housing, medical, and cost-of-living concerns, but also because of his solid grasp of Yard issues.[265]

Admiral Boorda returned to the Yard much sooner than expected. A crisis loomed on Wednesday, May 10, 1995, when the BRAC Com-

*During his October 1994 visit to the Yard, Admiral Jeremy Michael ("Mike")
Boorda, Chief of Naval Operations, personally awarded decorations and congratulated many U.S. Navy enlisted personnel. PNSY–Lashua Photo*

mission added Portsmouth to the closure list with a 4–2 vote. As the
news erupted throughout the seacoast, Portsmouth reaction was swift.
Anger quickly turned to resolve to save the Yard. Putting his office and
reputation on the line, Admiral Boorda flew up from Washington on
short notice on May 12 to defend the Yard. At the conclusion of a
change-of-command ceremony in the Yard auditorium, Boorda
appeared before the vast crowd—a filled-to-capacity auditorium with
standing room only in the balcony. He was wildly cheered at his introduction. "This yard needs to stay open," he said. Referring to the BRAC
Commission members, he commented, "Maybe they got confused. We
will unconfuse them." In conclusion, Boorda declared: "[The Navy]
made me CNO to have opinions. I will state my opinions. I will state my
opinions to the commission as clearly as I have stated [them] to you."[266]

With the lines of battle redrawn, Yard and seacoast interests
regrouped as they had done in the 1960s and in 1993 to head off yet

*Faced with the BRAC Commission deliberations on the Yard's future, Admiral
Boorda (in uniform) with Maine congressional delegation members (left to right)
James Longley Jr., William Cohen, and Olympia Snowe appeared at the Shipyard
on May 10, 1995, to provide their support for keeping the facility open. PNSY*

another potential closure order. With the BRAC Commission slated to
visit the Yard on June 2, 1995, to see the facility firsthand, the community rallied with meetings and sent contributions to the Seacoast
Shipyard Association. The Portsmouth City Council donated $10,000
to the cause, while the New Hampshire Legislature appropriated
$50,000 for the SSA. At stake were the jobs of 4,100 Yard workers and
an annual payroll of $220 million. On Friday, June 22, 1995, the eight-
member BRAC Commission, convening in Washington, took no action
on the Yard at 12:30 P.M. With the news transmitted instantly to the
Yard, victory whistles filled the air. "Shipyard stays open. Closure
panel ends 5-year ordeal"—the *Portsmouth Herald* "Extra," decorated
with stars, saluted the news. Many naval and civilian leaders on the
scene credited Admiral Boorda's bold stand for helping to win the battle. "I am very pleased with today's vote by the Base Realignment and
Closure Commission that agreed with the Navy and the Department
of Defense that Portsmouth Naval Shipyard should remain open,"
commented Boorda. "The tremendous support of all involved combined
to make this a winning effort."[267]

Toward the Bicentennial Celebration, 1995–2000

Even after managing to escape closure in 1995, the Portsmouth Naval Shipyard still struggled to adjust as its bicentennial neared. Downsizing continued in the Yard workload and the number of employees. In addition, issues never before fully considered, comprehended, or challenged in the Yard's history came to the forefront. A dispute over the Yard's location—in Maine or New Hampshire—affected the payment of state taxes for Yard workers. Maine has a state income tax; New Hampshire does not. Should underutilized Yard buildings and facilities be made available to private business—an action that could threaten the Yard's military compatibility? Notwithstanding these matters, the Yard prepared for a grand bicentennial celebration in the year 2000.

Less than a month after the BRAC nonclosure decision, the Yard savored another triumph. In early July 1995, the USS *Maine* (SSBN 741) arrived at the Yard for an extended visit and its commissioning. Built at Electric Boat in Groton, Connecticut, the *Maine* is one of the largest and most powerful submarines in the United States Navy, with a length of 560 feet and a displacement of 18,750 tons submerged. As an Ohio–class (Trident) submarine, the *Maine* carries twenty-four ballistic missiles, compared to sixteen on the earlier fleet ballistic-missile submarines. For twelve days, the seacoast hosted the *Maine*'s officers and crew with festivals, cookouts, and sporting events. In an almost-unprecedented relaxation of naval security, the *Maine*'s chief petty officers led tours of the sub, on deck and below, for many community members, Yard workers, and military personnel. The $1 billion submarine was so long, as the tour guides pointed out, that exercising crew members could jog from bow to stern within her compartments. On July 29, the *Maine* was commissioned, with 6,000 people in attendance, one of the largest ceremonies of its kind in the history of the Navy. Shortly afterward, the *Maine* departed for Kings Bay, Georgia, its home port. From Washington, Admiral Jeremy ("Mike") Boorda issued his best wishes, declaring: "While her technological capabilities and heritage combine to make her a fine ship, *Maine*'s true strength comes from the dedicated officers, chiefs, and sailors who proudly walk her decks."[268]

Balancing the pride and expectation of a new submarine joining the fleet, a decommissioning ceremony is also an honored tradition—one in which the submarine is retired with credit given to her gallant service to the nation. On October 5, 1995, the USS *Omaha* (SSN 692) was decommissioned at the Yard, the first inactivation of a Los Angeles–class submarine at the Portsmouth facility. At the ceremony, the *Omaha*'s commander relinquished custody of the ship to Shipyard Commander Captain Carl Strawbridge. The ship had served the Navy well for seventeen years. "This particular decommissioning ceremony is certainly an event of varied emotions," said Rear Admiral Richard A. Buchanan, a member of the official party. "The Navy and the submarine force can look back with pride on the success of the *Omaha*." After the Yard performed its inactivation work, the sub was towed to Puget Sound Naval Shipyard, Bremerton, Washington, for disposal and recycling; the crew members were reassigned to new duty stations.[269]

As the 1995 Christmas season approached, the Yard anxiously awaited, almost as a yearly ritual, the news from Washington in anticipating the future workload. Except for the year 1997, the Yard had submarines scheduled for rehabilitation for every year through 2002. Members of the Maine and New Hampshire congressional delegations met with Navy officials, including Admiral Boorda, in an effort to fill this gap. Their lobbying, in the words of the *Portsmouth Herald*, "has struck gold." To provide for the Yard, the Navy shifted work, earlier than scheduled, from Norfolk, Virginia, so that the USS *Oklahoma City* (SSN 723) in 1997 would undergo its "depot modernization period" (DMP) at Portsmouth. This transfer of work would involve an eleven-month project, supplying 120,000 man-days of labor. In addition, for the same year, the Navy added $3 million worth of work to the overhaul of the USS *Memphis*, then at the Yard. "The problem [of the delay in this announcement] was not that the Navy did not want to assign more work to Portsmouth," explained Maine Senator William S. Cohen. "The problem was that it [the Navy] needed to wait until an appropriations bill passed and made more money available. . . . The Navy is strongly committed to Portsmouth. The question is: Is Congress committed to a strong national defense?"[270]

With Cohen's rhetorical question answered by adequate congressional funding, the year of 1996 augured well, although the usual rumors circulated. Reacting to a military newspaper report that the Pentagon was asking Congress for another round of base closures, New Hampshire Senator Judd Gregg and others quashed such stories, saying there was no stomach in Washington for further base cuts. "The

Portsmouth compared to other shipyards

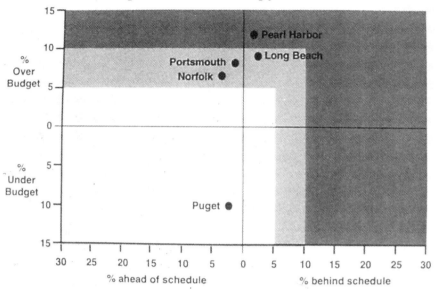

Portsmouth's ship performance

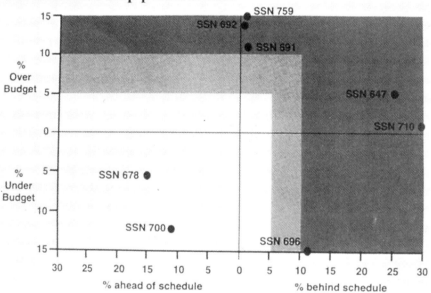

Two graphs from the January 5, 1996, issue of the Portsmouth Periscope *track the Portsmouth Naval Shipyard's record against other yards on budget and schedule issues. From official Washington's perspective, productivity, cost effectiveness, and other economic factors play an ongoing role in assessing the Yard's status.*

Located in the Recreation Center and supervised by an experienced staff, the library offers books, magazines, newspapers, on-line computers, and similar services to its many patrons. In anticipation of transfer to distant navy yards and bases, Internet users often search here for real estate information. PNSY–Lashua Photo

chances for another BRAC round in the foreseeable future," said Gregg, "are about the same as the chances of porpoises swimming up the Merrimack River." Other developments proceeded smoothly. In May, the Yard opened its new environmental facility, housed in Building 357 on Jamaica Island. Before the completion of the facility, hazardous-waste personnel had had to work outdoors at the mercy of the weather. Now all functions were under one roof. The building, designed in conjunction with the Maine Department of Environmental Protection, also included shower and decontamination rooms for the health and safety of the workers. A short time later, the Shipyard, as a member of the Piscataqua River Alliance, participated in a simulated oil spill in the Piscataqua, with 1,000 gallons of popcorn substituting for oil in the exercise. Within an hour, a Navy oil skimmer with 6,000 feet of boom was able to contain the mock spill. Finally, on Monday, April 29, the former USS *Omaha* left the Yard under tow for its ultimate destination via Norfolk and the Panama Canal to the Puget Sound Naval Shipyard. "They'll cut it [the sub] up, and recycle it," said the Yard spokesperson.[271]

As the spring of 1996 proceeded routinely at the Yard, a most unexpected shot rang out on Thursday, May 16, at the Washington (DC) Navy Yard, reverberating throughout the world. Outside his quarters, Admiral Boorda died of a self-inflicted gunshot wound to the chest. Called by many "a sailor's sailor," Mike Boorda was mourned throughout the Navy—indeed, throughout the United States and beyond. Just a year and five days earlier, Boorda had given his stirring speech at the Yard during the closure crisis. The seacoast area remembered Boorda as a champion of the Yard, and heartfelt tributes came from state and local politicians, Yard union leaders, and rank-and-file Yard workers. "Mike Boorda was directly responsible," said New Hampshire Senator Bob Smith, "for keeping the Portsmouth shipyard open." Secretary of the Navy John Dalton's tribute appeared in the *Periscope*. "We owe Mike Boorda a lot. To help us, he exposed himself to demands, difficulties, and sometimes criticism." It was learned after his death that Boorda, in a letter written to Senator Gregg on May 3, was wholeheartedly committed to using the Yard for submarine "depot modernization" work and overhauls. Boorda's successor, Admiral Jay L. Johnson, confirmed to the post of Chief of Naval Operations on August 2, carried out his predecessor's policies.[272]

This promise by Boorda and Johnson was realized when the USS *Oklahoma City* arrived at the Yard for the fiscal year 1997 workload on Wednesday, December 4, 1996—an excellent Christmas present. The depot modernization period (DMP) work was slated to begin in January 1997, with the upgrade requiring eleven months and costing $72 million. A participant in Operation Desert Shield action against Iraq, the *Oklahoma City* carried a crew of fourteen officers and 127 enlisted men. The sub's dimensions were most impressive: 360 feet long, 6,900-ton displacement, and a hull diameter of thirty-three feet.[273]

Just a day after the arrival of the *Oklahoma City*, President William J. Clinton nominated Maine Senator William S. Cohen as Secretary of Defense. With his twenty years in the U.S. Senate, Cohen knew the Portsmouth Naval Shipyard perhaps better than any other public official. He had been a participant in many sub commissionings

and a fervent supporter of the Yard during the many BRAC deliberations. Praise for the appointment was universal. "This is a great move
for the country," said former Yard Commander Peter Bowman. "It would
also give an advantage to the Portsmouth Naval Shipyard in the fact
that Senator Cohen is very knowledgeable about the yard."[274]

While the overall battle to save the Yard during the 1990s had been
largely won, one long-running skirmish remained unresolved, and shots
were being fired as 1996 drew to a close. The issue was: For state income-
tax purposes, was the Portsmouth Naval Shipyard in New Hampshire or
in Maine? Since 1969, the State of Maine has been collecting income
taxes from New Hampshire residents who worked at the Yard. On
December 15, 1996, the *Boston Globe* ran a major article, "Maine Takes
Taxes from N.H. Workers at Shipyard," detailing the frustration of Kurt
Wuelper of Strafford, New Hampshire, a twenty-year Yard veteran.
When he received his regular paychecks, Wuelper saw that a big chunk
always was missing. "They're ripping me off," complained Wuelper. "If I
owe Maine taxes, they can tax me. But this is straight larceny on their
part. I absolutely object to paying Maine taxes, because the shipyard is
in New Hampshire." While the border dispute between the two states
over the Piscataqua River islands had festered since colonial times, it
was not until 1988 that shipyarder Victor Bourre of Dover fired an opening salvo. In his April 1988 letter to the editor of the *Portsmouth
Periscope*, Bourre challenged the legality of the Maine tax, and urged a
"Portsmouth Tea Party," on April 9, 1988, to include a peaceful demonstration and march, with the participants dropping a symbolic tea bag
(harking back to the 1773 Boston Tea Party) into the river. Bourre's one-
man fight gradually gathered adherents through the years, and in
December 1996, New Hampshire Governor-elect Jeanne Shaheen added
her support, vowing to carry the fight to the United States Supreme
Court. Although the Shipyard took the official stance of neutrality in the
border and tax battles, the issue was hotly contested toward the end of
1996, a soon-to-be-filed legal case that would not go away.[275]

Notwithstanding the controversy swirling outside the gates, the
Yard community joined in celebrating the holiday season as Christmas
1996 drew near. Various Yard charities included the donation of approximately 700 pounds of nonperishable food for needy families. Through
the auspices of the Shipyard Chapel, "Operation Christmas Child"
reached out to needy children. Each donor filled an empty shoe with a

The 288-acre Portsmouth Naval Shipyard is served by land, sea, rail, and air transportation. The Memorial Bridge (bottom), completed in 1923, was built, in part, to displace the inefficient ferry system that transported Yard employees across the Piscataqua. PNSMVC

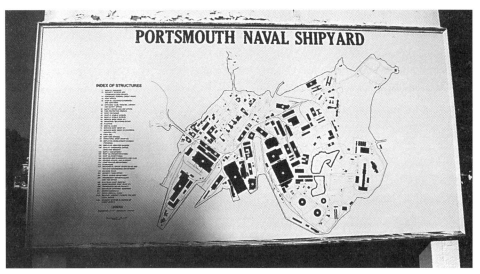

At Yard Gates No. 1 and No. 2, large wooden maps provide information and guidance for those entering the sprawling industrial complex. First-time visitors, truckers delivering supplies and materials, and others on official business utilize the map to find their way around the base. PNSY–Lashua Photo

On prominent display inside Building 86, near the entrance to the Shipyard commander's office, a "Sails to Atoms" logo sign and a ship's wheel symbolize the past traditions, current purposes, and future objectives of the Portsmouth Naval Shipyard. PNSY–Lashua Photo

variety of gifts for distribution overseas to a needy child. At the Child Development Center, Supply Department personnel gathered for a Christmas sing-along. "The kids were so receptive—it was really fun," said one adult participant. "They even asked us back next year." Capping the activities, Shipyard Commander Carl Strawbridge greeted the children and presented them with gifts.[276]

The new year of 1997 brought its own special challenges and frustrations. Reflecting the wish of many of the nation's dedicated naval-shipyard workers was the hoped-for recognition of their service to the United States in the form of a commemorative stamp honoring all shipyards. In preparation for the bicentennial of America's naval shipyards, the Naval Shipyard Bicentennial Support Group lobbied the U.S. Postal Service for such a stamp to be issued in the year 2000. In June 1997, the group presented a letter to the Postal Service stating that "no stamp has ever been issued to honor the yards and their workers." In addition, the group stated that Portsmouth, as the first public navy yard, should play host to a ceremony unveiling the new stamp. The proposal went unheeded. In December 1997, the Postal Service also decided not to issue a new stamp to honor the bicentennial of the Submarine Service, which would occur on April 12, 2000. This decision sparked outrage and indignation at Electric Boat, the U.S. Naval Submarine Base at Groton, Connecticut, and around the Portsmouth Yard area. "If we can have Elvis and Bugs Bunny stamps," said one retired submarine captain, "we should have a commemorative stamp for the submarine force."[277]

Two Yard projects fared better. In January 1997, the Shipyard Library went "on line" with four new multimedia computers. Under the direction of Librarian Dee Bissell, the library staff provided access and instruction to anyone, whether expert or a beginner, to explore the Internet. For Shipyarders, the Internet provided practical information on many topics, including the Code of Federal Regulations, technical information, the U.S. Navy home page, Navy on-line, ship regulations. "I'm transferring to Washington State in May," remarked an enlisted man from the USS *New York City*. "I utilized the Internet at the Shipyard library to look for real estate." That same month, the USS *Groton*, at the Yard for deactivation, entered into a partnership with the York Middle School in order to serve the host community of York, Maine. In this partnership, the officers and crew of the *Groton* volunteered to promote the school's education, health, and citizenship.

Eight or nine *Groton* personnel went to the school on a weekly basis, providing help with navigation and engineering projects and the school science fair. "Anytime you can help a student, it's beneficial," said a school coordinator. "It's great that the crew is willing to try something new and put their expertise to good use."[278]

On the national level, William S. Cohen was sworn in to head the Defense Department on January 24, 1997. Cohen's new position elevated him to respond to national and international concerns—not, as in the past, focusing primarily on local and state issues. Among others, Maine Senator Olympia Snowe and New Hampshire Senator Bob Smith assumed Cohen's mantle to protect the Yard's interests. "She's taking over where Cohen left off," remarked one of the Yard's union leaders. The Yard's workforce had dwindled, down 60 percent since 1991 to 3,500, and it was slated to be cut by another 454. "We didn't fight hard to save the Shipyard [only] to watch it bleed to death by having them peck away at it," contended Senator Smith. On February 19, 1997, Vice Admiral George Sterner of the Naval Sea Systems held a Yard press conference to explain what naval policies were in store for the future. Speaking in general terms, Sterner pledged that Portsmouth, as one of four government yards, would receive an equal share of submarine maintenance work. "[Open bidding] is not Navy policy today," concluded Sterner. "Navy policy today is: 'I have four shipyards. Sterner, you're supposed to manage them efficiently and balance the work load.' And I'm going to go back and look at better balance."[279]

The constant downsizing of the Yard's workforce followed a nationwide trend. From huge budgets during the Ronald Reagan presidency, eight naval shipyards dropped to just four, and the others closed. All the while, despite these reductions, the Portsmouth Yard was expected to "get the work done"—not only quickly but also "in an efficient and cost-effective manner." On July 22, 1997, Captain Vernon Thomas ("Tom") Williams took command of the Yard, replacing Captain Carl Strawbridge, who had absorbed the brunt of the downsizing for two years during economically pinched times. At the change-of-command ceremony, Williams entertained high hopes for the future, saying: "We must make ourselves indispensable to the submarine force and the Navy," by delivering "fully capable ships on time and on budget."[280]

A week later, at Williams's suggestion, the Maine and New Hampshire congressional delegations asked the Navy about the potential appropriations for Trident sub work, with eighteen Trident (Ohio–class) subs in the fleet. In October, the delegation announced positive results for the Yard, as the Navy agreed to provide $44 million worth of work through fiscal year 1998, thus assuring a stable employment level. "Workers at the shipyard can breathe easier," read the joint congressional delegation statement.[281]

With the approach of fall, as the fiscal battles continued, the seacoast community learned the fate of a long-lost sub and pondered the naming of a new one under construction at Electric Boat. On September 15, 1997, the University of New Hampshire's R/V *Gulf Challenger*, a research vessel using high-tech underwater sonar equipment, located the wreck of the submarine USS *0-9*, which had disappeared fifty-six years earlier off the Isles of Shoals. Utilizing this special equipment, naval and civilian officials were able to spot the sub's partially crushed hull in 420 feet of water seventeen miles off the New Hampshire coast. A floral wreath was flung into the ocean at the site in memory of the thirty-three men lost at sea. The official party decided to keep the exact location of the wreck a secret, with no plans to recover the sub. The area was designated an official naval burial ground.[282]

Familiar issues—some resolved, others stalemated—occupied the balance of 1997. In late September, one potential environmental hazard was addressed. Interred as landfill during the 1970s, two mercury burial vaults were excavated and removed from Jamaica Island and disposed of at a licensed off-yard facility. The vaults were discovered to be in excellent condition, and no contamination was detected in the soil or groundwater around the vaults.[283]

Interest in the naming of the third Seawolf–class submarine (SSN 23), under construction at Electric Boat, stimulated local pride. Since the state of Maine had been honored by the naming of a Trident submarine as the USS *Maine* in 1995, with her commissioning as cause for a statewide celebration, the state of New Hampshire lobbied for identical recognition. The last ship honoring the state was the battleship USS *New Hampshire*, which had been decommissioned in 1921. "Subs have been named after states as far inland as Ohio and Wyoming," noted the *Herald*, "but nothing for New Hampshire." Schoolchildren and citizens were urged to write supportive letters to the Navy Department. The suspense finally ended on April 8, 1998, when the Navy Department announced that the new sub would be named in honor of former President Jimmy Carter, an Annapolis graduate with distinguished submarine service. Disappointed New Hampshire politicians urged that this oversight be speedily corrected. Writing Navy Secretary John Dalton, New Hampshire Senator Judd Gregg asserted: "I think that you would agree that the USS *New Hampshire* is the appropriate name for the next Seawolf submarine."[284]

The thorny question as to the exact legal location of the Portsmouth Naval Shipyard continued unabated, with Victor Bourre, New Hampshire Governor Jeanne Shaheen, Maine Governor Angus King, and the congressional delegations of both states in the fray. A 1761 map, which surfaced in England, showed Seavey's Island on the New Hampshire side, and it was brought forward as evidence. A major *New York Times* article on Sunday, November 30, 1997, focused even more attention on the boundary dispute. The *Times* aired the particulars of the controversy for its national and international readers, including notice of the defeat in the U.S. Senate of a bill to win for New Hampshire shipyard workers an exemption from Maine income taxes.[285]

Throughout 1998, the border dispute festered, with Bourre retiring on January 1 from his Yard job as planner and estimator to devote full attention to his cause. The tax-revolt movement gradually gained momentum, with roughly a thousand New Hampshire–based Yard employees, as well as Bourre, filing a class-action suit against Maine and its tax system. Adding fuel to the fire was Maine's policy of taxing the spouses of Yard employees, even though they often worked in New Hampshire, Massachusetts, or elsewhere. In a major article, the *Boston Globe* articulated these grievances: "Nearly half the shipyard's 3,330 workers reside in New Hampshire, which has no income tax. Maine taxes these out-of state workers' incomes and figures their spouses' incomes into its tax rate even if they don't work in Maine. (The courts have allowed Maine to impose a tax rate based on total family income.) Maine's attorney general says New Hampshire shipyarders pay Maine $5 to $7 million in taxes a year. . . . By contrast, Massachusetts taxes New Hampshire residents working in the Bay State but leaves spousal income out of the picture."[286]

Behind the gates, the Yard moved forward as usual for the Navy. On February 25, it was announced that the USS *La Jolla* (SSN 701), a 688 Los Angeles–class attack submarine, would arrive at the Yard for a two-year engineered refueling overhaul (ERO). The Navy changed the home port of the *La Jolla* from San Diego to Portsmouth to provide more work for the Yard—estimated in the $200 million range, together with $5.9 million in salaries drawn by the *La Jolla* crew complement, during its twenty-four-month stay. On August 21, 1998, the *La Jolla* arrived, moving up the Piscataqua under its own power to Berth 6. Other submarine events during the year included the completion of the two-year overhaul of the USS *Dallas,* which then rejoined the U.S. Naval Fleet in Groton, Connecticut. The USS *Helena* also arrived in the Piscataqua for a $110 million DMP. On a historic, end-of-an-era note, the USS *Sand Lance,* with twenty-six years of service, was deactivated with appropriate ceremonies on Thursday, January 15, 1998, at Groton, Connecticut. Back in 1969, the *Sand Lance* had been the last (134th) Portsmouth-built submarine to be launched.[287]

Yard projects and activities continued. In March 1998, the Yard's power plant started conversion of its fuel from a very thick #6 fuel oil to a cleaner-burning natural gas; a gas supplier ran a pipe from Eliot, Maine, to the Yard. The potential emissions reduction in the conversion from oil to gas represented a significant environmental improvement: Annual waste eliminated from various pollutants included sulfur dioxide (961 tons), nitrogen oxides (492 tons), and carbon monoxide (73 tons). On January 5, 2000, the process was completed, with the Yard using natural gas. Radon detectors (1,700 instruments) were placed in 112 of the Yard's industrial buildings to check for levels of naturally occurring radon gas. Activities enlivened the recreational opportunities at the Yard. On April 17, about 400 Boy Scouts "invaded" the Yard for a weekend camporee. After pitching their tents on Jamaica Island and in front of the Marine Barracks, the Scouts participated in knot-tying, compass-reading, and model-rocketry classes. To learn more about the Yard's history, they embarked upon a hike with stops at the Fire Station, *Squalus* Memorial, Quarters A, the Peace Treaty Room in Building 86, and the chapel. In September, the newly renovated and air-conditioned Recreation Center in Building 22 (the former Officers Club) reopened with the sounds of bluegrass music. The facility, open to all—employees, officers, and enlisted personnel—included a movie theater, library, multimedia room, computer stations, and game room. In his speaking engagements around the community and in his "Captain's Corner" column in the *Periscope,* Shipyard Commander "Tom" Williams emphasized, often with a biblical reference, the Yard's proud record of delivering the work on time and on budget. "I will borrow a phrase from the Navy Seals training to express the concept differently," Williams stated, "'The only easy day was yesterday!'"[288]

In March 1998, great excitement greeted Senator Olympia Snowe's announcement that the two-century-old USS *Constitution*, the oldest commissioned ship in the U.S. Navy, would visit the Portsmouth Naval Shipyard—arriving August 7 and leaving August 10. The Department of the Navy had given its approval for this voyage, which would begin in Boston, stop in Gloucester, Massachusetts (August 4–7), then continue to the Portsmouth Yard. The visit was expected to be one of the focal points for Portsmouth's 375th anniversary celebration. Recently refurbished at a cost of $12 million, "Old Ironsides" had spent years at the Yard in the late nineteenth century as a training ship. To promote this banner tourist attraction, the town of Kittery decided to issue 15,000 free tickets. Before long, however, the Navy had second thoughts about the feasibility of such a voyage. Questions were raised about the old ship's seaworthiness, especially if a bad storm arose. "The Navy has no intention of endangering a national treasure," said a U.S. Navy spokesperson. "The safety of the ship and the crew is paramount." Despite talk of the ship's fragile condition, Gloucester, Kittery, and Portsmouth officials and organizers remained undaunted. "The only thing that will stop the *Constitution* from coming here," fumed one Gloucester organizer, "is a snow blizzard in August."[289]

While the Navy was assessing the situation, many seacoast organizers held firm and speculated that the number of visitors would surpass the crowd at the USS *Maine* commissioning in 1995, which drew between 300,000 and 500,000 people. "Once we get the final word from the Navy," said Portsmouth Mayor Evelyn Sirrell, "it's full steam ahead." All planning ended abruptly on Tuesday, June 9, when Chief of Naval Operations Admiral Jay L. Johnson announced his final decision on the *Constitution*'s status. "After weighing the benefits and associated risks of taking this priceless national treasure back to sea," said Johnson, "I decided the nation is best served by conducting any future operation of 'Old Ironsides' in close proximity to the Boston Harbor sea buoy in the sheltered waters of Massachusetts Bay." Maine Senator Snowe cited the disappointment of the organizers, but she

The 100,000-pound sail of the ex-Grayling submarine is the prime focus of the newly constructed (1999) Shipyard Workers Park, with Building 13 (left background). PNSY–Lashua Photo

Located in Building 86 near the Officers Row street entrance, a ship's wheel with American and U.S. Navy flags adorn the foyer. Ceremonial occasions are frequently held here. PNSY–Lashua Photo

Known as the General Stores Building during the 1905 Portsmouth Peace Conference, Building 86 serves as the administrative headquarters for the Portsmouth Naval Shipyard. Two third-floor rooms (upper center and facing street from wall corner) assigned to the Japanese delegation for conference meetings are now open for visitors. PNSY–Lashua Photo

supported Johnson's decision. "'Ironsides' Visit Dead in Water," was the *Herald*'s reaction.[290]

Although the *Constitution* visit was canceled, two other important developments, both with excellent prospects for success, were underway in mid-1998. On April 17, an agreement was signed by Shipyard Commander Tom Williams and Electric Boat President John Welch to create a joint working plan to pursue "a public–private partnership" to eliminate duplication and overlap. "The goal of this initiative," said a Yard spokesperson, "is to reduce the cost of submarine maintenance." Such an unprecedented agreement—linking a military base with a private company—was a totally new concept in United States naval history. Since both the Yard and Electric Boat Corporation (a subsidiary of General Dynamics Corporation) were hit hard with layoffs in the 1980s, this novel approach made sense: to reduce duplication and cost as long as there were no layoffs in either the public or the private sector. Shipyard Commander Williams made clear what the consolidation meant to the Yard: "The goal of this initiative is to reduce the cost of submarine maintenance in the Northeast region," he said. "There is *no* impact on employment levels at the Portsmouth Naval Shipyard as a result of this partnership effort."[291]

In keeping abreast of the changing economic realities of the times, the Navy moved even further, in the fall of 1998, to accommodate the private sector. "Yard Up for Rent. Empty Areas Set to Lease," read the *Herald* headline on September 1. With empty and underused facilities, the Yard advertised in the Department of Commerce's *Commerce Business Daily* that several buildings were available for lease. The deadline for submissions was September 21. On the list were two major Yard landmarks: Building 178, the chief construction facility, with its prominent big blue sign facing the river, and the prison complex. The Maine and New Hampshire congressional delegations endorsed this plan, hoping to make the Yard more cost-effective. American Fast Ferries showed an early interest in Building 178, inquiring about a five-year lease for building catamaran ferry vessels, which could result in the hiring of 1,200 workers. In early December, Shipyard Commander Williams articulated the merits of "outleasing"—a new word in the vocabulary of the Yard and indeed of the Navy: "Outleasing is a strategy to reduce costs borne by American taxpayers in maintaining the Department of Defense infrastructure used to win the Cold War, yet keep portions of this vital infrastructure available for future needs. The short answer is that successful outleasing will enable Portsmouth Naval Shipyard to be more competitive in the business of overhauling naval vessels. . . . In short, outleasing is a win-win situation."[292]

In 1999, the ongoing issues of outleasing, the boundary dispute, and the reopening of the museum—coupled with preparations for the Yard's bicentennial celebration—necessitated decisions. From an inspirational perspective, the year began most favorably. In his *Periscope* column, Captain Williams urged every Yard employee to do his or her best: "Each day's work either has a positive or negative impact. There are no neutral days. We are being provided many opportunities to succeed and demonstrate our value to the Navy—make the most of it, be the best!" On March 4, at the shipyard commander's annual 7 A.M. prayer breakfast at Tirante Tavern, the guest speaker was Meadowlark Lemon, the retired Harlem Globetrotters "Clown Prince of Basketball," who delivered an inspirational message. An ordained minister, Lemon elicited laughter and provoked reflection.[293]

The battle over the border continued. On Wednesday, March 18, the New Hampshire Legislature's Fiscal Committee approved an appropriation of $200,000 to pursue the state's claim that the Yard was, indeed, within the state's boundaries. Activist Victor Bourre, who had provided the state with numerous documents and maps, hailed the news. New Hampshire Attorney General Philip McLaughlin commented that the state would need this appropriation in order to cover the considerable legal costs of settling this issue with Maine. Since the United States Supreme Court is the nation's only court empowered to settle state boundary disputes, McLaughlin earmarked these funds "to have the U.S. Supreme Court resolve this long-disputed issue." For their part, Maine legislators awarded their attorney general $100,000 to mount a defense. At stake in this tussle were millions of dollars in Portsmouth Naval Shipyard wages and taxes. Praising Bourre's perseverance, the *Herald* editorialized: "Bourre is living proof that one man truly can make a difference. And if it turns out that he should be proven right, he himself becomes a part of New Hampshire history."[294]

While the possibility of an eventual Supreme Court decision remained for the future, the Yard's outleasing initiative gained momentum. On February 23, 1999, a Navy environmental-impact study concluded: "The leases would have no significant adverse impact

On June 21, 1999, at ceremonies outside the Naval Prison, Shipyard Commander Captain V.T. Williams announced the "outleasing" of the complex to the civilian sector to render the Yard more economically viable. PNSY–Lashua Photo

on the environment." On Thursday, June 17, the Naval Sea Systems Command announced a fifteen-year leasing agreement between the Portsmouth Naval Shipyard and the Seavey [sic] Island Limited Liability Corporation of New Castle, New Hampshire. This lease of the naval prison (also known as Building 93) was historic, the first such agreement between a public navy yard and a private corporation. Furthermore, such a business deal—involving an obsolete, decaying building—would have been considered utterly unthinkable and unworkable just a few years earlier. The Yard prison complex, long dismissed as awaiting the wrecking ball, was revived as the future headquarters of the Seavey Island Technology Center, with ten or eleven anticipated tenants. "The Castle" was to be renovated at a cost of more than $10 million. On Monday, June 21, at a press conference in front of the old prison, Captain Tom Williams and Joseph Sawtelle, the

*Recent (1990s) view of the Naval Prison, now undergoing renovation to become a
civilian technology center, thanks to a private-sector "outleasing" agreement by the
Yard. The most modern section, built in 1943 (extreme left), is the first part of the
complex being readied for occupancy. PNSMVC*

manager–partner of the private Seavey Island LLC, articulated their
aims. "Today is a great day," said Williams, "for the Navy, Portsmouth
Naval Shipyard, the Seacoast, and the American taxpayer. Outleasing
is in our interest." He added that leasing the 264,000-square-foot
prison was "recycling at the highest level." In absorbing the Yard's
overhead costs of maintaining the prison building, as well as paying
the utilities costs, the Seavey Island LLC also added $175,000 a year
in rent revenue. Most important, the lease respected the Yard's security, leaving intact the core military functions of the base. Ignoring the
boundary dispute for the moment, the New Hampshire and Maine
congressional delegations heartily endorsed the outleasing agreement. Predictions were made that perhaps 2,500 additional jobs and a
$69 million payroll would follow. At the conclusion of the press confer-
ence, Williams presented Sawtelle with a large key, symbolic of turning the prison over to private enterprise.[295]

In readiness for the Yard's Open House on June 10-11, 2000, the official bicentennial logo features a submarine (center), the mainstay of the facility for more than eighty years. Staying neutral in the controversy over the Yard's geographic location, the logo carries a Maine pine tree and New Hampshire's Old Man of the Mountain. PNSY

Concurrent with the outleasing developments, the Yard prepared to observe its bicentennial in the year 2000. On May 8, 1999, Captain Williams announced plans for the Yard's celebration, with an open house (the first at the Yard since 1976), to be held on June 10–11, 2000. The event would be organized to celebrate the Yard's two hundred years of "craftsmanship and service." Activities under consideration included visits of surface ships, submarines, and tall ships, as well as other festivities. Captain Williams then unveiled an official logo for the event— a silhouette of a nuclear-powered submarine in front of a Maine pine tree and New Hampshire's Old Man of the Mountain profile. A month later, on Saturday, June 12, 1999, the Portsmouth Naval Shipyard Museum and Visitor Center opened at its new location in Building 31. (Along with its altered name and site, this multipurpose facility housed

At the official opening of the Portsmouth Naval Shipyard Museum and Visitor Center on June 12, 1999, noted historian Joseph W.P. Frost, Portsmouth Ambassador Eileen Foley, Museum Director James Dolph, and Shipyard Commander Captain V.T. Williams cut the ribbon. Open to the public, the museum serves as an educational resource for the seacoast community. PNSY

not only the museum but also a library, an archival research room, a gift shop, and administrative offices.) After the ribbon cutting, Captain Williams looked ahead: "Today is our Shipyard's 199th birthday, and kicks off the celebration for our bicentennial a year from now. Our new museum will serve as a place where Shipyarders, students, organizations, and community members can come to learn about the history of our Shipyard and what it has meant to this area for the last 200 years."[296]

As the last half of 1999 moved toward the millennium, the Yard responded to old business and new challenges. The controversial state border dispute spawned a flurry of newspaper editorials and letters, with impassioned adherents on both sides. A judicial decision was stalled, pending the filing of the case before the U.S. Supreme Court by

Built as a powder magazine with massive granite construction in the 1840s, Building 31 later served as the Navy Exchange. On June 12, 1999, at a well-attended ribbon-cutting ceremony, the facility was dedicated as the new home of the Portsmouth Naval Shipyard Museum and Visitor Center, with its displays and library open to the public. PNSY–Lashua Photo

A proposed new logo for the Portsmouth Naval Shipyard features the NAVSEA (Naval Sea Systems Command) acronym with the location, "Portsmouth," underneath and a submarine profile to the right. Other navy yards—Norfolk, Puget Sound, Long Beach, and Pearl Harbor—would also be assigned the same standard logo. PNSY

New Hampshire Attorney General Philip McLaughlin. Victor Bourre continued to submit to McLaughlin old maps and especially a 1653 Portsmouth charter in which "one of Portsmouth's wards was made up solely of the harbor and all its islands." In a long editorial, "Maine Illegally Taking Funds from N.H. Workers," Walter V. Perkins, a Rochester, New Hampshire, resident, reviewed all the arguments (including Maine's "spousal tax") and concluded: "I am old, retired, and disabled. I hope I live long enough to see proper action in this case."[297]

In contrast to this legal quagmire, the concept of outleasing rested on solid ground. Unfortunately, however, the first effort fell through. American Fast Ferries, which proposed to build high-speed catamaran ferries, could not reach agreement with the Naval Sea Systems Command (NAVSEA), which makes the final decision on such leases. But development of the old naval prison moved ahead rapidly. Developer Joe Sawtelle, known for his success in refurbishing mills in Rochester and Dover, New Hampshire, commented: "It's very satisfying to transform a dilapidated mill into a first-class office space. If we're successful here [at the prison], I'm sure we'll have the same feeling." It was an ambitious undertaking. "This is one of the largest restoration projects in the state and maybe even New England," said Tim Shelton, director

Viewed from the shoreline of the Piscataqua River, the Castle is being readied for civilian offices. Under a pioneering agreement between the Yard and the private sector, this outleasing effort makes good use of the underutilized building and makes the Yard more competitive in an era of tight military budgets. PNSY–Lashua Photo

of development for the Seavey Island LLC. According to Shelton, the restoration would involve three phases. The first phase, concentrating on the 1943 relatively modern eight-story addition to Building 93, was slated to be ready for occupancy as "The Fortress" in spring 2000. (This section is located on the extreme left of the complex, viewed from the river.) The second and third sections, to be completed later, will be known as "The Castle" and "The Prison."[298]

Buoyed by this initial commercial response, the Yard announced a second round of outleasing opportunities in November 1999. Available for lease to civilian companies were six buildings and three parcels of land. The official announcement of the outleasing appeared on November 22 on the *Commerce Business Daily* Website.[299]

Concurrent with these promising business ventures, a bizarre financial problem commanded attention during the summer of 1999. From February 1998 through March 1999, Yard workers had performed $2.9 million worth of repairs and overhaul on the submarine USS *Helena*. When the headquarters of the Commander in Chief Pacific Fleet (CINCPAC) was billed for the work on the sub, which was assigned to that fleet, CINCPAC officials responded on July 26 that it did not have the money in its fiscal budget to pay the Portsmouth Naval Shipyard. Yard union leader Terry Eleftherion responded: "So we are stuck with a $3 million bill that is apparently not going to be paid." Three weeks later, news surfaced that the Navy was renovating three top admirals' quarters for $5.5 million. Eleftherion contacted the New Hampshire congressional delegation to seek redress, contending: "If we can afford to spend money to renovate the admirals' quarters, it seems to me the Navy could afford just bills owed to the shipyard." Finally, in early September, after prodding by New Hampshire and Maine representatives and senators in Washington, the Navy agreed to transfer $9 million to the Portsmouth Naval Shipyard to cover the sub's repairs as well as her refueling. "Just like any other customer," declared the New Hampshire and Maine congressional team in a joint statement, "even the Pentagon must fully pay for services requested and rendered." A positive aftermath of this incident resulted in the advent of reforms "in the way the Navy pays for work at its four public shipyards.[300]

As part of the larger naval picture, many admirals believed that, given the number of missions demanded of its submarine force, more subs should be built to ensure an adequate national defense leading up to the year 2015. Critics argued otherwise and urged tighter economic measures. Responding to this contretemps, Secretary of the Navy Richard Danzig declared: "[I] would likely support increasing the number of attack submarines beyond the current limit of 50 boats." A Navy study was underway to assess these needs. In early July, Rear Admiral Malcolm I. Fages, director of submarine warfare on the Chief of Naval Operations staff, predicted that the fifty-boat level would be increased. Fages further explained that eight submarines of the Los Angeles 688 class could be refueled instead of being deactivated. This policy of extending the service life of the older subs prompted speculation that work might be in store for the Portsmouth Naval Shipyard, the lead yard for such overhauls and refueling. To streamline such overhaul work, the Yard and Electric Boat at Groton, Connecticut, implemented a landmark public/private partnership for repair of these subs. In November, workers from both yards began working together on the USS *Memphis* and the USS *Annapolis* at the Submarine Base in Groton. Such a pooling of Yard and EB resources accomplished, according to one Yard official, "more work on both submarines through savings realized in teaming initiatives." Yard union leader Terry Eleftherion also endorsed the arrangement, saying: "Portsmouth cannot do all the repair work and neither can EB, but if both yards can do them and save the Navy money, that's good for everyone."[301]

At the Yard itself during the summer and fall of 1999, two important scientific projects were underway. To support a University of New Hampshire research experiment, the Yard made a dry dock available for one week in August to investigate the practicality of inaugurating an aquaculture industry. Two 50-foot cage systems were built to raise flounder and other finfish. Upon completion of the experiment, the cages were towed out of the dock and later attached to the Isles of Shoals mooring system. Another undertaking involved preventing lead-contaminated soil from eroding into the Piscataqua River. The project was spurred by high levels of lead found in a juvenile lobster in the river off the Shipyard. As an emergency measure, the Yard built a 600-foot retaining wall, at a cost of $370,000, to stabilize the slope and prevent additional erosion. Meanwhile, the larger environmental problem awaited a more permanent solution after consultation with federal and state environmental agencies.[302]

Another significant project had its beginnings when Shipyarder Amelia Canino, "on a cold, snowy, miserable day," noticed her fellow workers "walking to and from their job site[s]." It occurred to her that the Yard workers—unlike naval officers and enlisted men who were honored with plaques, commemorative tablets, and a sub superstructure in the Mall (or *Squalus* Memorial Park, as it is also known)—had not been appropriately recognized. "We wanted to do something for the bicentennial," said Canino, chairperson of the newly established Shipyard Workers Memorial Committee. "We settled on something to honor 200 years of shipyard workers who have labored here." The committee proposed creation of a memorial park on MacDonough Avenue across from the Mall, and the plan was accepted. On October 26, two crane operators lowered into a prepared site at the park the 100,000-pound

*On November 22, 1999, a groundbreaking ceremony officially dedicated the Ship-
yard Workers Park, located across the street from* Squalus *Memorial Park. Amelia
Canino (holding shovel in center) originally proposed the idea for this park, which
eventually will feature a statue, benches, picnic tables, and trees. PNSY*

sail of the *Ex-Grayling.* The sail was historically significant, since the
Grayling was the next-to-last of the 134 boats built at the Yard. On
November 22, at 11:30 A.M., about thirty people gathered at the park
for the groundbreaking ceremony. Along with Amelia Canino and Terry
Eleftherion, wielding gold-plated shovels, Captain Williams dug into
the earth with his own shovel, gave a short speech, and posed for photographs. Once completed, the park will feature benches, picnic tables,
trees, and, most important, a life-size statue of a Shipyard worker.
Funds to pay for the monument are being raised by the sale of special
bricks, which will be placed in the park. "We've been cut in size," Captain Williams said during his speech, referring to the Yard's reduced
employment level, "but we haven't been cut in spirit."[303]

The same day the park ceremony was being held, the latest issue
of the *Maine Times,* a liberal newspaper with a reputation for addressing the state's pressing issues in blunt language, was hitting the news-
stands. Its lead article, "Saving the Shipyard: For Portsmouth It May

Be Convert or Die," bore the subtitle, "Where have all the welders gone? Peace dividend finally takes hold in Kittery." The report tackled the issues confronting the Yard: BRAC decisions, outleasing, layoffs, an aging workforce, and a reduced employment level. Once dubbed "the gravy yard" for its high wages and a relatively certain guarantee of career-long job security during and after World War II, the Yard now found it increasingly difficult to attract and retain young blue-collar workers. Many opted to receive free apprenticeship training and to gain experience, but given the uncertainty of a long-range working career, they often elected to leave the Yard and start their own businesses. As the older employees were nearing retirement, the Yard thus needed to recruit and keep its younger workers in order to be able to provide the increasingly sophisticated skills of repairing, refueling, and decommissioning nuclear subs. Once the dominant and leading employer in Maine, the Yard had seen its civilian workforce drop to roughly 3,400 employees in 1999, trailing Hannaford Brothers (7,200–7,400 in food distribution and supermarkets), Bath Iron Works (7,000–7,200 in shipbuilding), L.L. Bean (5,400–5,600 in outdoor clothing and gear), and Wal-Mart (4,000–4,200 in retail stores in Maine). As the year 2000 approached, the Yard clearly recognized the realities contingent on its survival: remain competitive, cut costs, rejuvenate its workforce, and cultivate excellent relations with future BRAC commissions. Longtime Yard employees, moreover, continued to view their workplace with pride. "It's a great place to work," said rigger Frank Coleman after thirty-four years of service. "You're always learning something. I do all the work on my home and my car—electrical, plumbing. You just don't learn your own trade, you learn others."[304]

Notwithstanding the journalistic speculation about the Yard's status, work went on as usual within the Shipyard gates. As the holiday season kicked off, the Yard held its forty-ninth annual Christmas Caravan of Toys on December 4. "I want to give back something, especially at Christmas," said Linda Muise, chairperson for the Christmas Caravan Committee. Captain Williams himself was Santa, handing out candy canes and loading gifts into vehicles. A caravan of trucks and automobiles rolled out the gates to deliver 3,000 toys worth $10,000 to twenty-five agencies in the tri-state area.[305]

As the New Year approached, the Yard geared up to meet any potential problems connected with the arrival of Y2K (Year 2000). The

Yard's Y2K Midnight Crossover Plan had been devised to forestall any computer glitches. In mid-November, the *Periscope* devoted its entire front page to the details of the plan, aimed to ward off Y2K problems. On December 30, two days before confronting this electronic uncertainty, a Yard spokesperson stressed that every precaution had been taken: "The Portsmouth Naval Shipyard is Year 2000 compliant." After more than a year of work on the issue, the Yard's comprehensive review lent assurance that "no problems associated with the date [would] occur. . . . The Shipyard is ready for the Year 2000." As almost everywhere else, however, the new year at the Yard approached, arrived, and began without a hitch—leading to the widespread conclusion that fears of the Y2K disease had been highly exaggerated.[306]

Optimism prevailed as the year 2000 began, with the Yard stepping up its efforts to publicize its November outleasing announcement. If a lease could be arranged for the Building Ways, as many as 1,200 shipbuilding jobs would be created. Site tours were scheduled for interested parties, along with preproposal conferences. Civilian businesses merely needed to log on to the NAVSEA Contracts Directorate Website at http://www.contracts.hq.navsea.navy.mil to find out the details.[307]

As the Portsmouth Naval Shipyard's bicentennial celebration approaches, it's inevitable to reflect on the establishment of the Yard two hundred years ago. In many ways, the Yard's purpose has remained the same from the day the facility was founded to the present moment: the need to protect and defend the interests of the United States. The weapons of war may have changed, but the mission and the military responsibility have remained exactly the same. In 1800, the threat came from European privateers and Barbary Coast pirates; in 2000, vigilance is required to deal with international terrorism, brushfire wars, interventions, and rogue nations with nuclear capabilities.

As the northernmost American navy yard on the Atlantic Ocean, the Portsmouth Naval Shipyard is strategically poised, ever ready in an age of military preparedness, a pre–World War I–era watchword as relevant today as it was then. Herbie Grimes's 1989 advice, "Do Your Job!" has been the appropriate exhortation for faithful service during the last two centuries for everyone from the shipyard commander to a new, first-day-on-the-job civilian employee. Each person, whatever his or her responsibility, has responded to do his or her job: to win wars, to prevent them, to host peace conferences, and to develop inventions and techniques for both military and peaceful purposes.

What is the future of the Portsmouth Naval Shipyard, and will it remain open? Of the innumerable books, articles, pamphlets, and reports pertaining to this issue as it affects the United States Navy and its Yards, an unsigned article, "PENNY WISE, POUND FOOLISH," which appeared in the *Portsmouth Journal* on May 27, 1876, assessed this question as logically as if it were printed in today's *Portsmouth Herald* or *Portsmouth Periscope*. Referring to the proposal to close the Yard during 1876, the unnamed journalist provided a timeless answer:

> The United States has no standing army, worth mentioning, because it trusts to volunteers. This is risk enough for the nation. The Navy cannot be built up at short notice; it must retain a certain degree of strength and power, not as a threat to foreign nations, but as an insurance against attack.
>
> What proportion of this actual value of the land and buildings does the House [of Representatives] think could be realized, if the navy yards were sold this year under the [auctioneer's] hammer? They would probably be bought by speculators for a song, and sold back to the government three or four years hence.[308]

The Portsmouth Naval Shipyard in the year 2000 is an industrial complex serving both the national defense and an increasingly civilian enterprise in a "Penny Wise, Pound Wise" partnership. Perhaps not too far in the future, there shall be a public toast offered at a function in Building 86, Tirante Tavern, or in Quarters A: "To the Portsmouth Naval Shipyard: Two Hundred Years of Service, and May It Continue This Proud Tradition Long Into the Future."

Appendices

Based on official and semiofficial sources, the following appendices update lists that originally appeared in *Cradle of American Shipbuilding* (1978).

Appendix 1.
Civilian Employees at Portsmouth Naval Shipyard

1818	50	1846	13	1870	758	1924	1,850
1819	57	1847	24	1871	697	1925	2,623
1820	70	1848	143	1872	870	1926	2,200
1821	114	1849	150	1873	680	1927	1,850
1822	111	1850	105	1874	700	1928	1,850
1827	90	1851	69	1875	417	1929	1,900
1828	74	1852	73	1876	160	1930	1,601
1829	9	1853	112	1877	71	1931	1,552
1830	16	1854	241	1903	510	1932	1,477
1831	24	1855	351	1904	492	1933	1,595
1832	43	1856	265	1905	456	1934	1,811
1833	51	1857	357	1906	418	1935	2,579
1834	42	1858	557	1907	435	1936	3,300
1835	70	1859	348	1908	440	1937	3,200
1836	74	1860	207	1909	840	1938	3,300
1837	90	1861	589	1915	1,150	1939	3,968
1838	45	1862	1,160	1916	1,450	1940	7,587
1839	179	1863	1,460	1917	5,100	1941	11,142
1840	104	1864	1,766	1918	5,500	1942	18,326
1841	169	1865	1,861	1919	5,100	1943	20,466
1842	188	1866	876	1920	3,600	1944	17,102
1843	164	1867	977	1921	2,850	1945	10,133
1844	63	1868	697	1922	2,200	1946	5,542
1845	18	1869	837	1923	1,750	1947	5,433

1948	5,971	1961	9,496	1974	6,095	1987	7,771
1949	4,054	1962	9,197	1975	6,591	1988	8,042
1950	4,047	1963	8,539	1976	6,701	1989	8,322
1951	10,018	1964	7,180	1977	7,248	1990	8,262
1952	10,559	1965	7,325	1978	7,421	1991	7,347
1953	8,270	1966	7,805	1979	7,665	1992	6,563
1954	8,000	1967	8,313	1980	7,603	1993	5,983
1955	6,984	1968	8,528	1981	7,930	1994	5,050
1956	6,865	1969	7,614	1982	8,444	1995	4,100
1957	7,210	1970	6,813	1983	8,674	1996	3,836
1958	7,500	1971	5,991	1984	8,587	1997	3,338
1959	8,410	1972	5,582	1985	8,505	1998	3,336
1960	9,335	1973	5,511	1986	8,407	1999	3,474

1820–76: yearly averages of mechanics and laborers only
1903–8: Construction and Repair Department only

Appendix 2. Ships Built at Portsmouth Navy Yard

Name	Class		Year
WASHINGTON	Ship		1814
ALABAMA	Ship	1817	1819
(New Hampshire 1864 1863		Granite State 1904)	
PORPOISE	Schooner		1820
SANTEE	Frigate		1820
	(Launched)		1855
CONCORD	Sloop	1827	1828
PREBLE	Sloop		1839
CONGRESS	Frigate		1841
SARATOGA	Sloop		1842
PORTSMOUTH	Sloop		1843
SARANAC	Steam Frigate		1848
	(Launched)	1855	1848
JAMESTOWN	Sloop		1857
MOHICAN	Steam Sloop	1857	1859
OSSIPEE	Steam Sloop		1861
KEARSARGE	Steam Sloop		1861
SEBAGO	Steam Sloop		1861
MAHASKA	Steam Sloop		1861
SACRAMENTO	Steam Sloop		1862
SONOMA	Steam Sloop		1862
CONEMAUGH	Steam Sloop		1862
SASSACUS	Steam Sloop	1863	1862
FRANKLIN	Steam Frigate		1863
	(Laid 1854; Launched 1864)		
PAWTUXET	Sidewheel	1863	1864
NIPSIC	Sidewheel		1863
SHAWMUT	Sidewheel		1863
DECOTA	Sidewheel		1863
PASSACONAWAY	Ironclad		1864
(Thunderer 1869;	Massachusetts 1869) (Never Commissioned)		
PORT FIRE	Tug		1864
BLUE LIGHT	Tug		1864
AGAMENTICUS	(Terror)	Ironclad	1864
PISCATAQUA (Delaware) Sloop of War 1864			1866
MINNETONKA (California) Sloop of War 1864			1867
ILLINOIS (Never Commissioned)			1864

CONTOOCOOK	(Albany) Sidewheel	1864
ALGOMA	(Benicia 1869 1865) Sidewheel	1868
RESACA	Screw Steamer	1865
ENTERPRISE	Steam Sloop 1873	1874
ESSEX	Steam Sloop	1874
#132	Steam Ferry	1891
BOXER	Training Brig	1904
PATAPSCO	Tug	1908
#1048	Ferry	1912
HUDSON	Coast Guard Cutter	1934

Appendix 3. Submarines Built at Portsmouth Navy Yard

Hull No.	Name		Commissioned
SS48	L-8		8-30-17
SS62	O-1		11- 5-18
SS107	S-3		1-30-19
SS109	S-4		11-19-19
SS110	S-5		3- 6-20
SS111	S-6		5-17-20
SS112	S-7		7- 1-20
SS113	S-8		10-1-20
SS114	S-9		2-21-21
SS115	S-10		9-21-22
SS116	S-11		1-11-23
SS117	S-12		4-30-23
SS118	S-13		7-14-23
SS163	BARRACUDA	(SF-4, B-1, V-1)	10-1-24
SS164	BASS	(SF-5, B-2, V-2)	9-26-25
SS165	BONITA	(SF-6, B-3, V-3)	5-22-26
SS166	ARGONAUT	(U-4, A-1, SF-7, SM-1, APS-1)	4- 2-28
SS167	NARWHAL	(V-5, N-1, SF-8, SC-1)	5-15-30
SS169	DOLPHIN	(V-7, D-1, SF-10, SC-3)	6- 1-32
SS170	CACHALOT	(V-8, C-1, SF-11, SC-4)	12-1-33
SS172	PORPOISE	(P-1)	8-15-35
SS173	PIKE	(P-2)	12- 2-35
SS179	PLUNGER	(P-8)	11-19-36
SS180	POLLACK	(P-9)	1-15-37
SS185	SNAPPER	(S-4)	12-15-37
SS186	STINGRAY	(S-5)	3-15-38
SS191	SCULPIN	(S-10)	1-16-39
SS192	SQUALUS	(S-11)	3- 1-39
SS192	SAILFISH		5-15-40
SS196	SEARAVEN	(S-15)	10- 2-39
SS197	SEAWOLF	(S-16)	12- 1-39
SS201	TRITON		8-15-40
SS202	TROUT		11-15-40
SS205	MARLIN		8- 1-41
SS209	GRAYLING		3- 1-41
SS210	GRENADIER		5- 1-41

SS228	DRUM		11- 1-41
SS229	FLYING FISH		12-10-41
SS230	FINBACK		1-31-42
SS231	HADDOCK		3-14-42
SS232	HALIBUT		4-10-42
SS233	HERRING		5- 4-42
SS234	KINGFISH		5-20-42
SS235	SHAD		6-12-42
SS275	RUNNER		7-30-42
SS276	SAWFISH		8-26-42
SS277	SCAMP		9-18-42
SS278	SCORPION		10- 1-42
SS279	SNOOK		10-24-42
SS280	STEELHEAD		12- 7-42
SS285	BALAO		2- 4-43
SS286	BILLFISH		4-20-43
SS287	BOWFIN		5- 1-43
SS288	CABRILLA		5-24-43
SS289	CAPELIN		6- 4-43
SS290	CISCO		5-10-43
SS291	CREVALLE		6-24-43
SS298	LIONFISH	(completed at PNS)	11- 1-44
SS 299	MANTA	(completed at PNS)	12-18-44
SS 308	APOGON		7-16-43
SS 309	ASPRO		7-31-43
SS 310	BATFISH		8-21-43
SS 311	ARCHERFISH		9- 4-43
SS 312	BURRFISH		9-14-43
SS 381	SAND LANCE		10- 9-43
SS 382	PICUDA		10-16-43
SS 383	PAMPANITO		11- 6-43
SS 384	PARCHE		11-20-43
SS 385	BANG		12- 4-43
SS 386	PILOTFISH		12-16-43
SS 387	PINTADO		1- 1-44
SS 388	PIPEFISH		1-22-44
SS 389	PIRANHA		2- 5-44
SS 390	PLAICE		2-12-44
SS 391	POMFRET		2-19-44
SS 392	STERLET		3- 4-44
SS 393	QUEENFISH		3-11-44

SS 394	RAZORBACK	4- 3-44
SS 395	REDFISH	4-12-44
SS 396	RONQUIL	4-22-44
SS 397	SCABBARDFISH	4-29-44
SS 398	SEGUNDO	5- 9-44
SS 399	SEA CAT	5-16-44
SS 400	SEA DEVIL	5-24-44
SS 401	SEA DOG	6- 3-44
SS 402	SEA FOX	6-13-44
SS 403	ATULE	6-21-44
SS 404	SPIKEFISH	6-30-44
SS 405	SEA OWL	7-17-44
SS 406	SEA POACHER	7-31-44
SS 407	SEA ROBIN	8- 7-44
SS 408	SENNET	8-22-44
SS 409	PIPER	8-23-44
SS 410	THREADFIN	8-30-44
SS 417	TENCH	10- 6-44
SS 418	THORNBACK	10-13-44
SS 419	TIGRONE	10-25-44
SS 420	TIRANTE	11- 6-44
SS 421	TRUTTA	11-16-44
SS 422	TORO	12- 8-44
SS 423	TORSK	12-16-44
SS 424	QUILLBACK	12-29-44
SS 475	ARGONAUT	1-15-45
SS 476	RUNNER	2- 6-45
SS 477	CONGER	2-14-45
SS 478	CUTLASS	3-17-45
SS 479	DIABLO	3-31-45
SS 480	MEDREGAL	4-14-45
SS 481	REQUIN	4-28-45
SS 482	IREX	5-14-45
SS 483	SEA LEOPARD	6-11-45
SS 484	ODAX	7-11-45
SS 485	SIRAGO	8-13-45
SS 486	POMODON	11-9-45
SS 487	REMORA	1- 3-46
SS 488	SARDA	4-19-46
SS 489	SPINAX	9-20-46
SS 490	VOLADOR	1-10-48

AGSS555	DOLPHIN	10-17-68
SS 563	TANG	10-25-51
SS 565	WAHOO	5-30-52
SS 567	GUDGEON	11-21-52
AGSS569••	ALBACORE	12- 5-53
SSR572#	SAILFISH	4-14-56
SSR573	SALMON	8-25-56
SSG577##	GROWLER	8-30-58
SSN579•	SWORDFISH	9-15-58
SS580	BARBEL	1-17-59
SSN584	SEADRAGON	12- 5-59
SSN593	THRESHER	8- 3-61
SSBN602••	ABRAHAM LINCOLN	3-11-61
SSN605	JACK	3-31-67
SSN606	TINOSA	10-17-64
SSBN620••	JOHN ADAMS	5-12-64
SSBN636	NATHANAEL GREENE	12-19-64
SSN646	GRAYLING	10-11-69
SSN660	SAND LANCE	9-25-71

#—R designates radar picket

##—G designates guided missile

•—N designates nuclear propulsion

••—B designates ballistic missile submarine

•••—AG designates research submarine

Appendix 4.
History Of Nuclear Submarine

New Construction, Overhauls And Scheduled Maintenance Availabilities

Nuclear Sub Name	Sub No.	Type Availability	Avail. Start Date	Avail. Comp Date
USS SWORDFISH	SSN 579	New Construction	10/01/55	09/15/58
USS THRESHER	SSN 593	New Construction	04/04/58	08/01/61
USS ABRAHAM LINCOLN	SSBN 602	New Construction	08/01/58	03/08/61
USS SEADRAGON	SSN 584	New Construction	04/01/59	12/01/59
USS NAUTILUS	SSN 571	Refueling Overhaul	06/03/59	08/10/60
USS TINOSA	SSN 606	New Construction	08/03/59	11/28/64
USS JACK	SSN 605	New Construction	04/01/60	04/21/67
USS JOHN ADAMS	SSBN 620	New Construction	02/06/61	05/16/64
USS NATHANIEL GREENE	SSBN 636	New Construction	02/01/62	12/23/64
USS SKIPJACK	SSN 585	Regular Overhaul	02/09/62	09/19/62
USS THRESHER	SSN 593	Post Shakedown Availability	07/12/62	04/10/63
USS GRAYLING	SSN 646	New Construction	03/04/63	12/01/69
USS NAUTILUS	SSN 571	Regular Overhaul	01/20/64	05/01/66
USS SANDLANCE	SSN 660	New Construction	06/29/64	10/02/71
USS JOHN ADAMS	SSBN 620	Post Shakedown Availability	08/23/64	09/26/64
USS SEAWOLF	SSN 575	Refueling Overhaul	05/05/65	08/21/67
USS DACE	SSN 607	Post Shakedown Availability	09/08/65	11/22/65
USS TULLIBEE	SSN 597	Refueling Overhaul	12/20/65	11/28/68
USS TINOSA	SSN 606	Post Shakedown Availability	04/01/66	06/18/66
USS SAM HOUSTON	SSBN 609	Refueling Overhaul	08/24/66	11/22/67
USS NAUTILUS	SSN 571	Refueling Overhaul	08/15/67	12/09/68
USS JACK	SSN 605	Restricted Availability	10/11/67	12/10/67
USS ANDREW JACKSON	SSBN 619	Refueling Overhaul	03/14/68	06/14/69
USS JACK	SSN 605	Post Shakedown Availability	11/01/68	03/17/69
USS TINOSA	SSN 606	Regular Overhaul	05/06/69	12/16/71
USS SAM RAYBURN	SSBN 635	Refueling Overhaul	01/19/70	09/02/71
USS JACK	SSN 605	Restricted Availability	02/28/70	03/13/70
USS JACK	SSN 605	Regular Overhaul	02/06/71	04/27/72
USS GEORGE BANCROFT	SSBN 643	Refueling Overhaul	04/28/71	07/31/72
USS LAPON	SSN 661	Regular Overhaul	10/26/71	10/13/72
USS SAM RAYBURN	SSBN 635	Post Conversion Availability	01/11/72	02/17/72
USS HAMMERHEAD	SSN 663	Regular Overhaul	03/14/72	02/09/73
USS GREENLING	SSN 614	Restricted Availability	04/04/72	06/25/73

USS SANDLANCE	SSN 660	Post Shakedown Availability / Restricted Availability	06/19/72	08/28/72
USS DACE	SSN 607	Restricted Availability	07/07/72	07/30/72
USS WILL ROGERS	SSBN 659	Refueling Overhaul	10/10/72	02/08/74
USS GEORGE BANCROFT	SSBN 643	Post Conversion Availability	12/21/72	01/31/73
USS TREPANG	SSN 674	Restricted Availability/ Intermediate Dry Docking	01/10/73	02/07/73
USS TULLIBEE	SSN 597	Refueling Overhaul	03/01/73	08/30/74
USS SEA DEVIL	SSN 664	Restricted Availability/ Intermediate Dry Docking	05/07/73	06/29/73
USS STURGEON	SSN 637	Restricted Availability	06/05/73	04/16/74
USS GRAYLING	SSN 646	Regular Overhaul	07/02/73	05/28/74
USS GEORGE C. MARSHALL	SSBN 654	Post Conversion Availability	07/09/73	08/13/73
USS GEORGE W. CARVER	SSBN 656	Post Conversion Availability	08/20/73	09/27/73
USS FRANCIS S. KEY	SSBN 657	Post Conversion Availability	10/15/73	11/13/73
USS FLYING FISH	SSN 673	Regular Overhaul	11/15/73	11/16/74
USS JOHN ADAMS	SSBN 620	Refueling Overhaul	02/01/74	04/15/76
USS MARIANO G. VALLEJO	SSBN 658	Post Conversion Availability	05/09/74	06/12/74
USS WILL ROGERS	SSBN 659	Post Conversion Availability	06/28/74	08/09/74
USS SEA DEVIL	SSN 664	Regular Overhaul	07/01/74	06/22/75
USS TUNNY	SSN 682	Post Shakedown Availability	08/20/74	10/09/74
USS TREPANG	SSN 674	Regular Overhaul	10/15/74	10/24/75
USS BILLFISH	SSN 676	Regular Overhaul	01/13/75	12/11/75
USS GEORGE W. CARVER	SSBN 656	Restricted Availability	03/28/75	05/20/75
USS HENRY CLAY	SSBN 625	Refueling Overhaul	04/29/75	07/29/77
USS JACK	SSN 605	Refueling Overhaul	10/01/75	01/23/78
USS TECUMSEH	SSBN 628	Technical Availability	10/22/75	11/30/75
USS TREPANG	SSN 674	Restricted Availability	10/25/75	11/04/75
USS DANIEL BOONE	SSBN 629	Regular Overhaul	03/23/76	03/24/78
USS WHALE	SSN 638	Refueling Overhaul	09/15/76	07/07/78
USS JOHN ADAMS	SSBN 620	Post Shakedown Availability	09/29/76	11/03/76
USS JOHN C. CALHOUN	SSBN 630	Regular Overhaul	01/17/77	12/22/78
USS WILLIAM H. BATES	SSN 680	Selected Restricted Availability	03/07/77	05/02/77
USS RICHARD B. RUSSELL	SSN 687	Selected Restricted Availability	05/09/77	06/29/77
USS CAVALLA	SSN 684	Selected Restricted Availability	06/13/77	08/07/77
USS JAMES MADISON	SSBN 627	Extended Refit Period	09/11/77	11/07/77
USS TECUMSEH	SSBN 628	Regular Overhaul	09/27/77	06/27/79
USS HENRY CLAY	SSBN 625	Post Shakedown Availability	01/06/78	02/23/78
USS SAM RAYBURN	SSBN 635	Regular Overhaul	02/01/78	10/23/79
USS VON STEUBEN	SSBN 632	Extended Refit Period	03/10/78	05/06/78
USS CASIMIR PULASKI	SSBN 633	Extended Refit Period	05/18/78	07/17/78

USS STONEWALL JACKSON	SSBN 634	Regular Overhaul	08/07/78	03/28/80
USS SIMON BOLIVAR	SSBN 641	Regular Overhaul	03/02/79	12/28/80
USS NATHAN HALE	SSBN 623	Extended Refit Period	04/24/79	06/20/79
USS ARCHERFISH	SSN 678	Selected Restricted Availability	07/30/79	10/01/79
USS TULLIBEE	SSN 597	Refueling Overhaul	08/18/79	10/04/82
USS ALEXANDER HAMILTON	SSBN 617	Extended Refit Period	09/01/79	10/28/79
USS BENJAMIN FRANKLIN	SSBN 640	Regular Overhaul	11/12/79	09/18/81
USS TINOSA	SSN 606	Selected Restricted Availability	01/07/80	3/22/80
USS PARGO	SSN 650	Selected Restricted Availability	02/20/80	04/19/80
USS GEORGE C. MARSHALL	SSBN 654	Extended Refit Period	03/31/80	05/27/80
USS BILLFISH	SSN 676	Selected Restricted Availability	04/18/80	06/15/80
USS GEORGE BANCROFT	SSBN 643	Regular Overhaul	06/01/80	03/05/82
USS GEORGE W. CARVER	SSBN 656	Extended Refit Period	06/17/80	08/11/80
USS WHALE	SSN 638	Selected Restricted Availability	07/29/80	09/26/80
USS TREPANG	SSN 674	Regular Overhaul	11/17/80	11/16/82
USS GREENLING	SSN 614	Selected Restricted Availability	01/21/81	03/17/81
USS KAMEHAMEHA	SSBN 642	Regular Overhaul	04/01/81	12/09/82
USS PHILADELPHIA	SSN 690	Selected Restricted Availability	04/20/81	06/17/81
USS ARCHERFISH	SSN 678	Selected Restricted Availability	08/05/81	09/29/81
USS JAMES MONROE	SSBN 622	Extended Refit Period	09/20/81	11/16/81
USS JAMES K. POLK	SSBN 645	Regular Overhaul	09/30/81	04/21/83
USS TINOSA	SSN 606	Selected Restricted Availability	01/08/82	03/08/82
USS GATO	SSN 615	Selected Restricted Availability	03/09/82	05/06/82
USS BILLFISH	SSN 676	Regular Overhaul	05/19/82	11/05/83
USS ANDREW JACKSON	SSBN 619	Extended Refit Period	06/17/82	08/21/82
USS GROTON	SSN 694	Selected Restricted Availability	06/17/82	09/28/82
USS PARGO	SSN 650	Selected Restricted Availability	10/01/82	11/19/82
USS JACK	SSN 605	Regular Overhaul	10/04/82	04/08/85
NAVAL RESEARCH ONE	NR-1	Regular Overhaul	11/10/82	08/29/83
USS GREENLING	SSN 614	Selected Restricted Availability	01/11/83	03/13/83
USS DANIEL WEBSTER	SSBN 626	Extended Refit Period	02/13/83	04/09/83
USS ARCHERFISH	SSN 678	Regular Overhaul	03/01/83	10/14/84
USS WHALE	SSN 638	Selected Restricted Availability	04/15/83	06/10/83
USS TINOSA	SSN 606	Regular Overhaul	07/13/83	09/30/85
USS DACE	SSN 607	Selected Restricted Availability	10/01/83	11/30/83
USS DALLAS	SSN 700	Selected Restricted Availability	01/07/84	03/07/84
USS JAMES MONROE	SSBN 622	Extended Refit Period	03/07/84	05/05/84
USS GATO	SSN 615	Selected Restricted Availability	04/09/84	06/09/84
USS BOSTON	SSN 703	Selected Restricted Availability	06/15/84	08/15/84
USS PHILADELPHIA	SSN 690	Regular Overhaul	06/25/84	01/21/86
USS GREENLING	SSN 614	Regular Overhaul	10/01/84	10/09/87

USS ALEXANDER HAMILTON	SSBN 617	Extended Refit Period	11/07/84	01/09/85
USS ULYSSES S. GRANT	SSBN 631	Refueling Overhaul	12/01/84	06/11/87
USS SNOOK	SSN 592	Special Availability	01/15/85	03/27/85
USS SIMON BOLIVAR	SSBN 641	Refueling Overhaul	02/01/85	11/20/87
USS HENRY CLAY	SSBN 625	Extended Refit Period	03/03/85	04/28/85
USS ANDREW JACKSON	SSBN 619	Extended Refit Period	06/21/85	08/18/85
USS TREPANG	SSN 674	Selected Restricted Availability	08/01/85	09/28/85
USS DACE	SSN 607	Selected Restricted Availability	09/30/85	12/02/85
USS GROTON	SSN 694	Regular Overhaul	10/01/85	05/20/88
USS JAMES K. POLK	SSBN 645	Refueling Overhaul	01/15/86	11/29/88
USS DANIEL WEBSTER	SSBN 626	Extended Refit Period	02/28/86	04/25/86
USS BILLFISH	SSN 676	Selected Restricted Availability	05/01/86	06/28/86
USS GATO	SSN 615	Regular Overhaul	05/28/86	02/26/86
USS ARCHERFISH	SSN 678	Selected Restricted Availability	09/30/86	12/05/86
USS KAMEHAMEHA	SSBN 642	Refueling Overhaul	11/30/86	12/23/89
USS BOSTON	SSN 703	Selected Restricted Availability	01/22/87	03/22/87
USS JAMES MONROE	SSBN 622	Extended Refit Period	03/12/87	05/10/87
USS AUGUSTA	SSN 710	Selected Restricted Availability	05/22/87	07/22/87
USS LAFAYETTE	SSBN 616	Extended Refit Period	05/31/87	07/28/87
USS TINOSA	SSN 606	Selected Restricted Availability	08/03/87	10/15/87
USS SKIPJACK	SSN 585	Selected Restricted Availability	09/30/87	12/21/87
USS TULLIBEE	SSN 597	Inactivation	09/30/87	07/01/88
USS BLUEFISH	SSN 675	Extended Refit Period	12/01/87	06/17/90
USS SCULPIN	SSN 590	Selected Restricted Availability	01/05/88	03/12/88
USS CITY OF CORPUS CHRISTI	SSN 705	Selected Restricted Availability	01/18/88	03/10/88
USS SHARK	SSN 591	Selected Restricted Availability	05/02/88	07/28/88
USS SANDLANCE	SSN 660	Regular Overhaul	06/01/88	08/08/90
USS ALBUQUERQUE	SSN 706	Selected Restricted Availability	06/13/88	08/19/88
USS PHILADELPHIA	SSN 690	Selected Restricted Availability	09/07/88	11/06/88
USS DALLAS	SSN 700	Depot Modernization Period	10/03/88	09/27/89
USS DANIEL WEBSTER	SSBN 626	Intermediate Dry Docking	02/24/89	03/20/89
USS TREPANG	SSN 674	Refueling Overhaul	03/01/89	11/01/91
USS BOSTON	SSN 703	Depot Modernization Period	06/15/89	05/18/90
USS JACK	SSN 605	Inactivation	10/01/89	07/27/90
USS GEORGE W. CARVER	SSBN 656	Extended Refit Period	10/18/89	12/16/89
USS GREENLING	SSN 614	Selected Restricted Availability	01/10/90	03/18/90
USS CITY OF CORPUS CHRISTI	SSN 705	Depot Modernization Period	03/01/90	03/10/91
USS TINOSA	SSN 606	Selected Restricted Availability	03/12/90	05/06/90
USS L. MENDEL RIVERS	SSN 686	Refueling Overhaul	05/07/90	06/05/93
USS LAFAYETTE	SSBN 616	Extended Refit Period	06/05/90	08/03/90
USS PITTSBURGH	SSN 720	Selected Restricted Availability	09/04/90	10/18/90

USS ALBUQUERQUE	SSN 706	Depot Modernization Period	10/01/90	07/19/91
NAVAL RESEARCH ONE	NR-1	Refueling Overhaul	11/06/90	11/29/92
USS NORFOLK	SSN 714	Depot Modernization Period	02/27/91	05/01/92
USS WILL ROGERS	SSBN 659	Extended Refit Period	06/24/91	08/21/91
USS DANIEL BOONE	SSBN 629	Extended Refit Period	07/12/91	09/05/91
USS TECUMSEH	SSBN 628	Extended Refit Period	09/09/91	11/01/91
USS FINBACK	SSN 670	Selected Restricted Availability	09/30/91	11/27/91
USS MINNEAPOLIS/ST. PAUL	SSN 708	Depot Modernization Period	9/30/91	09/01/92
USS SILVERSIDES	SSN 679	Selected Restricted Availability	11/20/91	02/07/92
USS PARGO	SSN 650	Selected Restricted Availability	01/06/92	02/29/92
USS GATO	SSN 615	Selected Restricted Availability	03/02/92	04/29/92
USS HAMMERHEAD	SSN 663	Selected Restricted Availability	03/23/92	05/19/92
USS CINCINNATI	SSN 693	Selected Restricted Availability	05/19/92	07/21/92
USS AUGUSTA	SSN 710	Depot Modernization Period	06/01/92	10/23/93
USS GREENLING	SSN 614	Selected Restricted Availability	06/30/92	08/27/92
USS PHOENIX	SSN 702	Selected Restricted Availability	8/10/92	11/01/92
USS PHILADELPHIA	SSN 690	Engineered Refueling Overhaul	10/01/92	12/23/94
USS WHALE	SSN 638	Selected Restricted Availability	03/01/93	04/25/93
USS PITTSBURGH	SSN 720	Depot Modernization Period	05/03/93	08/29/94
USS ARCHERFISH	SSN 678	Selected Restricted Availability	06/01/93	07/24/93
NAVAL RESEARCH ONE	NR-1	Restricted Availability	08/09/93	10/12/93
USS MEMPHIS	SSN 691	Engineered Refueling Overhaul	02/07/94	08/06/96
USS TREPANG	SSN 674	Selected Restricted Availability	10/03/94	12/01/94
USS GRAYLING	SSN 646	Selected Restricted Availability	01/09/95	03/08/95
USS ALEXANDRIA	SSN 757	Selected Restricted Availability	01/09/95	03/15/95
USS OMAHA	SSN 692	Inactivation	02/07/95	01/31/96
USS ASHEVILLE	SSN 758	Selected Restricted Availability	03/10/95	05/23/95
USS LA JOLLA	SSN 701	Selected Restricted Availability	05/10/95	07/20/95
USS SALT LAKE CITY	SSN 716	Selected Restricted Availability	06/28/95	09/25/95
USS JEFFERSON CITY	SSN 759	Selected Restricted Availability	08/16/95	11/14/95
USS DALLAS	SSN 700	Engineered Refueling Overhaul	10/23/95	02/12/98
USS ARCHERFISH	SSN 678	Selected Restricted Availability	01/22/96	03/25/96
USS POGY	SSN 647	Selected Restricted Availability	02/01/96	04/01/96
USS BOISE	SSN 764	Intermediate maintenance Availability	02/26/96	03/28/96
USS NEW YORK CITY	SSN 696	Inactivation	03/19/96	07/10/97
USS AUGUSTA	SSN 710	Selected Restricted Availability	04/08/96	06/15/96
USS MONTPELIER	SSN 765	Intermediate maintenance Availability	06/06/96	07/15/96
USS PHOENIX PHASE I	SSN 702	Intermediate maintenance Availability	06/11/96	06/25/96

USS MINNEPOLIS ST. PAUL	SSN 708	Intermediate maintenance Availability	07/15/96	08/16/96
USS PHOENIX PHASE II	SSN 702	Intermediate maintenance Availability	07/22/96	08/23/96
NAVAL RESEARCH ONE	NR-1	Selected Restricted Availability	08/06/96	10/18/96
USS SCRANTON	SSN 756	Intermediate maintenance Availability	08/12/96	09/13/96
USS ALBANY	SSN 753	Intermediate maintenance Availability	09/16/96	10/25/96
USS GROTON	SSN 694	Inactivation	10/01/96	03/30/98
USS TREPANG	SSN 674	Selected Restricted Availability	10/15/96	12/13/96
USS PROVIDENCE	SSN 719	Selected Restricted Availability	10/17/96	12/21/96
USS ATLANTA	SSN 712	Intermediate maintenance Availability	10/28/96	11/22/96
USS OKLAHOMA CITY	SSN 723	Intermediate maintenance Availability	10/28/96	11/22/96
USS OKLAHOMA CITY	SSN 723	Depot Modernization Period	01/06/97	03/18/98
USS RICKOVER	SSN 709	Intermediate maintenance Availability	01/13/97	03/13/97
USS MINNEAPOLIS /SAINT PAUL SSN 708		Intermediate maintenance Availability	01/27/97	02/28/97
USS SPRINGFIELD	SSN 761	Selected Restricted Availability	02/03/97	04/04/97
USS CITY OF CORPUS CHRISTI SSN 705		Selected Restricted Availability	04/01/97	05/31/97
USS NARWHAL	SSN 671	Intermediate maintenance Availability	05/26/97	06/30/97
USS NORFOLK	SSN 714	Intermediate maintenance Availability	05/27/97	06/30/97
USS HOUSTON	SSN 713	Selected Restricted Availability	06/30/97	09/29/97
USS SAN JUAN	SSN 751	Intermediate Dry Docking	08/01/97	09/24/97
USS ALBUQUERQUE	SSN 706	Selected Restricted Availability	10/01/97	12/08/97
USS PHOENIX	SSN 702	Inactivation	10/01/97	03/17/99
USS MIAMI	SSN 755	Selected Restricted Availability	10/15/97	01/23/98
USS PITTSBURGH	SSN 720	Selected Restricted Availability	11/15/97	02/04/98
USS NORFOLK	SSN 714	Selected Restricted Availability	03/02/98	05/13/98
USS HELENA	SSN 725	Depot Modernization Period	03/09/98	04/01/99
USS PHILADELPHIA	SSN 690	Selected Restricted Availability	06/09/98	10/08/98
USS NAVAL RESEARCH ONE NR-1		Selected Restricted Availability	08/05/98	11/03/98
USS LA JOLLA	SSN 701	Engineered Refueling Overhaul	10/01/98	
USS ALEXANDRIA	SSN 757	Selected Restricted Availability	10/05/98	12/02/98
USS MINNEAPOLIS SAINT PAUL SSN 708		Selected Restricted Availability	01/28/99	04/22/99
USS SALT LAKE CITY	SSN 716	Selected Restricted Availability	03/02/99	05/02/99

USS HARTFORD	SSN 768	Selected Restricted Availability	05/01/99
USS SPRINGFIELD	SSN 761	Intermediate maintenance Availability	05/10/99
USS TOLEDO	SSN 769	Selected Restricted Availability	
USS HAMPTON	SSN 767	Intermediate maintenance Availability	
USS SAN JUAN	SSN 751	Intermediate maintenance Availability	

Appendix 5. Chronological Record of Commanders

Commandant of the Navy Yard

Commodore Isaac Hull	1812–1815
Capt. Thos. MacDonough	1815–1818
Capt. Charles Morris	1818–1823
Capt. Wm. M. Crane	1823–1825
Capt. C.G. Ridgely	1825–1826
Capt. J.O. Creighton	1826–1828
Capt. J.O. Henley	1828–1832
Capt. Wm. M. Crane	1832–1840
Capt. J.D. Sloat	1840–1843
Capt. G.W. Storer	1843–1846
Comm. Daniel Turner	1846–1849
Capt. T.W. Wyman	1849–1852
Capt. Joseph Smoot	1852–1855
Comm. J.T. Newton	1855–1857
Capt. John Pope	1857–1860
Comm. G.F. Pearson	1860–1864
Radm. Theodorus Bailey	1864–1867
Comm. Joseph Lanman	1867–1869
Comm. J.A. Winslow	1869–1870
Comm. A.M. Pennock	1870–1872
Comm. J.C. Howell	1872–1874
Comm. Andrew Bryson	1874–1876
Capt. Earl English	1876–1877
Comm. John Guest	1877–1879
Radm. J.C. Beaumont	1879–1881
Comm. C.H. Wells	1881–1884
Comm. P.C. Johnson	1884–1887
Capt. R.F. Bradford	1887–1889
Comm. J.S. Skerrett	1889–1890
Capt. C.C. Carpenter	1890–1894
Capt. Montgomery Sicard	1894
Capt. A.V. Reed	1894–1896
Capt. G.C. Remey	1896–1898
Radm. C.C. Carpenter	1898
Radm. G.C. Remey	1898–1900
Radm. B.J. Cromwell	1900
Radm. J.J. Read	1900–1903
Radm. C.F. Goodrich	1903–1904

Radm. W.W. Mead	1904–1907
Radm. G.W. Bicknell	1907–1908
Radm. E.K. Moore	1908–1909
Capt. F.A. Wilner	1909–1911
Radm. C.C. Rogers	1911–1914
Capt. Thomas Snowden	1915
Capt. W.L. Howard	1916–1917
Radm. C.L. Boush	1917–1918
Radm. A.S. Halstead	1919–1920
Capt. L.R. de Steiguer	1920–1921
Capt. N. E. Irwin	1921–1922
Radm. D.E. Dismukes	1923–1925
Radm. W.D. McDougall	1925–1928
Radm. W.W. Phelps	1928–1931
Radm. W.C. Watts	1931–1932
Radm. C.S. Kempff	1932–1934
Radm. C.P. Snyder	1934–1935
Radm. C.W. Cole	1936–1940
Radm. J.D. Wainwright	1940–1942
Radm. Thomas Withers	1942–1945

In 1945, the Navy Yard was reorganized in accordance with General Order 19. A U.S. Naval Base was established, with the Naval Shipyard as a component activity. The Commander, U.S. Naval Base, was the Commandant, First Naval District, with headquarters in Boston. He had a Chief of Staff assigned who resided at the Base and was designated Acting Base Commander when the Commander was not present. In 1963, Base Commander became Shipyard Commander.

Acting Commander, U.S. Naval Base

Radm. J.H. Brown	1945–1949
Capt. L.N. Blair	1949–1953
Capt. G.E. Peterson	1953–1954
Capt. E. Olsen	1954–1957
Capt. A.B. Banister	1957–1958
Capt. C.A. Johnson	1958–1960
Capt. J.B. Grady	1960–1962

Manager, Portsmouth Navy Yard

Capt. L.S. Adams	1915–1921
Capt. C.P. Snyder	1921–1922

Capt. W.M. Hunt	1923–1925
Capt. D.A. Weaver	1925–1928
Capt. Louis Shane	1928–1931
Capt. J.W. Woodruff	1931–1932
Capt. B.T. Bulmer	1932–1935
Capt. H.R. Greenlee	1935–1940
Capt. H.F.D. Davis	1940–1944
Capt. S.E. Dudley	1944–1945

Commander, Portsmouth Naval Shipyard

Capt. S.E. Dudley	1945–1946
Capt. R.S. McDowell	1946–1949
Radm. R.E. McShane	1949–1950
Capt. E.C. Craig	1950–1952
Capt. R.E. Cronin	1952–1954
Capt. C.S. Seabring	1954–1956
Radm. R.L. Moore, Jr.	1956–1959
Capt. H.P. Rumble	1959–1961
Radm. C.J. Palmer	1961–1964
Radm. W.C. Hushing	1964–1969
Capt. D.H. Kern	1969–1971
Radm. E.T. Westfall	1971–1974
Capt. W.D. McDonough	1974–1979
Radm. H.L. Young	1979–1981
Capt. J.F. Yurso	1981–1984
Capt. L.L. Lammers	1984–1987
Capt. P.B. Bowman	1987–1990
Radm. L.A. Felton	1990–1993
Capt. L.C. Horne	1993–1995
Capt. C.N. Strawbridge	1995–1997
Capt. V.T. Williams	1997–

Notes

1. *DAB*, 9:62-63; *NHG*, January 30, 1799.

2. For standard books on the history of the Portsmouth Navy Yard, see Fentress (1876); Preble (1892); and *Cradle of American Shipbuilding* (1978); *NHG*, February 24, 1801.

3. *NHG*, April 14, 1801.

4. *Ibid.*, September 14, 1802.

5. Dudley, 1:555-56.

6. *NHG*, March 23, 1813, with first quotation excerpted from *British Quarterly Review*, September 1812.

7. *Ibid.*, April 6, 1813.

8. Dudley, 2:91-92, 195-98, 265-69 (quotation on p. 197).

9. Fentress, p. 40.

10. *Ibid.*, pp. 37-38; *NHG*, December 28, 1813.

11. *NHG*, January 4, 1814.

12. *Ibid.*, October 4, 1814; *DANFS*, 4:578-80; 8:123-24.

13. *PC*, March 7, 1870 (no. 9 of a special series, "The Portsmouth Privateers in the War of 1812").

14. *NHG*, April 4, 1815.

15. Winslow, *Portsmouth-Built*, pp. 16-18; *Portsmouth Oracle*, July 19, 1817 (reprinted in *PJ*, May 11, 1878); *NGH*, July 21, 1817.

16. *PJ*, February 26, 1825; September 2, 1837 ("Portsmouth Navy Yard," emphasizing construction history).

17. *DANFS*, 5:353; Boyd, *Extracts*, entries for December 2, 1820, and May 8, 1823.

18. Long, pp. 49, 60-62; Love, pp. 135-39.

19. *PJ,* February 16 (with quotations from Ramage's report, "dated off the North side of Cuba, Jan. 20, 1822," to Secretary of the Navy Smith Thompson), 1822.

20. *Ibid.,* March 2, 1822.

21. *Ibid.,* September 27, 1828.

22. *DAB,* 10:488-89; *PJ,* May 28, October 15, 1831; August 24, 1839 ("The Navy Yard at Portsmouth," excerpted from *Philadelphia North American).*

23. *PJ,* February 27, 1836; September 2, 1837; August 24, 1839 (with quotation).

24. *Ibid.,* October 15, 1831; September 14, 1839.

25. Love, p. 164; *PJ,* February 20, June 11, 1836.

26. *PJ,* June 11, July 9, 1836 ("SAILOR SOLDIERS," excerpted from *Talla-hassee Floridian*, June 13).

27. *Ibid.,* August 20, 1836, excerpted from *Charleston Courier,* August 10, 1836.

28. *Ibid.,* August 14, 21 (with quotation), 1841; July 9, September 24 (with quotation), 1842; March 22, 1845.

29. *Ibid.,* December 31, 1842; January 14, March 18, 25 (with quotation; three articles including quotation from *New York American),* June 10, 1843; Boyd, *Extracts,* entries for January 7, March 16-19, May 2, 1843.

30. *PJ,* January 14 ("Flogging in the Navy," with quotation), January 28, March 4, 1843; November 23, 1844.

31. *Ibid.;* Boyd, *Extracts,* entry for February 2, 1843; Abbott, pp. 24-25.

32. *Ibid.,* November 28, 1840 ("Blasting Rocks Under Water"); November 25, 1843.

33. *Ibid.,* July 17, 1841 ("The American Navy"); *DNB,* 3:202-3.

34. *PJ,* April 5 (letter dated, "U.S. Ship *Preble,* Porto Grande, St. Vincent, February 2d 1845"), May 31, 1845.

35. Beach, pp. 159-60; Love, pp. 188-211; *PJ,* March 28, 1846.

36. Rogers, *passim* (quotation on p. 63).

37. Long, pp. 218, 249; *PJ,* August 23, 1849, with excerpt from Hong Kong *China Mail.*

38. Long, pp. 242-48; *PJ,* April 23, November 12, 1853; June 17, 1854 ("Opening of Japan").

39. *PJ,* November 11, 18, 25, 1848; January 26 (with quotation), March 9, April 6, 1850.

40. Abbott, pp. 24-25; *PJ,* September 28, 1850; June 21, 1856 (obituary of Watson G. Haynes).

41. *Ibid.,* January 25 (excerpted from *Norfolk* (VA) *Herald*), July 4 (excerpted from *Boston Courier),* 1851.

42. *Ibid.,* January 1, 1853 ("Spirit Rations and Flogging in the Navy"); April 28, 1855; May 17, 1856.

43. Winslow, *Constructing Munitions of War,* pp. 11-15, 52-56; *PJ,* January 16, August 21, September 4 (with quotation), 1858; February 11, 1860; *PH,* August 16, 1916, with full text of the Treaty of Ambrizette.

44. *PJ,* March 8, 1856, reprinted from *Philadelphia Inquirer,* August 29, 1857 ("The Navy Yard"), September 4, 1858 ("Portsmouth Navy Yard," with quotation); May 24 ("Portsmouth Navy Yard," with quotation), June 2 (with quotation), 23, November 26, 1860.

45. *PJ,* August 25, 1855; August 8, 29, 1857; Boyd, *Extracts,* entries for June 2, 14, 1855;

 August 10-11, 1857; May 27-29, 1858; August 1, 1860.

46. *PC,* November 7, 1859, excerpted from *New York News.*

47. Winslow, *Constructing Munitions of War, passim*; *PC,* January 28, May 6 (with quotation), June 5, 15, July 18, 30, September 9, 23, October 4, 7, 17-18, 24, December 6, 18, 28 (with quotation), 1861; *PJ,* August 24 (with quotation), September 7 ("An Hour at the Navy Yard"), 1861.

48. *Marblehead* (MA) *Ledger,* May 10, 1862; *PC,* November 7, 1862; *PJ,* October 11, 1862, excerpted from *New York Tribune.*

49. *PC,* September 26, 1862, excerpted from *Portsmouth Ballot.*

50. *PC,* October 17, 1862 (with quotation).

51. *PC,* March 31, June 10 ("What they have done, and how quickly they did it," with quotation), October 29, 31, December 19, 29, 1863 (with quotation, excerpted from *Boston Journal); PJ,* October 31 ("Operations at the Navy Yard"), 1863.

52. *PJ,* January 26 ("Our Navy"), 1864.

53. *Ibid.,* September 3 ("An Hour at Portsmouth Navy Yard," with quotation), November 12 (excerpted from *Newburyport Herald,* with quotation), 1864; *PC,* February 16, 1864.

54. Marvel, *The Alabama and the Kearsarge,* pp. 244-65; C[arsten] B. DeWit, "Dover, England, July 1864," to William [DeRochemont, Newington, New Hampshire, with quotation], *Kearsarge* folder, Frost Collection; Edward E. Preble, "U.S. Steamer *Kearsarge,* Cherbourg, France, June 20th 1864," to his mother [Portland, Maine], with quotation, *Portland* [ME] *Daily*

Press, July 12, 1864; "Carleton," *Stories of Our Soldiers,* p. 207 (with quotation); *PC,* July 16, 1864 (with quotation); Engineer William Miller, "U.S. Ship *Kearsarge,* Cherbourg, France, June 24, 1864," *Kennebec Journal* (Augusta, Maine), July 29, 1864; *Holyoke* [MA] *Transcript,* July 30, 1864 ("The *Kearsarge* and the *Alabama"),* letter of James S. Thornton, dated June 23-25, 1864 [Cherbourg, France], describing the sea battle and its aftermath.

55. *PC,* May 16, December 24 (with quotation), 1864; *PJ,* May 21, 1864, two articles, with quotation.

56. *PC,* April 11 (with quotation), 1865; *PJ,* May 27, 1865 ("Navy Yard Affairs").

57. *PC,* August 24, 1865 (with quotation).

58. *PJ,* May 27, 1865 (reprinted from *PC,* with quotation).

59. *Ibid.,* March 26, 1870 (with quotation).

60. *Ibid.,* May 16, August 29, 1868; May 15, 1869 (with quotation).

61. *Ibid.,* September 16, 1871; October 2, 1897 (obituary of George M. Robeson); Nevins, p. 281, with quotation on Robeson's abilities; *DAB,* 8:31-32.

62. *PJ,* May 21, 1870 (with quotation); November 24, 1877 ("Ex-Secretary Robeson," with quotation); Love, pp. 341-44; Nevins, pp. 815-16.

63. *PJ,* July 18, 1868; June 5, 1869; May 25, 1872.

64. *Ibid.,* October 4, November 29, 1873; January 31, June 20, 1874.

65. *PJ,* November 29, 1873; June 17, 1876 (with quotation); Fentress, p. 79 (with quotation); *PT,* June 14, 1876.

66. *PJ,* March 14, 1874; January 30, 1875; January 8, 15, February 19, 1876; *CAB,* 5:492-93.

67. *PJ,* May 27 ("Penny Wise, Pound Foolish," with excerpt from *Worcester Gazette),* July 15, 1876.

68. *PJ,* December 9, excerpted from the Annual Report of the Secretary of the Navy, December 16, 30, 1876; *Cradle of American Shipbuilding,* p. 76, with table of statistics, "Civilian Employees at Portsmouth Naval Shipyard."

69. Love, pp. 341, 346, 351-56; *PJ,* January 20, May 5 ("Present Condition of Our Navy," excerpted from *New York Tribune),* 1877.

70. *PJ,* January 19, 1878.

71. Love, pp. 345, 349-53; *DAB,* 3:616-18; *PJ,* January 21, March 25 ("Building a New Navy"), April 15 ("The New Secretary of the Navy"), 1882.

72. *PJ,* January 21, May 27 (letter of E.H. Rollins to William H. Sise, mid-May 1882), September 16, 1882; Boyd, *Extracts,* entry for October 27, 1882.

73. *PJ*, September 9, 16, October 7 (excerpted from *Army and Navy Register)*, December 30, 1882.

74. *PJ*, July 26, August 2, 9, 16, 23, 30, September 24, 1884; *DAB*, 11, Supplement Two, pp. 252-55; Love, pp. 353-56.

75. *PJ*, January 10 (excerpted from *New York Sun* of January 6, with *PJ* quotation), July 4, 1885; January 1, August 13, 27, 1887; May 26, 1888; *DAB*, 10:165-66; Love, pp. 356-58.

76. *PJ*, August 13, 1887; *DAB*, 10:165.

77. *Ibid.*, April 6, 13, 1889, both with quotations.

78. *Ibid.*, April 20, November 30, 1889; February 1 (with quotation), June 20 (with quotation), 1896.

79. *Ibid.*, July 22, 1893 (excerpted from *Boston Journal*, with quotation); June 30, 1894, with quotation from Hilary A. Herbert's form letter.

80. *Ibid.*, July 24, 1875 (excerpted from *Boston Globe);* April 14, July 21 (with quotation), 1888; July 20, August 10, 1889; June 2, December 29, 1894; January 11, 1896; January 2, 23, 30, July 24, August 4, September 18, 25, October 9, November 20, 1897.

81. *Ibid.*, September 25 (with quotation), October 9, November 20, 1897.

82. *Ibid.*, June 5 (with quotation), 26 (with quotation), July 3 (with quotation), 1897; Love, p. 383.

83. *Ibid.*, September 18 (with quotation), October 30, 1897.

84. *Ibid.*, February 19, 1898.

85. Richard Hovey, "Unmanifest Destiny," one-page typescript with handwritten corrections, with commentary in unknown hand (MS #898,422, Special Collections, Baker Library, Dartmouth College, Hanover, New Hampshire, the poem printed in Hovey, *Along the Trail,* pp. 16-17). For Hovey, see *DAB*, 5:273-74, with critique in Linneman, pp. 122-23.

86. *PC*, February 19, 1898; *PJ*, March 5, April 16, 1898.

87. *PJ*, April 23, 30, 1898; Brighton, "Old Tom," *Naval History 1* (April 1987): 67; Baysden,
pp. 38-39.

88. *PJ,* April 30, 1898, reprinting telegram, George A. Ramsdell [April 1898] to John D. Long, and a letter, William E. Chandler, Washington, DC, April 23, 1898, to John S. Tilton, Portsmouth, New Hampshire.

89. *PC,* May 4, 6, 10, 1898; *PJ*, May 14, June 11 (with quotation), 1898.

90. *PJ*, January 22, April 30, May 7 (three articles), 14, 28, June 4, 1898; Love, pp. 390-92; Beach, pp. 342-50.

91. *PJ,* May 28, June 4 (excerpted from *Boston Herald),* 11, July 9, 1898; *DANFS,* 2:451-52.

92. Brighton, "Old Tom," p. 67; *PJ,* June 18, September 3, 1898; *PH,* June 13, June 28 (with quotations), 1898; March 14, 1922, obituary of Elizabeth W. Huntington; *NYT,* November 6, 1917; and *PH,* November 12 ("Married a Portsmouth Woman"), 1917 (obituaries of Robert W. Huntington); Metcalf, pp. 256-60; Pierce and Hough, pp. 138-40; Baysden, pp. 38-41; Varner and Koze, pp. 3-5.

93. Barker, "The Peaceful Prisoners," pp. 28-30; Estes and Goodman, pp. 155-60; "List of Spanish Prisoners Transferred to Camp Long, Seavey's Island, New Hampshire from USS *Harvard,*" pp. 1-31, PNSMVC; *PJ, PC, PH,* July–October 1898, *passim*; *PJ,* July 16 (with quotation), 23, 30, August 6, 13, 20, 27, September 3, 10, 17, 24, 1898.

94. *PH,* August 22, 1898; Howells, "Confessions of a Summer Colonist," pp. 747-48.

95. Brighton, "Old Tom," p. 67; *PJ,* September 3, 10, 17, 24, October 24, 1898; *NCAB,* 27:384-85, biographical sketch of Charles Heywood.

96. *PJ,* September 17, 1898 (with quotation); Beach, p. 385; Baysden, pp. 43-44.

97. *PJ,* October 8, November 26, 1898; Doyle, "Spanish Graves," three-page typescript, PNSMVC.

98. *PH,* June 11-12, 1907; Baysden, p. 54, photograph of tablet.

99. Bailey, 2:669; *PJ,* November 12, 1898, letter of John D. Long, "Navy Department, Washington, Oct. 14, 1898," with quotation.

100. *Ibid.*, January 4, 1899 (with quotation); April 28, June 23, 1900 (two articles, one excerpted from *Manchester* (NH) *Mirror,* with quotation).

101. *PH,* January 4, 1900; August 10 (obituary of Frank W. Hackett), 11, 1926; *DAB,* 8:71-72; *PJ,* November 11, 25, December 9, 23, 1899; February 10, 1900 (with quotation); Sullivan, pp. 64-88.

102. *PJ,* May 26 (two articles), June 9, October 27, November 11, December 22, 1900; Winslow, "Frank Jones of New Hampshire," p. 194.

103. *PJ,* March 24 (with quotation), November 24, 1900; *PH,* November 16, 1916 (obituary of William Henry Jaques); Love, pp. 452-53; Healy and Kutner, p. 275.

104. Love, p. 453; Winslow, *Portsmouth-Built,* pp. 23-24; *PH,* January 5, June 28, July 24 (with quotation), September 5 (with quotation), December 17 (with quotation), 1900.

105. *PJ,* June 16, 1900 ("Centennial Anniversary"), excerpted from *Boston Sunday Herald; PH,* June 12 (two articles), 13-14, 1900.

106. Love, pp. 416-43; O'Gara, pp. 28-29 (with quotations on p. 31); *DAB,* 102-4.

107. Sullivan, pp. 65-73; *PH,* June 10, 1901.

108. Sullivan, pp. 74-88; *PH,* February 17, 1902; July 18 (two articles), 24, 1905.

109. *Ibid.,* July 21, 24, 25, 1905.

110. *Ibid.*

111. Randall, *There Are No Victors Here!* pp. 20-24; *PH,* July 13, 20, August 5 (with quotation), 8, 1905.

112. *PH,* July 15, 1905, excerpted from the *Army and Navy Journal.*

113. *Ibid.,* September 8, 1905.

114. *Ibid.;* Randall, pp. 82, 91, 92, the last two with photographs and captions.

115. *Castle Courier,* April 1l, 1958, May [no date], 1960; *DANFS,* 6:569; *PH,* January 28 (with quotation), February 10, 14, March 31, April 13 (with quotation), 1908.

116. *PH,* May 4 (with quotation), 5, 7, 8, 1908.

117. *Ibid.* , July 29, 1908 (with quotation); *Castle Courier,* April 11, 1958 (with quotation).

118. Openo, *Tugboats on the Piscataqua,* pp. 24-32, 128-29, with a detailed account of the USS *Nezinscot* sinking and investigation.

119. *PH,* September 21, 28, 29 (with quotation), 1909; *NYT,* February 18, 1943, obituary of John G. Tawresey.

120. Love, pp. 444-56; *PH,* September 26, October 4, 1912.

121. *Ibid.,* October 23, 1912: "AT THE NAVY YARD."

122. *DAB,* Supplement Four, pp. 215-18 (biography of Josephus Daniels); Williams, pp. 7-9; Burns, pp. 49-52; *PH,* April 22, June 18 (with quotation), 1913; October 26, 1914; August 17, 26, 27 (with quotation), 28, 1915.

123. *Ibid.,* September 8, 1913; July 10, 1914 (with quotation); October 15, 1915; August 26, 1916.

124. *Ibid.,* March 12-13, 18, April 12, July 9, 1913; April 7, 1914; December 29 (two articles), 1915; February 8, 1916.

125. *Ibid.,* April 10, September 3 (with quotation), 1913; April 30, 1915; May 6, 8, 1916.

126. *Ibid.,* April 13, June 16, July 9, 1913; April 7, 1914; December 29, 1915.

127. *Ibid.*, December 17, 1913; January 5, 1914; November 29, 1915 (with quotation).

128. *Ibid.*, August 16 (with quotation), 26, September 8, 1915; August 29, October 3, 1916.

129. *Ibid.*, October 20, 1914; September 30, December 8, 1915; January 31, May 12 (with quotation), 1916.

130. *Ibid.*, August 26, 28, 30, September 1-2, 5, 15, 19, November 2, 1916.

131. Winslow, *Portsmouth Built,* pp. 24-31; *PH,* March 11, 12 (two articles), July 11, December 30, 1914; January 18, February 24, April 1 (with quotation), 9, 23, 1915; October 6, November 2, 23 (with quotation), 1916.

132. *Ibid.*, April 23, 28, July 22 (with quotation), 1914; April 19, May 27 (with quotation), December 9, 1915; February 8, April 25, June 29, November 6, 10, December 27 (with quotation), 1917.

133. *Ibid.*, October 14, 1916; February 10, 13 (with quotation), 1917.

134. *Ibid.*, March 26, 29, April 3, 4, 7, 1917.

135. Winslow, *Portsmouth*-Built, pp. 29-35; *PH,* April 6, 25, 30, July 5 (with quotation), 1917.

136. *Ibid.*, July 30, September 22, December 21, 1917.

137. *Ibid.*, April 3, 10, May 4, 7, November 15 (with quotation), 17, 1917.

138. *Ibid.*, April 11, June 28 (with quotation), September 1 (with quotation), 1917; May 15, 1918.

139. *Ibid.*, January 15, 18, May 17 (with quotation), 1918.

140. *Ibid.*, April 11-12, 23, 1917.

141. *DAB,* 7:75-76 (biography of Thomas Mott Osborne); *PH,* January 18, July 28, August 3, 18, September 25, December 22, 1917. For the "Trust and Be Trusted" motto, see *PH,* April 3, 1920.

142. *Cradle of American Shipbuilding,* p.76; *PH,* December 31, 1917.

143. Love, pp. 493-515.

144. *PH,* February 1, 1918 (with quotation).

145. *Ibid.*, June 3, July 24, 1918.

146. *Ibid.*, March 5 (with quotation), April 12, May 24, June 22, July 8-9, 27, November 14, 1918.

147. *Ibid.*, January 14, March 1, 27, April 6, July 3, August 6, 8, 22 (with quotations), 28, September 24, October 26, 29, November 26, 1918.

148. *Ibid.*, September 25-26 (the latter with quotation), 1918; *DAB,* 4:355-57 (biography of George W. Goethals), *DAB,* 11(Supplement One): 70-71 (biography of William S. Benson).

149. *PH,* October 25, 31, November 1 (with quotation), 19, 1918.

150. Sullivan, *Our Times,* 5:652-54; *PH,* September 11 (with quotation), 17-18, 20, 23-24, 26, October 1, 5, November 2, 1918.

151. Winslow, *Portsmouth-Built,* p. 35; *PH,* November 12, 1918.

152. *PH,* November 16 (two articles), 18-19, 30 (with quotation), December 16, 1918. For Bogart anecdote, see Benchley, pp. 17-19.

153. *Ibid.,* December 17 (with quotation), 23 (two articles), 1918.

154. Coletta, pp. 167-73; Love, pp. 516-83; Winslow, *Portsmouth-Built,* pp. 37-58; *Cradle of American Shipbuilding,* p. 76.

155. *PH,* January 3 (two articles with quotation), 1919.

156. *Ibid.,* February 4 (with quotation), March 10, May 13, 22, August 7, September 4, October 6, 1919.

157. *Ibid.,* January 29, July 1, 1919; August 17, 1923.

158. *Ibid.,* March 4 (photograph with caption), November 10, 1919.

159. *Ibid.,* March 15 (with quotations), 16, 1920.

160. *Ibid.,* April 21, June 17, 1920.

161. *Ibid.,* February 12, 19, March 8 (with quotation), 10 (with quotation), March 23, May 27, 1920.

162. Boyd, "Continuation of Preble's *History* . . . 1878–1930," p. 37; Love, pp. 528-33; Coletta, pp. 168-71; *PH,* February 10 (with quotation), 13 (with quotation), 15, July 7, 1922; *DANFS,* 5:56-57.

163. *PH,* October 26-28, 1922; October 25 (two articles), 26-27, 1923.

164. *Ibid.,* July 17 (with quotation), 18 (with photograph), 1924; Boyd, *Extracts,* entry of July 17, 1924.

165. *PH,* July 17, 1924; Winslow, *Portsmouth-Built,* p. 51.

166. *Ibid.,* pp. 46-49; Boyd, "Continuation of Preble's *History* . . . 1878–1930," pp. 39 (with quotation), 41-42; Boyd, *Extracts,* entries of January 29-30, February 7, 1925; February 3, 1927; September 4, 1928.

167. Coletta, pp. 180-81; Love, pp. 558-85; *PH,* July 6, 1931.

168. *Ibid.,* November 8, 1932 (with quotation).

169. *Ibid.,* November 8, December 5 (with quotation), 1933.

170. *Ibid.,* November 18, 21, December 13, 1933.

171. *Ibid.,* January 21, February 14 (with quotation), 28, March 2, 7 (with quotation), 8, 1933.

172. Winslow, *Portsmouth-Built,* pp. 58-74; Love, pp. 584-654; Coletta, LaVO, pp. 3-87, *PH,* June 29, 1934; July 2, 1940.

173. *PH,* March 8 (with quotation), August 3-4, 1933; January 5, 1934; July 7, 1939 (obituary of Claude A. Swanson); *DAB,* vol. 11, part 2: 641-42.

174. *PH,* April 14, June 19-24, 1933. *Extracts . . . 1929-1963,* entries for June 21-22, 1933.

175. *PH,* October 10, 19, 26-27, December 1, 1933.

176. *Ibid.,* December 4, 22, 1933.

177. *Ibid.,* January 4, 8, April 26, May 13, 1937; July 17, 1940.

178. *Ibid.,* May 5, 17, 1937.

179. Winslow, *Portsmouth-Built,* pp. 59-62; *PH,* March 10-11, 1936; June 10 (with quotation), 1937.

180. *PH,* July 23, 1936, August 24, October 25, 27, 1937; *Manchester Union,* May 4, 1938; Maas, pp. 40-44, 67-80; Winslow, *Portsmouth-Built,* p. 49-50; *NYT,* May 26, 1967 (obituary of Charles B. Momsen); *Shipmate* (May 1978), p. 86 (obituary of Allan Rockwell McCann).

181. Material on the *Squalus/Sailfish* includes books by Barrows (1940); Mass (1967), with an updated, revised study (1999); and LaVO (1994). See also the Portsmouth Scrapbooks, 1939-40; Winslow, *Portsmouth-Built,* pp. 64-66; Bachelder, pp. 151-84; *PH,* May 23–June 5, 1939 (quotation in June 3 issue).

182. PH, February 2, 15, May 6, 14-15, 1940.

183. *Ibid.,* April 6, 1937; January 2, 20 (with quotation), July 10 (with quotation), August 15, September 3, 9, October 28, 1940. For Frank Knox, see *DAB,* Supplement Two, Vol. XI, part 2: 641-42; *ANB,* 12: 831-33; *PH,* July 3, 8, 12 (with photograph), 1940; October 22, 1941.

184. *Ibid.,* August 12 (with quotation), 1940.

185. *Ibid.,* January 24, 28-29, March 20, May 23, 1941. For the *O-9* sinking, see Bachelder, pp. 183-96; *PH,* June 20-21, 23, September 18, 1941.

186. *Ibid.,* September 19, October 22, 27, 1941.

187. *Ibid.,* November 5 (with Yarnell quotation reconstructed from text), December 3, 4 (with photograph), 1941. *NYT,* July 8, 1959 (obituary of Harry Ervin Yarnell); Winslow, *Portsmouth-Built,* pp. 73-74.

188. Winslow, *Portsmouth-Built,* pp. 75-91. For an excellent contemporary assessment of the Yard war years, see *PH,* August 15, 1945 (two articles, one poem).

189. *PH,* December 8, 1941, with quotations.

190. *Ibid.,* December 15 (with quotation), 17, 19 (with quotation), 22, 27, 29, 1941.

191. *Ibid.*, January 15-16, 1942.

192. *Ibid.*, January 13, 24 (with quotations), 1942.

193. *Ibid.*, January 29, March 12, 27-28, 1942.

194. *NYT,* October 5, 1942, with quotation.

195. Winslow, *Portsmouth-Built,* p. 84; *PP*, September 16, 1942 (with quotation).

196. *PH,* April 14, 1942; *DANFS,* 6:422-23.

197. *PH,* July 15, 21, December 24, 1942.

198. *Ibid.*, February 23, June 16 (with quotation), 1943.

199. *Ibid.*, April 3, 5, 1943.

200. Winslow, *Portsmouth-Built,* pp. 86-89; *Cradle of American Shipbuilding,* p. 81; *PH,* April 26, 28 (with photograph), 1944.

201. *Ibid.*, June 9, 1944; July 28, 1987 (article, "A Castle to Everyone but Those Who Were Inside").

202. *PH,* April 29, May 1-2, 1944.

203. *PH,* August 10, 1944; August 10, 1994 (postwar reunion anniversary article); *DANFS,* 7:210-11; 79th Submarine Birthday Ball, USS *Tirante* (SS420), on April 28, 1979, for dedication of Tirante Tavern, pamphlet, *Tirante* file, PNSYMVC

204. *PH,* April 13, 1945.

205. Winslow, *Portsmouth-Built,* pp. 91-95; Kinkead, "The Surrender of the U-805," *New Yorker* (July 21, 1945): 35-41; *Time,* 45 (May 28, 1945): 32; Scalia, "The Failed Voyage of *U-234";* manuscripts and documents, Frank A. Jackson Collection, Weymouth, MA, with copies in possession of the author; *PH,* July 28, 1987.

206. *PH,* May 7, 1945.

207. *Ibid.*, May 31, 1945.

208. *Ibid.*, August 14 (two articles), 15, 17, 1945.

209. Winslow, *Portsmouth-Built,* pp. 127-73.

210. Furer, pp. 540-43; *Cradle,* p. 60; *PH,* November 14, 1945.

211. Winslow, *Portsmouth-Built,* pp. 106-8; *PH,* September 21, October 5, 27, 30, November 4, 21, 1945; November 12, 1946; May 4, 1948.

212. Winslow, *Portsmouth-Built,* pp. 134-38; *PH,* November 2, 1948, with quotation.

213. *Ibid.*, November 9, 1948.

214. *PP,* July 25, August 8, 1952.

215. *Ibid.*, October 23, 1952; Winslow, *Portsmouth Built,* pp. 137-38.

216. Winslow, *Portsmouth-Built,* pp. 138-47; *PP,* March 21, 1952 (with quotation reconstructed from text) , December 5, 1953 (with reconstructed quotation); April 1, 1955; *PH,* August 1, December 5, 1953; November 23, 1960; March 1, 1963; February 14, 1964.

217. *PP,* March 13, June 5, 1953; *PH,* December 5, 1953.

218. Winslow, *Portsmouth-Built,* pp. 147-48; *PP,* September 21, 1956; January 18, March 18, April 5, 1957; January 10, July 18, 1958.

219. *Ibid.,* August 23, September 6, 1957.

220. Winslow, *Portsmouth-Built,* pp. 148-52; *PP,* August 15, 1958; May 13 (with quotation), June 24, August 5, September 2, 1960; March 8, 1968; *PH,* August 2, 25, 1960.

221. *PP,* June 13, 1958; October 30, 1959; May 13, July 8, 22 (with quotation), 1960.

222. *Ibid.,* April 17, 1963, with quotation of John F. Kennedy, and with excerpt and quotation from *NYT.*

223. *PP,* April 24 (with quotation), December 1, 1964 (with quotation reconstructed from text); *PH,* November 19, 20, 1964.

224. *PP,* April 24, May 8, 15, 1964; *PH,* May 12, 13, 1964; *DANFS,* 3:532, 5:21.

225. Winslow, *Portsmouth-Built,* pp. 161-62; *PP,* May 15, July 24, October 23 (with quotation reconstructed from text), 30, November 6, 1964.

226. *PP,* September 6, 1968; September 19, 1969 (with quotation).

227. Winslow, *Portsmouth-Built,* pp. 165-68; *PP,* August 23, 1968; February 7 (with quotation), December 27, 1968.

228. *PP,* January 15, 29, 1965; *PH,* November 29, 1969, with quotation.

229. Winslow, *Portsmouth-Built,* pp. 172-73, with Nixon quotation on p. 173; *PP,* June 12, 1970 (with quotation); January 8, 22 (with quotation), 1971.

230. *Cradle,* pp. 71-72, 76; *PP,* September 15, 1972; August 17, 1973.

231. Newspaper coverage of the Yard prison is extensive. See *PH,* March 10-11, 1948; May 5, 1967; July 28, 1987; May 29, 1990; Jordan, pp. 8-11, 48-49; *Portsmouth Press,* December 31, 1992; *Boston Sunday Globe,* September 20, 1987; *Portland* (ME) *Sunday Telegram,* December 12, 1968.

232. *Portland Press Herald,* April 28, 1983, with quotation; *PH,* April 30, 1983, with quotation; *Boston Sunday Globe,* September 20, 1983; *New Hampshire Sunday News* (Manchester, NH), April 23, 1978. For letters on the prison's status, see William S. Cohen, Washington, DC, August 3, 1983, to Joseph F. Yurso, PNSY, Portsmouth, NH; Yurso to Cohen, August 24, 1983, with quotation;

Donald L. Allen, Augusta, ME, September 23, 1982, to James V. Connor, PNSY; Yurso to Allen, October 8, 1982; L[ennis] L. Lammers, PNSY, Portsmouth, NH, October 17, 1987, to John P. McKernan, Washington, DC; P[eter] E. Bowman, PNSY, Portsmouth, NH, October 27, 1988, to Bill Johnson, Washington DC. All in the Navy Yard Prison folder, PNSYMVC, Portsmouth, NH.

233. *PP,* October 18, November 15 (with quotation), 1975.

234. *Ibid.*, April 25, June 13 (with quotation), 1975; May 18, 1979, with photographs.

235. *Ibid.*, June 11, 25 (with complete schedule of events), July 23, 1976.

236. *Ibid.*, February 18, May 13, 27, June 24 (with quotations), July 15 (with quotation from Fletcher plaque), 1977; *PH,* March 2, 1977 (obituary of C. Douglass Fletcher).

237. *PP,* June 10, 1977, with quotation; January 13, February 10, 1978.

238. *Ibid.*, February 24, 1978, with quotation and photographs.

239. *Ibid.*, March 24, 1978, with quotation.

240. *Ibid.*, March 23, 1979, with quotation and a reprinting of "A Message to Garcia."

241. *Ibid.*, October 1, 1982; February 4, September 30, October 14, 1983, the latter with a quotation and a reprinting from *PH,* October 9, 1983.

242. *PP,* February 1, 1985, with quotation and the Cohen poem.

243. *Ibid.*, April 10, 1987; *PH,* April 7-8, 1987.

244. Winslow, *Portsmouth-Built,* p. 167; *PP,* December 2, 1966, with quotation; March 19, July 23, 1982; February 18, 1983, with quotation; February 17, 1984, with quotation.

245. Winslow, *Portsmouth-Built,* pp. 154-55; *PP,* March 16, June 22 (with quotation), 1984.

246. *PP,* October 17, 1980; July 22 (with quotation), September 16, 1983.

247. *Ibid.*, May 10, August 2, 1985; April 10, 24, May 22, 1987.

248. *Ibid.*, August 8, 1980; April 30, 1982; January 20, 1984; August 14, September 25, 1987.

249. *Ibid.*, August 14, 1987, with quotation.

250. *PH,* September 4, 18 (with quotation), 19, 1987.

251. *PP,* November 6, 1987, with quotation.

252. *Ibid.*, April 8, 1988; January 24, May 15 (with quotation), July 10, 1992.

253. *Ibid.*, April 1, May 13, October 28 (with quotation), 1994; June 9, 1995.

254. *Ibid.*, May 11, 1984; July 29, 1988; November 3, 1989; April 6, 1990; Octo-

ber 4, 1991.

255. *Ibid.*, October 4, 1991; January 10, 1992.

256. *Ibid.*, April 17, 1992; April 16 (with quotation), July 23, 1993.

257. *Ibid.*, January 16, September 11(with quotation), 1987; January 27, June 16, 1989; January 12, 1990 (two-page summary of important events during the 1980s); Official Program, "Groundbreaking Ceremony, ENGINEER-ING/MANAGEMENT FACILITY," *PP* file folder for August 1987, PNSYMVC.

258. *PP,* February 12, 1988; January 12, 1990.

259. Winslow, *"Constructing Munitions of War,"* pp. 411-12; *PP,* January 13, June 30, 1989; December 27, 1991; February 19, 1993; April 28, 1995.

260. *PP,* January 29, 1988; June 16 (with quotation), October 20 (with quotation), 1989.

261. *Ibid.*, January 13, 1989; August 24 (with quotation), September 7, 1990.

262. *Ibid.*, December 27, 1991; January 10, 1992.

263. *Ibid.*, January 10, 1992, with quotation.

264. *Ibid.*, June 25, 1993; *PH,* June 26, 1993, with quotation.

265. *Ibid.*, October 14, 1994.

266. *Ibid.*, May 26, 1995; *PH,* May 12, 13 (with quotation), 1995.

267. *PP,* June 9, 23, July 7 (with quotation), 1995; *PH,* May 17-18, 20, June 22-23, 1995; *Boston Globe,* June 24, 1995.

268. *PP,* July 7, 21, August 4 (with quotation), 1995.

269. *Ibid.*, October 13, 1995, with quotation.

270. *PH,* November 30, 1995, with quotation.

271. *Ibid.*, March 27 (with quotation), 28, April 30 (with quotation), 1996; *PP,* April 12, May 10, 1996.

272. *PP,* May 24, 1996 (with quotation); *NYT,* May 17-18, 1996; *PH,* May 17-18, August 6, 1996; *Boston Globe,* May 20, 1996.

273. *PH,* December 5, 1996; *PP,* December 6, 1996.

274. *PH,* December 6, 1996, with quotations.

275. *PP,* April 8, 1988; Victor Bourre, Letter to the Editor (with quotation), *Boston Globe,* December 15, 1996, with quotations; *Seacoast Scene* (Hampton, NH), December 18, 1996; *Washington Post,* May 22, 1999, providing an excellent summary of the dispute.

276. *PP,* January 3, 1997, with quotation.

277. *PP,* June 10 1997; *Boston Globe*, December 19, 1997.

278. *PH,* January 17, 31, 1997, both with quotations.

279. *PH,* January 27, 31 (with quotation), February 18, 19 (with quotation), 1997.

280. *Ibid.,* March 21-22, April 30, May 1, July 20 (with quotation), 23 (with quotation), 29, 1997; *PP,* August 1, 1997, with quotation.

281. *PH,* August 1, 1997; *Boston Globe,* October 26, 1997.

282. *PH,* September 17, 1997; *Boston Globe,* October 26, 1997.

283. *PP,* November 7, 1997.

284. *PH,* November 9 (with quotation), 19, 1997; February 4, April 9 (with quotation), 1998.

285. *PH,* August 12, October 7, 15-16, 18, 25, November 6, 13, 1997; *FDD,* October 26, November 24, 1997; *NYT,* November 30, 1997.

286. *PH,* January 2, 18, February 28, December 20, 1998; *Boston Globe,* January 11, 1998, with quotation.

287. *PH,* February 1 (USS *Dallas),* 8 (USS *Helena),* 26, August 22 (USS *La Jolla),* 1998. For the deactivation of the USS *Sand Lance,* see *PH,* January 20, 1998.

288. *Ibid.,* January 13, 20 (with quotation), August 18, 1998; *PP,* April 24, May 8, July 31, September 11, November 20 (with quotation), 1998.

289. *Boston Globe,* March 5, 1998; *PH,* March 5, April 14, 15 (with quotation), 1998.

290. *PH,* May 17 (with quotation), 21, June 10 (with quotation), 1998.

291. *Wall Street Journal,* May 20, 1998, with quotation; *PH,* May 21 (with quotation), 24 (with cartoon), July 5, 1998.

292. *PH,* September 1 (with quotation), December 31, 1998; *PP,* December 4, 1998 (with quotation).

293. *PP,* February 26 (with quotation), March 12, 1999.

294. *FDD,* April 21, 28, 1999; *PH,* March 17, 18 (with quotation), 28, April 4, May 5 (with quotation), 1998; *Washington Post,* May 22, 1999.

295. *PH,* February 9, 24 (with quotation), 26, March 18, June 10, 18, 22 (with quotation), 1999.

296. *PH,* May 8, June 12, 1999; *PP,* May 21, June 18 (with quotation), 1999; *FDD,* June 12, 1999.

297. *PH,* August 8, 10 (with mention of the 1969 Maine state income tax law applying to New Hampshire–resident Yard workers), 12, 16, 17, September 5, October 30 (with quotation), November 4, December 5 (with quotation), 1999.

298. *Ibid.,* July 24, September 17, 1999; *FDD,* September 14, 16 (with quotation), 1999; *Boston Globe,* October 3, 1999, with quotation; *Maine Times,*

November 18-24 (one issue), 1999.

299. *PH,* November 19, 22, 1999.

300. *Ibid.,* July 27 (with quotation), 29, September 3 (with quotation), 1999; *FDD,* July 27, August 13 (with quotation), 1999; *PP,* October 8, 1999.

301. *PH,* July 3 (with quotation), August 20, September 30 (with Eleftherion quotation reconstructed from text), 1999; *Boston Globe,* June 27, 1999, with quotation.

302. *PP,* August 13, 1999; *PH,* September 5, November 11, 1999; *FDD,* December 20, 1999.

303. *PP,* September 10, November 5, December 3, 1999; *PH,* September 5 (with quotation), November 24 (with quotation), 1999; *FDD,* August 27, 1999.

304. *Maine Times,* November 18-24 (one issue), 1999, with quotations.

305. *PH,* December 5, 1999, with quotation.

306. *PP,* November 19, 1999; *PH,* December 31, 1999, with quotation.

307. *PH,* January 3, 2000.

308. *PJ,* May 27, 1876, with quotation.

Bibliography

FOR ANYONE CONTEMPLATING RESEARCH ON ANY ASPECT of the Portsmouth Naval Shipyard, Portsmouth Naval Shipyard Museum and Visitor Center (including its library) is the place to begin. There is so much material that one could search indefinitely. "We have so much here," says Director Jim Dolph, "more than people might think." Having examined this vast collection myself, I fully agree that this research bonanza could keep any hard-working historian busy for several lifetimes.

Since the museum was established in 1985, the continual acquisition of artifacts, books, manuscripts, reports, images, photographs, maps, charts, and models has necessitated increasingly larger quarters to house this huge and still-growing collection. With items arriving almost daily, Dolph and his volunteer staff are busy processing, filing, and boxing these materials. The museum's resources are consulted not only by historians and others interested in the past, but also by naval engineers, scientists, officers, enlisted men, and civilians within the Yard in the everyday execution of their professional duties. From the shipyard commander on down, this working archive plays a vital role in advancing the Yard's interests, whether pertaining to future planning or to maintenance, safety, and any number of other current objectives.

Without any pretense of completeness, I venture to present an inventory of the research holdings, omitting the numerous artifacts in the larger museum hall and display area. Three rooms have been devoted to research purposes. The library room houses books, bound *Portsmouth Periscope* volumes, and related journals. The main research office is furnished with a long table, chairs, two computers, and a photocopier providing free copies. The third room, the storage area, houses materials that can be requested and withdrawn for use. Items are often transferred back and forth depending on their use. The office and storage rooms house the following classifications: PNSY Hospital (four boxes); Public Works (one box); Navy Registers (three boxes); Public Works Contracts (two boxes); Carpenter Shop (four boxes); Harbor Defense (two boxes); Electrical Manufacturing, World War II, at Somersworth,

New Hampshire (one box); Yard Cemetery (two boxes); World War II records (three boxes); Ships' Files (four cabinet drawers); submarine files (three cabinets, consisting of twelve drawers); *Portsmouth Periscope,* the Yard newspaper (two cabinets, or eight drawers); Trades and Professions (one drawer); and piles, cases, and shelves of books, pamphlets, manuals, scrapbooks, magazine runs—anything and everything.

In the main office are the photographs, many unpublished except in back issues of the *Periscope,* filed in folders and preserved in drawers labeled: "Buildings," "People, Events, and other Areas," "Portsmouth Shipyard: Views and Areas," "Submarines," "Surface Ships," and "Miscellaneous."

The storage room contains approximately 140 boxes. Labeled holdings include: "Vessel Planning and Construction," "Sub Launchings," "Preble Papers," "Joe Copley Collection," "Yards & Docks," "Construction and Repair," "German U-boats," "Payroll Records," "Muster Records," "USS *Thresher* Board of Inquiry Records," "Environmental Affairs," "Buildings," "'Quarters' Buildings," "Biographies," "Historic Events," "Miscellaneous Facilities (Dry Docks, Berths, Quay Walls, etc.)," "PNS Annual Reports," "Inspection & Command Histories," "Surface Ships," "World War II Personnel Records," "Vessel Planning and Construction," "Submarine *Squalus,*" "Dry Dock #1," "Navy Dept., Washington," "*Portsmouth-Built* research materials," "*Wealth and Honour* privateering research materials," "Docking Operations and Launch Preparations," and "Yard Craft." The approximately 100 PNSY logs (with gaps) cover the years 1822 through 1970.

The museum collection—much of it unrestricted and open to the public under supervision—contains ample resources for dozens of books on myriad subjects. But the above inventory is fluid, constantly being augmented, so researchers should check in advance to ascertain the availability of materials in this massive collection.

Above and beyond the Yard's holdings, this book could have been written, for all intents and purposes, by using materials readily available in public libraries, archival depositories, and historical societies. As a key source, complete runs of the area's newspapers are available on microfilm. Taken together, these microfilm reels cover the entire span of the Yard's existence. Almost every issue of the *New-Hampshire Gazette, Portsmouth Oracle, Portsmouth Journal of Literature and Politics, Portsmouth Morning Chronicle,* Portsmouth *Evening Times, Portsmouth Herald,* and *Foster's Daily* Democrat (of Dover, New Hampshire) features articles, interviews, documents, and public notices pertaining to the Yard. Along with other federal agencies and departments, the Navy has long realized the value of public relations, utilizing the public press to keep readers informed on naval issues. Even during the selective news blackouts on classified military information during the two world wars, the Yard released news to promote the war effort and to dispense practical information. The two in-house Yard newspapers—the *Life Buoy* (published during World War I and available now on microfilm) and the *Periscope,* the current paper that began publication during World War II—are also indispensable sources.

Numerous books, pamphlets, reports, scientific papers; articles on the United States Navy and the Submarine Service; and biographies of admirals, submarine skippers, Navy Department secretaries, presidents, diplomats, and other public officials provide much background material and supplement the Portsmouth Naval Shipyard story.

Much essential and often-hard-to-get material is found in vertical files, or thick library file folders, which contain Yard-originated booklets: Navy Day open-house guides, prison newsletters, change-of-command and commissioning ceremony programs, special-events programs, and other ephemera. Such files are housed at the Portsmouth Public Library; Rice Public Library, Kittery, Maine; and Special Collections, Dimond Library, University of New Hampshire, Durham.

For those who may elect to follow me in pursuing this topic, I recommend research at the Naval Historical Center, Library of Congress, and the National Archives, all in Washington, DC; the National Archives in Waltham, Massachusetts; and the Nimitz Library, United States Naval Academy, Annapolis, Maryland. Also requiring scrutiny are the papers of many key Maine and New Hampshire political figures prominent in the Yard's recent history. These manuscript collections include the following individuals (listed with the depository): William E. Chandler, New Hampshire Historical Society, Concord; Thomas McIntyre and Norris Cotton, Dimond Library, University of New Hampshire, Durham; George Mitchell and William Cohen, Hawthorne-Longfellow Library, Bowdoin College, Brunswick, Maine; and Edmund Muskie, Ladd Library, Bates College, Lewiston, Maine.

The photography collections whose images grace this book are located at the following institutions: the Portsmouth Naval Shipyard Museum; Dimond Library, University of New Hampshire, Durham; Portsmouth Athenaeum; National Archives, College Park, Maryland; Naval Historical Center, Washington, DC; and the Peabody Essex Museum, Salem, Massachusetts.

The selective bibliography for this book lists the materials consulted and also provides a handy reference for future studies of the Portsmouth Naval Shipyard.

Books

Allmendinger, David F., Jr. *Ruffin: Family and Reform in the Old South*. New York and Oxford: Oxford University Press, 1990.

American National Biography. John A. Garraty and Mark C. Carnes, eds. 24 vols. New York and Oxford: Oxford University Press, 1999.

Appendix to the Report of the Chief of the Bureau of Navigation. Washington, DC: Government Printing Office. Includes "Naval Prisoners of War," pp. 701-2.

Appletons' Cyclopaedia of American Biography. James Grant Wilson and John Fiske, eds. 6 vols. New York: D. Appleton, 1889.

Bachelder, Peter Dow. *Shipwrecks and Maritime Disasters of the Maine Coast*. Portland, ME: Provincial Press, 1997. Includes chapter 9, "Disaster at Seventy-Two Fathoms," accounts of the USS *Squalus* and *0-9* sinkings, pp. 151-96.

Bardwell, John D. *Images of America: Old Kittery*. Dover, NH: Arcadia, 1995.

Barrows, Nathaniel A. *Blow All Ballast! The Story of the* Squalus. New York: Dodd, Mead, 1940.

Baysden, Philip S. *A History of the Marine Barracks, Portsmouth Naval Shipyard, Portsmouth, New Hampshire, 1776–1978*. N.p.: 1978. 91-page pamphlet. Copy at the Portsmouth Room, Portsmouth Public Library Portsmouth, New Hampshire.

Beach, Edward L. *The United States Navy: 200 Years*. New York: Henry Holt and Company, 1986.

Beale, Howard K. *Theodore Roosevelt and the Rise of America to World Power*. Baltimore: Johns Hopkins Press, 1956.

Benchley, Nathaniel. *Humphrey Bogart*. Boston and Toronto: Little, Brown, 1975.

Benson, Henry P. *A Record of War Activities*. New York: Bartlett Orr Press, 1919. Includes chapter entitled "Odd Jobs for the Navy: New York and Kittery Point, Me.," pp. 33-35, with photographs.

Boyd, David F., comp. *Extracts from the Daily Log Book, U.S. Navy Yard, Portsmouth, New Hampshire, October 15, 1819 –December 17, 1929*. "Printed at the UNITED STATES NAVAL PRISON, Portsmouth New Hampshire, 31 March 1931."

Brighton, Ray. *Clippers of the Port of Portsmouth and the Men Who Built Them*. Portsmouth, NH: Portsmouth Marine Society, 1985.

———. *Frank Jones: King of the Alemakers*. Hampton, NH: Peter E. Randall Publisher, 1976.

———. *The Prescott Story*. New Castle, NH: Portsmouth Marine Society, 1982.

———. *Rambles about Portsmouth*. Portsmouth, NH: Portsmouth Marine

Society, 1994.

———. *Tall Ships of the Piscataqua, 1830–1877*. Portsmouth, NH: Portsmouth Marine Society, 1989.

Brown, John H., Jr. *Portsmouth Navy Yard, 1800,—and her early Commandants*. Princeton, NJ: Princeton University Press; New York: Newcomen Society of England, American Branch, 1947.

Buker, George E. *Swamp Sailors in the Second Seminole War*. Gainesville: University Press of Florida, 1997.

Burleigh, John H. *Remarks of Hon. J.H. Burleigh of Maine, in Defense of His Course in Regard to the Kittery Navy Yard*. Washington, DC, 1876. 8-page pamphlet, extracted from the *Congressional Record*. Copy at the Maine Historical Society, Portland, Maine.

Burns, James MacGregor. *Roosevelt: The Lion and the Fox*. New York: Harcourt, Brace, 1956.

Carey, Roland E. *Brief History of the U.S. Naval Disciplinary Command*. N.p.: ca. 1965. 14-page pamphlet.

"Carleton" [Charles Carleton Coffin] and the Soldiers of New England. *Stories of Our Soldiers: War Reminiscences*. Collected from the Series Written Especially for the *Boston Journal*. Boston: Journal Newspaper Company, 1893. Includes "How We Sank the *Alabama*," by Austin Quimby [usually Quinby], pp. 204-7, and "The *Kearsarge* and the *Alabama*," by John Albee, p. 207.

Chadwick, French Ensor. *The Relations of the United States and Spain: The Spanish American War*. Vol. 2. New York: Russell and Russell. Reissued edition, 1968.

Coletta, Paolo E. *The American Naval Heritage*. 4th ed. Lanham, New York, Oxford: University Press of America, 1997.

Dictionary of American Biography. 20 vols. Allen Johnson, ed., vols. 1-3; Allen Johnson and Dumas Malone, eds., vols. 4-7; Dumas Malone, ed., vols. 8-20. New York: Charles Scribner's Sons, 1928–36.

Dictionary of American Naval Fighting Ships. James L. Mooney et al., eds. 8 vols. United States Naval History Division. Washington: Government Printing Office, 1959–81.

Dudley, William S. *The Naval War of 1812: A Documentary History*. Vol. 1, 1812; vol. 2, 1813. Washington, DC: Naval Historical Center, 1985, 1992.

Estes, J. Worth, and David M. Goodman. *The Medical Biography of an American Town, 1623-1983*. Boston: Francis A. Countway Library of Medicine, 1986.

Fentress, Walter E.H. *Centennial History of the United States Navy Yard, at Portsmouth, N.H.* Portsmouth, NH: O.M. Knight, 1876.

Friedman, Norman. *U.S. Submarines Through 1945: An Illustrated Design*

History. Annapolis: Naval Institute Press, 1995.

Furer, Julius Augustus. *Administration of the Navy Department in World War II.* Washington, DC: [Government Printing Office?], 1959.

Gray, Charlie. *Surrender at Sea: A Compilation of the Stories of the Surrender of the Nazi Submarines [U-805, U-873, U-1228, and U-234] as Presented over WHEB.* [Portsmouth, NH]: WHEB, Inc., and Colonial Laundry, 1945.

Hart, Robert A. *The Great White Fleet: Its Voyage Around the World, 1907–1909.* Boston and Toronto: Little, Brown, 1965.

Healy, Laurin Hall, and Luis Kutner. *The Admiral.* Chicago and New York: Ziff-Davis, 1944. Biography of Admiral George Dewey.

History of the Portsmouth Naval Shipyard 1800–1958.

Hovey, Richard. *Along the Trail.* New York: Duffield, 1907. Includes Hovey's war poems, especially "Unmanifest Destiny," pp. 16-17.

Langley, Harold D. *Social Reform in the United States Navy, 1798–1862.* Urbana, Chicago, and London: University of Illinois Press, 1967.

LaVO, Carl. *Back from the Deep: The Strange Story of the Sister Subs* Squalus *and* Sculpin. Annapolis: Naval Institute Press, 1994.

Linneman, William R. *Richard Hovey.* Boston: Twayne, 1976.

Long, David F. *Gold Braid and Foreign Relations: Diplomatic Activities of U.S. Naval Officers, 1798–1883.* Annapolis: Naval Institute Press, 1988.

Love, Robert W., Jr. *History of the U.S. Navy, 1775–1941.* Vol. 1. Harrisburg, PA: Stackpole Books, 1992.

Maas, Peter. *The Rescuer.* New York, Evanston, and London: Harper and Row, 1969.

———. *The Terrible Hours: The Man Behind the Greatest Submarine Rescue in History.* New York: HarperCollins, 1999.

Maloney, Linda M. *The Captain from Connecticut: The Life and Naval Times of Isaac Hull.* Boston: Northeastern University Press, 1986.

Martin, Tyrone G. *A Most Fortunate Ship: A Narrative History of* Old Ironsides. Annapolis: Naval Institute Press, 1997.

Marvel, William. *The* Alabama *and the* Kearsarge: *The Sailor's Civil War.* Chapel Hill and London: University of North Carolina Press, 1996.

Metcalf, Clyde H. *A History of the United States Marine Corps.* New York: G. P. Putnam's Sons, 1939.

Mitchell, Betty L. *Edmund Ruffin: A Biography.* Bloomington: Indiana University Press, 1981.

Morison, Samuel Eliot. *"Old Bruin": Commodore Matthew C. Perry, 1794–1858.* Boston and Toronto: Little, Brown, 1967.

The National Cyclopaedia of American Biography. Vol. 27. New York: James T. White and Company, 1939.

Nevins, Allan. *Hamilton Fish: The Inner History of the Grant Administration.*

New York: Dodd, Mead, 1937. Includes material on Secretary of the Navy George M. Robeson.

New Hampshire: A Guide to the Granite State. Boston: Houghton Mifflin, 1938.

O'Gara, Gordon Carpenter. *Theodore Roosevelt and the Rise of the Modern Navy.* New York: Greenwood, 1969.

Openo, Woodard D. *Tugboats on the Piscataqua: A Brief History of Towing on One of America's Toughest Rivers.* Portsmouth, NH: Portsmouth Marine Society, 1992.

Pierce, Philip N., and Frank O. Hough. *The Compact History of the United States Marine Corps.* Rev. ed. New York and London: Hawthorn Books, 1964.

The Portsmouth Book. Boston: n.p., ca. 1899. Includes article, "The Navy Yard," by Theodore H. Low.

Portsmouth Naval Shipyard. *Cradle of American Shipbuilding.* Introduction by "W[illiam] D. McDonough, Captain, USN, Shipyard Commander, December 1978." Portsmouth, NH: Portsmouth Naval Shipyard, 1978. Rev. ed. (1999), with updated list of commanders, PNSY, 1974–1999, and other information.

Portsmouth Naval Shipyard. Fact Sheets, 1999. Included:

"History of Nuclear Submarines: New Construction, Overhauls, and Scheduled Maintenance Availabilities," four pages; "Navy Wide Submarine Major Depot Overhaul Completion History by Shipyard (6/99)," one page; "68 Nuclear Submarine Major Depot Overhauls Completed by Portsmouth Naval Shipyard (6/99)," one page; and "Portsmouth Naval Shipyard," two pages. These information sheets contain pertinent information on the history of the Portsmouth Naval Shipyard's recent overhaul work. Copies at PNSMVC.

Preble, Geo[rge] Henry. *History of the United States Navy-Yard, Portsmouth, N.H.* Washington, DC: Government Printing Office, 1892.

Randall, Peter. *There Are No Victors Here!: A Local Perspective on the Treaty of Portsmouth.* Portsmouth, NH: Portsmouth Marine Society, 1985.

Read, Thomas Buchanan. *The Poetical Works of Thomas Buchanan Read.* 3 vols. Philadelphia: J.B. Lippincott, 1866. Includes "The Eagle and Vulture," 3: 287-89.

Rogers, Fred Blackburn. *Montgomery and the* Portsmouth. Portsmouth, NH: Portsmouth Marine Society, 1990. Reprint of orig. 1948 ed.

Rusbridger, James. *Who Sank* Surcouf? *The Truth About the Disappearance of the Pride of the French Navy.* London, Sydney, Auckland, and Johannesburg: Century, 1991.

Scarborough, William Kauffman, ed. *The Diary of Edmund Ruffin.* 3 vols. See especially Vol. 2, *The Years of Hope: April 1861–June 1863,* and Vol. 3, *A*

Dream Shattered: June 1863–July 1865. Baton Rouge and London: Louisiana State University Press, 1976, 1989.

Smith, Margaret Chase. *Declaration of Conscience.* William C. Lewis, Jr., ed. Garden City, NY: Doubleday, 1972.

Spector, Ronald. *Admiral of the New Empire: The Life and Career of George Dewey.* Baton Rouge: Louisiana State University Press, 1974.

Sperber, A.M., and Eric Lax. *Bogart.* New York: William Morrow, 1997.

Stephen, Leslie, and Sidney Lee, eds. *Dictionary of National Biography.* Vol. 3. New York: Macmillan, 1908.

Sullivan, Mark. *Our Times: The United States, 1900–1925.* Vol. 5, *Over Here, 1914–1918.* New York and London: Charles Scribner's Sons, 1933.

Tyler, Patrick. *Running Critical: The Silent War, Rickover, and General Dynamics.* New York: Harper and Row, 1986.

U.S. Submarine Losses: World War II. N.p.: Prepared by the Commander, Submarine Force, U.S. Pacific Fleet, 1946.

Varner, B.D., and Daniel Koze. The History of Guantanamo Bay. 3d ed. Guantanamo Bay: U.S. Naval Base, publisher, 1964. Ca. 102-page pamphlet.

Weir, Gary E. *Building American Submarines, 1914–1940.* Washington, DC: Naval Historical Center, 1991.

———. *Forged in War: The Naval–Industrial Complex and American Submarine Construction, 1940–1961.* Washington, DC: Naval Historical Center, 1993.

Whittaker, Robert H., comp. *Portsmouth–Kittery Naval Shipyard in Old Photographs.* Dover, NH: Alan Sutton, 1993.

Winslow, Richard E., III, *"Constructing Munitions of War": The Portsmouth Navy Yard Confronts the Confederacy 1861–1865.* Portsmouth, NH: Portsmouth Marine Society, 1995.

———. *Portsmouth-Built: Submarines of the Portsmouth Naval Shipyard.* Portsmouth, NH: Portsmouth Marine Society, 1985.

———. *"Wealth and Honour": Portsmouth During the Golden Age of Privateering, 1775–1815.* Portsmouth, NH: Portsmouth Marine Society, 1988.

Wysong, Jack P. *The World, Portsmouth and the 22nd Coast Artillery: The War Years, 1938–1948.* Missoula, MT: Pictorial Histories Publishing Co., 1997.

Public Documents

Letter from the Secretary of the Navy . . . with certain Documents relating thereto, dated 30th January 1802. Washington, DC: Printed by William Duane, 1802.

Articles

Abbott, Collamer M. *"White-Jacket* and the Campaign Against Flogging in the

Navy." Melville Society, *Extracts,* number 89 (June 1992): 24-25.

"Allan Rockwell McCann." *Shipmate* (May 1978): 86. Obituary of McCann, U.S. Naval Academy, Class of 1917, in the U.S. Naval Academy alumni magazine.

Barker, Shirley. "The Peaceful Prisoners." *New Hampshire Profiles* (June 1958): 28-30, with photographs. Description of the Spanish-American prisoners of war at Camp Long, Portsmouth Navy Yard, in 1898.

"Battle of the Seas: Gangsters' End." *Time* 45 (May 28, 1945): 32. Surrender of U-boats at the Portsmouth Navy Yard.

Brighton, Ray. "Old Tom." *Naval History* 1 (April 1987): 67.

Heintze, James R. "'Tyranny and Despotic Violence': An Incident Aboard the U.S.S. *Washington*." *Maryland Historical Magazine* 94 (spring 1999): 31-54.

Howells, W[illiam] D[ean]. "Confessions of a Summer Colonist." *Atlantic Monthly* 82 (December 1898): 742-50. Description of mock bullfight by Spanish prisoners of war at the Portsmouth Navy Yard on Sunday, August 21, 1898.

Hull, R.R. "Signal Encounter at Guantanamo." *Naval History* 12 (May/June 1998): 18-23.

Jordan, Ralph A. "The Castle." *Our Navy* (July 1, 1946): 8-11, 48-49. Photocopied sheets, U.S. Naval Prison folder, PNSMVC.

Kinkead, Eugene. "The Surrender of the *U-805*." *New Yorker* 21 (July 25, 1945): 35-41.

Mason, Robert. "She Died a Noble Death." *Naval History* 11 (January/February 1997): 30-35. Eyewitness testimony on the *Kearsarge–Alabama* sea battle of 1864, from a Confederate agent in France.

Newman, Richard J. "Breaking the Surface." *U.S. News & World Report* 124 (April 6, 1998): 28-42.

O'Connor, Daniel. "Muzzle to Muzzle with the *Merrimack*." *Civil War Times Illustrated* 35 (June 1996): 20-22, 64-70.

Preble, Geo[rge] Henry. "Vessels of War Built at Portsmouth, New Hampshire, 1690–1868." *New England Historical and Genealogical Register* 22 (October 1868): 393-402.

Sloan, Edward W. "The U.S.S. *Kearsarge,* Sixteen Irishmen, and a Dark and Stormy Night." *American Neptune* 54 (fall 1994): 259-64.

Sullivan, Timothy P. "The Portsmouth Navy Yard, the New Dry Dock, and Henderson's Point." *Granite Monthly* 36 (February 1904): 64-88.

Tusler, Floyd A. "The Salvage of the U.S.S. *Squalus*." *Journal of the American Society of Naval Engineers* 52 (May 1940): 157-87. United States Naval History Division.

Vizard, Frank. "Shadow in the Shallows." *Popular Science* (May 1999): 58-62.

Description of future submarine USS *Virginia*.

Williams, William J. "Josephus Daniels and the U.S. Navy's Shipbuilding Program During World War I." *Journal of Military History* 60 (January 1996): 7-38.

Newspapers/Periodicals

Boston Globe

The Economist (London, England). Contains "The Protection of Maritime Commerce," June 25, 1864, pp. 798-99.

Foster's Daily Democrat (Dover, New Hampshire)

Holyoke Transcript (Massachusetts): July 30, 1864. Contains James S. Thornton's letter of June 23-25, 1864, and the poem "Hail to the *Kearsarge,*" by George W. Bungay, the latter originally published in the *New York Independent.*

Kennebec Journal (Augusta, Maine): July 29, 1864.

Maine Times (Bangor, Maine): November 18-24, 1999. Contains "Saving the Shipyard: For Portsmouth It May Be Convert or Die," pp. 1, 4-9.

Manchester Guardian (Manchester, England): June 21, 22, 23, 27, 29, July 2, 1864. Articles on the *Kearsarge–Alabama* sea battle.

Marblehead (Massachusetts) *Ledger:* May 10, 1862.

New-Hampshire Gazette (Portsmouth, New Hampshire)

New Hampshire Sunday News (Manchester, New Hampshire): April 23, 1978.

New York Daily Tribune: August 31 ("Obituary: Raphael Semmes"), September 1, 1877 ("The Late Admiral Semmes: Personal Reminiscences").

The New York Times

The Oracle (also *Oracle of the Day)* (Portsmouth, New Hampshire)

Portland (Maine) *Daily Press:* July 12, 1864.

Portland (Maine) *Press Herald:* April 23, 1983.

Portland (Maine) *Sunday Telegram:* December 12, 1968.

Portsmouth Chronicle

Portsmouth Evening Times

Portsmouth Herald

Portsmouth Journal of Literature and Politics

Portsmouth Scrapboooks, Clippings from PH, *1939-1940,* Portsmouth Room, Portsmouth Public Library, Portsmouth, NH.

Seacoast Scene (Hampton, New Hampshire): December 18, 1996.

The States and Union (Portsmouth, New Hampshire): June 15 ("A Seaman's War Story: An Incident of the *Kearsarge's* First Cruise"), June 22 ("War Story: The *Kearsarge–Alabama* Naval Duel off Cherbourg"), 1893. Two reminiscences by Martin Hoyt, Landsman on the USS *Kearsarge* and

Newington, New Hampshire, resident.

The Wall Street Journal (New York): May 20, 1998.

Washington Post: May 22, 1999.

Manuscripts

Alden, John D. Letter, one page, July 11, 1979, from Pleasantville, New York, to "Don" [William D. McDonough, Portsmouth Naval Shipyard, Portsmouth, New Hampshire]. A critique of *Cradle of American Shipbuilding,* with minor corrections. *Cradle* folder, PNSMVC.

Badger, Oscar C. Papers. 1868–69. One folder. Joseph W.P. Frost Collection, Eliot, Maine. Badger was equipment officer at the Portsmouth Navy Yard.

Bailey, Theodorus. Papers. One folder. Joseph W.P. Frost Collection, Eliot, Maine.

Boyd, David F., Captain, USN, "Continuation of Preble's History of the United States Navy Yard, Covering the Years 1878-1930." 45-pages, with various appendices. (Typescript with handwritten corrections and additions.) Original in the Maine Room, Rice Public Library, Kittery, Maine; copy in possession of the author.

Bradford, Robert F. Naval papers, 1852–1890. One box. Manuscript MS-686, Special Collections, Baker Memorial Library, Dartmouth College, Hanover, New Hampshire. Baker, a career naval officer, was the ordnance inspector at the Portsmouth Navy Yard from 1872 to 1875.

Creighton, J.O. Portsmouth Navy Yard bills and naval supply documents, 1828. One folder. Joseph W.P. Frost Collection, Eliot, Maine.

Dickinson, M. Letter, May 30, 1836, Navy Department, Washington, DC, to Capt. Will[iaml M. Crane, Portsmouth Navy Yard, Portsmouth, New Hampshire. New Hampshire Historical Society, Concord, New Hampshire.

Domina, Walter E. "A Brief History of the Portsmouth Naval Disciplinary Command." 17-page typescript. Copy in the Joseph Copley Library, Portsmouth Athenaeum, Portsmouth, New Hampshire.

"Extracts from the Daily Log Book, U.S. Navy Yard, Portsmouth, New Hampshire: December 18, 1929–March 3, 1963." 76-page typescript. Copy in the Portsmouth Athenaeum, Portsmouth, New Hampshire, and in the Portsmouth Public Library, Portsmouth, New Hampshire.

Hovey, Richard. "Unmanifest Destiny." Poem in typescript with inked-in corrections. MS 898,422, Special Collections, Baker Memorial Library, Dartmouth College, Hanover, New Hampshire. Date of library acquisition: "July 22, 1898."

Hughes, Paul F., Sr. Navy Yard records, photos, and papers. Looseleaf notebook, with "Navy Yard" on spine. 1920–62. In possession of Paul F. Hughes, Jr., Greenland, New Hampshire.

Kearsarge. Miscellaneous papers pertaining to the Portsmouth-built vessel USS *Kearsarge.* Includes Carsten B. DeWit's letter of July 1864 to "William," describing the *Kearsarge–Alabama* sea battle of June 19, 1864. One folder. Joseph W.P. Frost Collection, Eliot, Maine.

Long, John D. Collection. Massachusetts Historical Society, Boston, Massachusetts. Long was Secretary of the Navy during the 1898 Spanish–American War.

Morris, Charles. Six letters to John F. Parrott re U.S. Navy, 1820–25. One folder. John F. Parrott Collection, New Hampshire Historical Society, Concord, New Hampshire.

Navy Prison Yard. Collection, one folder, with many letters between shipyard commanders and Maine politicians regarding the status and potential use of the prison. PNSMVC.

Porter, David D. Collection. One folder relating to Porter's official naval duties as public works officer, 1858–60. Ca. 30 items. Joseph W.P. Frost Collection, Eliot, Maine.

Rodgers, John. Papers. In light blue notebook. Joseph W.P. Frost Collection, Eliot, Maine. Commodore Rodgers was in charge of the Navy Commissioners' Office, Washington, DC, from 1815 to 1831.

"Rodgers Letters and MacDonough" Collection. One notebook. John Rodgers letters to Thomas MacDonough and to Charles Morris. Joseph W.P. Frost Collection, Eliot, Maine.

Scalia, Joseph Mark. "The Failed Voyage of *U-234:* The Intelligence Value of Germany's Final Technical and Diplomatic Mission to Japan, 1945." Unpublished master's thesis, Louisiana Tech University, Ruston, Louisiana, 1997.

Southard, Samuel L. Papers. One folder. Joseph W.P. Frost Collection, Eliot, Maine. Southard was Navy Secretary from 1823 to 1829.

White, D[eborah] M. Letter, from Public Affairs Office, PNSY, Portsmouth, New Hampshire, August 16, 1999, one page, to Richard E. Winslow III, Rye, New Hampshire. Original in possession of the author. Statistics on PNSY employment levels, 1978–99.

Winslow, Richard E., III. "Frank Jones of New Hampshire: A Capitalist and a Politician during the Gilded Age." Unpublished master's thesis, University of New Hampshire, Durham, New Hampshire, 1965.

Index

This index is arranged using word-by-word alphabetization. Illustrations, including maps and photographs are indicated by the use of bold typeface.

About the Author

With this latest book for the Portsmouth Marine Society (PMS), Richard E. Winslow III senses that he may be in line for a promotion. During his long friendship with the late Ray Brighton, a most prolific PMS historian, Dick and Ray often joked that each PMS book earned the author a step up in (honorary) rank. Thus, Dick's first book, *The Piscataqua Gundalow: Workhorse for a Tidal Basin Empire* (1983), earned him the honorary rank as captain; the second book, *Portsmouth-Built: Submarines of the Portsmouth Naval Shipyard* (1985), bumped him to commodore; the third, *"Wealth and Honour": Portsmouth during the Golden Age of Privateering 1775–1815* (1988), made him a rear admiral; the fourth, *"Constructing Munitions of War": The Portsmouth Navy Yard Confronts the Confederacy 1861–1865* (1995), earned him the title of vice admiral; and this fifth effort promotes him to full admiral. Thus, after eighteen years with the Portsmouth Marine Society, Dick has finally joined Ray in achieving this unofficial distinction within the combined USN/PMS command hierarchy.

Winslow was born in Boston in 1934 and obtained his academic training at Union College, the Universities of New Hampshire and Maryland, and Penn State. His field is nineteenth-century American history, with special interests in the Civil War and marine-maritime-naval subjects.

As a "Navy junior," Dick grew up in naval shipyards and bases around the country, until his father's last tour of duty at the Portsmouth Naval Shipyard, 1957–60. From childhood, Dick absorbed the Navy's lingo, lore, and customs. Along with this background, Winslow holds memberships in the Portsmouth Naval Shipyard Museum, the Naval Historical Foundation, the Portsmouth Athenaeum, and the Civil War Round Table of New Hampshire—all of which have promoted the contacts and enriched the research involved with the writing of this book.

Along with hundreds, if not thousands, of others, Dick has proudly worn a souvenir "Bicentennial Portsmouth Naval Shipyard 2000" button-badge pinned on his shirt in anticipation of the June 9-11, 2000, celebration. Winslow is confident that in the year 2100, the Yard will still be operational as a naval facility, and a century from now, another historian will publish an updated account of the Portsmouth Naval Shipyard's uninterrupted saga of accomplishment and service.